RADICAL PHILOSOPHY

2.13
Series 2 / Autumn 2022

Radical Philosophy turns 50
Jonathan Rée, Sean Sayers, Christopher J. Arthur, Kate Soper, Diana Coole and Stella Sandford — 3

Philosophy as cultural form
Interview with Peter Osborne — 15

Anti-abortion feminism
Victoria Browne — 27

Tutelage or assimilation?
Marie Louise Krogh — 43

The Red Pill
William Clare Roberts — 57

Producing the intolerable
Martina Tazzioli — 66

Untimely Media
Amit S. Rai — 77

Reviews — 89

Tom Holert, *Knowledge Beside Itself*
Nicolas Helm-Grovas — 89

Matthew T. Huber, *Climate Change as Class War*
Casey Williams — 92

Susan Buck-Morss, *Year One: A Philosophical Recounting*
Nasrin Olla — 96

Dipesh Chakrabarty, *Climate of History in a Planetary Age*
Regan Burles — 99

Willem Styfhals, *No Spiritual Investment in the World*
Daniel Fraser — 103

Oxana Timofeeva, *Solar Politics*
Isabel Jacobs — 107

Paul K. Jones, *Critical Theory and Demagogic Populism*
Morelock, ed, *How to Critique Authoritarian Populism*
Mike Makin-Waite — 110

Sebastian Truskolaski, *Adorno and the Ban on Images*
Hedy Cohen — 115

Jack Z. Bratich, *On Microfascism: Gender, War, and Death*
Takin Raisifard — 117

'Marx and Capitalism', Deutsches Historisches Museum
Rachel Pafe — 121

Editorial collective
Claudia Aradau
Brenna Bhandar
Victoria Browne
David Cunningham
Peter Hallward
Stewart Martin
Lucie Mercier
Daniel Nemenyi
Hannah Proctor
Rahul Rao
Martina Tazzioli
Chris Wilbert

Engineers
Daniel Nemenyi
Alex Sassmanshausen

Cover image
Panda Mery, *The hole*, 2021,
https://gizmonaut.net/ .

Creative Commons BY-NC-ND
Radical Philosophy, Autumn 2022

ISSN 0300-211X
ISBN 978-1-914099-02-1

Radical Philosophy turns 50

Jonathan Rée, Sean Sayers, Christopher J. Arthur, Kate Soper, Diana Coole and Stella Sandford

It's 50 years since the first issue of *Radical Philosophy* was published in 1972. To mark the occasion, we asked a selection of former editors to share their recollections and reflections on their time on the job. We wanted to hear from those involved in the early years, without neglecting those who had participated in subsequent developments. There are memoirs by Jonathan Rée, Sean Sayers, Christopher J. Arthur, Kate Soper and Diana Coole, and an interview with Stella Sandford, by Victoria Browne. There is also an extended interview in this issue with Peter Osborne, the journal's longest-serving editor, by David Cunningham. (A further interview with Mark Neocleous will appear in *RP* 214.) They all offer important contributions to a history of *RP*, with valuable insights into the experiences that founded and sustained it, the ambitions and challenges, the continuities and breaks, not ignoring the crucial, often glamourless and comical practicalities of its production and distribution. Readers will find testimony to the generational solidarity underpinning *RP*'s exceptional endurance, but they will also discover some of the conflicts and disappointments that are perhaps belied by the image of a half-century old journal. *RP* has survived because of the extraordinary commitments of its editors, and sometimes despite them.

The selection of perspectives here is obviously partial and inadequate to a comprehensive retrospective. In preparing for this anniversary, some of us trawled through past issues to produce a complete list of editors: we counted 83. And that doesn't include the dedicated writers who have helped in no small measure to make the journal what it is. The editors we ended up inviting have been gracious enough to expose the personal character of their perspectives, and readers should keep that in mind, not only in considering how they relate to one another but also how they might relate to all those who didn't get a say on this occasion.

Perhaps the most conspicuous absentees are the current editors. For a variety of reasons, we decided to remain silent or wait for another day. That would be an occasion to describe the major changes that took place since all these former editors left, especially the crisis that the journal went through between issues 200 and 2.01 when it nearly folded. It emerged transformed, as the new production, distribution and financing apparatus that it is today – namely, a freely accessibly online publication, funded through sales of print-on-demand issues and donations, and combined with an archive of issues 1–200 overseen by former editors. This crisis was largely practical, rather than one of 'ideological direction', however it was accompanied by a significant change of staff that has had an undoubted impact on the content of the journal since 2016. Whether *RP* today can still be understood in terms of its founding aims, or perhaps subsequent shifts in those aims, or whether it is now fundamentally different, despite the same name, is a question answered variously by the former editors in this anniversary issue. But, after reading them, it's a question worth asking anew.

Jonathan Rée, 1972–1994

As far as I remember, my involvement started early in 1971 with a conversation with Tony Skillen, who was a friend of a friend, a lecturer at the University of Kent, an anarchic socialist, and extremely funny. I was a graduate student at Oxford University at the time, and – having previously studied at the relatively free-spirited University of Sussex – I was appalled by the conservatism and complacency of the place. Most of my fellow students seemed to think they were the cleverest people in the greatest department at the world's top university, and their only aim in life was to suck up to the dons, emulate their tics, mannerisms and put-downs, and follow them into gilded academic careers. I was shocked, and Tony seemed to understand.

Over the next few months there were further conversations, in Canterbury and London, involving – if I remember right – Chris Arthur, Jerry Cohen, Richard Norman and Sean Sayers. The main thing that united us, I think, was a generalised feeling that British philosophy was in the doldrums. It had contrived to isolate itself from the turbulent world around it – from student unrest, from the peace movement, from the politics of anti-capitalism and colonial liberation, and above all from feminism. (The fact that we were all male perhaps confirmed this analysis.) But we knew that we were ourselves victims of the system, having been reared on a one-sided philosophical diet – bits of analytical philosophy and Wittgenstein, with some perfunctory history of philosophy on the side. We were embarrassed about knowing very little – in my case next to nothing – about Hegel, Marx, Husserl, Heidegger, Sartre, Althusser, Derrida and Foucault, not to mention Simone de Beauvoir.

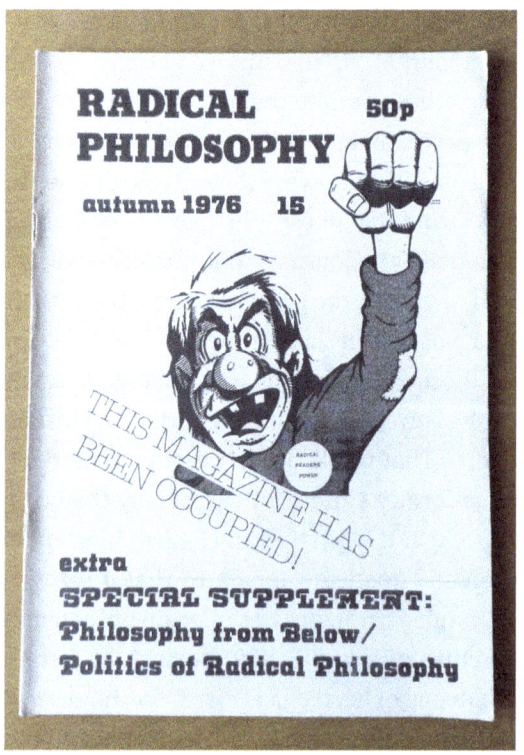

I was not alone, I think, in thinking that our main task was to liberate ourselves from our brainwashing and – in the idiom of the time – to 'raise consciousness' about the arrogance, aggression and narrow-mindedness of the philosophical culture which had shaped us. The idea of producing a regular publication was something of an afterthought, and we envisaged *RP* not as a vehicle for our favourite philosophical doctrines but as a means of mutual self-education. We thought of ourselves as a 'collective' rather than a committee, and strove to make the editorial process open, non-hierarchical and collaborative. After a while some of us became quite proficient in the shared labour of (literally) cutting and pasting bits of shiny typescript onto A1 boards, with the help of scalpels, set squares, drawing boards, drafting machines, Cow gum, Letraset and Rotring pens. The first issue came out in January 1972, and we had no firm expectation that it would continue for more than a year.

But it went on, and on and on. There were debates, not always good tempered, over

Chinese communism, Marxist dialectics, Althusser and Foucault, but as far as I was concerned they were beside the point: the finest exercises in progressive or revolutionary theory were not going to serve much purpose, I thought, if they reproduced the haughty exclusiveness and chilly impersonality of mainstream philosophy. My position was that philosophy needed to escape from the social and intellectual deformations that go with being a modern academic discipline, and I thought that the magazine should model itself not on *Mind* or *Philosophy and Phenomenological Research*, nor yet on *New Left Review* or the even more rebarbative *Theoretical Practice*, but on the recently founded *Spare Rib* and *Gay News*.

In 1978 I resigned from the position of 'secretary and co-ordinator of the editorial collective' and contributed a valedictory editorial to *RP* 20, in which I lamented what I saw as a drift from the attempt to construct a 'counter-culture' to the pursuit of 'theoretical excellence'. But I remained part of the collective, and took on the semi-detached role of reviews editor, until 1993.

Looking back I would describe my involvement in the early years of *RP* as the most decisive intellectual experience of my life. It opened my eyes to the fact that philosophy – like every other theoretical and literary practice – is not only a body of ideas but also a set of social relations which, for better or for worse, shape people's lives. After a few years I realised that my approach did not have much resonance within the editorial collective, or much support outside it – that if I wanted to pursue it, I would have to do so on my own. And I came to the conclusion that *RP* had been captured by the universitarian forces which, as far as I was concerned, it was supposed to resist. That at least is what my memory tells me.

Sean Sayers, 1972–2001

RP was a child of the 1960s. At the time, philosophy in universities was unutterably conservative and complacent. Analytic and ordinary language philosophy, as well as empiricism, of the driest, dullest sort, had a total stranglehold. For young teachers and students this was intolerably blinkered and constricting. An explosion of radical and critical ideas was occurring in the wider world. A group of us in Canterbury arranged a small meeting of some like-minded teachers and graduate students. We decided to create a group to organise meetings around the country and publish a journal, to be called '*Radical Philosophy*'.

Some urged us to reject philosophy altogether as bourgeois academicism, but we were committed to doing philosophy, and to the highest intellectual standards. We wanted to transform philosophy, not to abandon it. We were politically committed to the left and to the reform of the universities. We recognised the central importance of Marxism to radical thought, but many wanted to remain open to other philosophies as well. Some wanted to reject analytic philosophy altogether, others to use it for critical purposes. After considerable discussion, we decided not to commit to a particular philosophy or political line. Rather our aim would be to provide a forum for ideas and debate. Let a hundred flowers blossom! We were determined to avoid jargon and technicality in so far as possible, and to be read by students. Our policy was proclaimed in our 'Founding Statement'. (See *RP* 1.)

The first issue appeared in January 1972. We worried that we would be left with boxes of unsold copies, but the journal was an immediate success. We had to reprint the first issue twice. It created enthusiastic interest from the outset. Local 'Radical Philosophy groups' sprang up in universities all around the country. These distributed the journal and organised meetings at which the editors often spoke. We also put on some large and lively conferences.

A movement developed.

At first, the established world of philosophy was indifferent or positively hostile, but our impact was so great that it could not ignore us. Mary Warnock wrote a foolish piece in the popular weekly, *New Society*, arguing that 'radical philosophy' had nothing to do with philosophy properly so called, and complacently claiming that the commonsensical British were immune to Marxism. However, there were also some supportive responses from established figures. Roy Edgley at the University of Sussex stood out in encouraging us from the outset. Soon it became possible to discuss political issues in philosophy departments, and to mention Sartre, Freud and even Marx.

The main editorial and production work for the first five issues was done in Canterbury by Richard Norman, Tony Skillen and me. Editorial decisions were in the hands of a wider collective that met regularly in London. The success of the journal soon led to demands for the editors to circulate. From issue 6, main control was handed over to Jonathan Rée and a group in London (not without misgivings on my part).

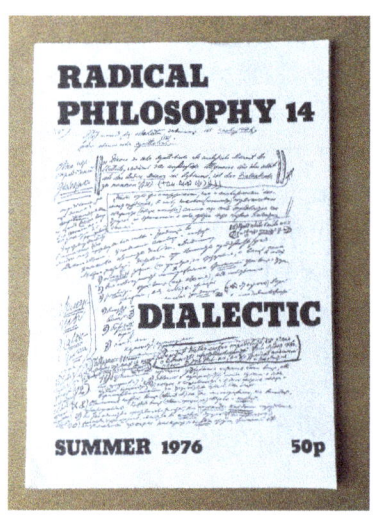

The policy of providing a forum worked well at first, but we soon needed to specify what we stood for positively. We were determined to be open to new forms of philosophy, but we did not want to simply import ideas and jargon from the continent. We fought off attempts to make us into a journal of Foucauldian or structuralist dogma. We were committed to working out our own ideas in our own language. Structuralist Marxism and analytical Marxism were the most influential forms of left philosophy in 1970s and they were discussed critically in the journal. By the mid 1970s some distinctive ideas began to crystallise. Perhaps the most influential was Epistemological Realism. A number of Hegelian Marxists were also closely associated with the journal. (They later formed the nucleus of the Marx and Philosophy Society). With the right resurgent under Thatcher, the left was thrown onto the defensive. The most dynamic forces on the left developed outside traditional socialist political groups in the women's, peace and environmental movements. All these gave rise to important philosophical debates which provided the main focus of work in *RP* in these years.

One by one the early editors began to drop out. In the 1980s the journal's original aims were largely abandoned. Mainstream Marxism was excluded, the focus turned to cultural topics. It became a journal of continental cultural theory. I regretted the direction things were going, but I had no clear alternative to propose nor the energy to fight for it. I was reviews editor in the 1990s and then ceased to be actively involved altogether, one of the last of the old guard.

Philosophy in Britain and in the English-speaking world went through enormous changes in the aftermath of the 1960s. Even a field as sleepy and conservative as academic philosophy was forced eventually to acknowledge and reflect them. *RP* can claim some of the credit for this. It was not the primary cause of these changes – larger forces were at work – but it provided an effective and influential place where they could be aired and discussed. It appeared at the right place and at the right time with the right means to facilitate them. It was rewarding and exciting to be part of this.

Christopher J. Arthur, 1972–2001

I was involved in the inception of *RP*. Having become intellectually excited by Marx in my student days, I was extraordinarily fortunate to get a job at the University of Sussex that included teaching an option on Marxist Philosophy – probably the only one in the country – and later introducing one on Hegel. (I joined Sussex in 1965, the same year as John Mepham, another founding member of *RP*, who taught philosophy of science.) So I naturally joined in the project of *RP* and the editing of its journal.

RP was originally conceived as an intervention in the stagnant philosophy of the time, as a space for everything heterodox. It soon became dominated by Marxism, but it was just as much an intervention of philosophy in Marxism. It is important to stress that we never discussed – still less imposed – a particular 'line', either in philosophy or politics: our approach was very much to 'let a hundred flowers bloom'. The content reflected what we and our supporters were doing at the time. Jonathan Rée thought most readers valued the reviews above all. Obituaries were also well received. Tony Skillen was keen that we include humour, for instance, the cartoons.

It was hard to figure out who the readers of *RP* were, especially because many copies were sold through bookshops. I think they were not so much professionally engaged with philosophy, but perhaps from outside the academy, or in other disciplines. Interdisciplinarity interests were characteristic of the left at that time. We attended one another's conferences. (For example, John Mepham and I were active in the Conference of Socialist Economists.) It was disappointing we never achieved much penetration in the US.

In the early days, the layout of the journal would be rotated between editors in Kent, Sussex and London. My floor in Lewes, and Mepham's in Hove, would be awash with Letraset etc. I recall John's young son wanted to help. Eventually a more professional layout was negotiated with specialist production editors from Russell Press. One interesting feature of *RP* in the early years was that the whole collective never appeared on the mast-head. Instead, the editors listed in each issue included only those present at the meeting to decide (on the basis of internal referees' reports) what was to go in that issue, thereby taking responsibility for its particular content.

I regard *RP* as a great success, as it made space for philosophers who were radical to engage not only with each other but with a wider constituency. It is worth noting the existence of an off-shoot of *RP*, namely the founding of Marx and Philosophy by ex-*RP* editors (myself, Sean Sayers, Joe McCarney, together with Andrew Chitty) to provide a space for specifically Marx scholarship, although still under the general rubric of philosophy.

Kate Soper, 1974–1998

RP was one of several publications to emerge in response to the student movements of the 1960s and their calls for less insular and conservative approaches in the academy. Its aims were multiple and not always easily reconcilable. Certainly, it wanted to transform philosophy teaching in Britain, to redefine and broaden its remit, exposing in the process the limited and a-historical stance of the Anglo-American analytic tradition and engaging with more continental philosophy. It also aimed to provide philosophers, and intellectuals more generally, with a higher public profile, more akin to that of their continental counterparts. At the same time, it adhered to Marx's view that philosophy's role was to change rather than merely contemplate the world, a position deemed absurdly presumptuous by mainstream opponents, but one that inspired a heady engagement with ideas among those more sympathetic, and for which there seems little equivalent today.

The journal was initially produced and distributed by its editorial collective and their friends – and using methods that by today's digital standards were primitive. I remember day-long sessions in editors' houses, where we did the lay-out and pasting up. Errors had to be corrected with bits of Letraset delicately tweezered into place. Illustration was pretty ad hoc. (The images, for example, of the article in issue 11 on 'Peter Rabbit and the Grundrisse' were extracted – causing some discontent – from my three year old's Beatrix Potter books). The first issues were thought too expensive at 35 pence each. But they quickly sold out and *RP* soon became a bestseller in the philosophy magazine market.

During the first two *RP* decades, and in the context of the seemingly permanent fixture of the Cold War, left theory was preoccupied with the issue of who makes history and the role of human agency in it. Within *RP*, this sparked the early disputes between a pro-Althusserian, anti-humanist reading of Marx and the socialist humanism of those retaining allegiance to 'early' Marx and the theory of alienation. Subsequently, it was played out in the opposition between structuralist and phenomenological approaches, and was a still lingering concern of the later post-structuralist critiques.

By the 1980s, feminism had become a major influence, there was more writing on gender and identity politics, and on ecological issues. Aesthetics and cultural politics also began to figure more prominently in *RP*'s pages, and many articles assumed a more scholarly –

sometimes even quite scholastic – tone. Some of the political edge was lost in the process, but a flexibility of coverage in the journal has almost certainly been essential to its extraordinary longevity. And the forms of political expression in the earliest issues were, in any case, often crude and contestable in their claims.

That said, one has to applaud the initiative of its founding editors, the energy and imagination they brought to the project, their commitment to a collective ethos and their independence from commercial patronage or sponsorship. It is difficult now to convey what it was like to be involved in the intellectual ferment of that period, with the importance it attached to critical thinking, its confidence in the power of ideas to shape the future, the solidarities and counter-cultural networks it generated, its relative disengagement from more instrumental and careerist concerns. When I think back to the time when the *RP* groups flourished throughout the country, when *RP* conferences were attended by hundreds and addressed by academics without a thought for how this would enhance their research profile or university promotion, I can't help but lament its passing. The world now is arguably more dangerous and unequal than ever before: in many ways it has changed for the worst, and our optimism has proved – at least to date – unfounded. But *RP* did transform the philosophical climate in this country, and it has managed, against the odds and thanks to the efforts of its successive editorial teams, to continue to shape the philosophical culture of our times. May it continue to continue. I wish it all the best for the next half century.

Diana Coole, 1996–2002

I'd published an article in *RP* in 1996, entitled 'Is Class a Difference that Makes a Difference?' (*RP* 77), and perhaps that was the catalyst for inviting me to join, although I was also the beneficiary of a decision to expand. When my name first appeared on the contents page, in issue 81, I was one of 17 editors, whereas a year earlier there had only been eight.

I remember feeling incredibly honoured, but also a little intimidated, by the invitation to join some of the 1990s' most provocative theorists. In 1996 the group included the likes of Peter Dews, Gregory Elliott, Jean Grimshaw, Peter Osborne and Kate Soper, all of whom were publishing important books in the field. *RP*'s signature, as a socialist and feminist journal, was still relatively straightforward in those days. It spoke not only to a wide, progressive audience, but also to a substantial section of academic social scientists for whom Marxist and (second wave) feminist approaches still retained theoretical primacy. Psychoanalysis was another important aspect of our repertoire. During my tenure, such theoretical identifiers became more complicated and contested, due especially to critiques from poststructuralism and critical race theory that we felt compelled to accommodate.

I'd moved from teaching at Leeds University to Queen Mary during 1996, so it felt apt to join a London-based group that held its meetings in Fitzrovia. We met at the Fitzroy Tavern, a venue redolent of Bohemian lifestyles and a former haunt of writers such as Orwell, Woolf, Shaw and Dylan Thomas. We'd assemble downstairs, monthly, on Saturday mornings before the day's drinkers arrived. Smoking in pubs was still legal and our discussions were accompanied by the smell of smoke and beer, and the clatter of barrels and hoovers. In summer we'd adjourn to tables outside on Windmill Street.

The enlarged collective was actually quite unwieldy, but we prided ourselves in managing the entire output ourselves and that required all hands on deck. The production process was utterly different from the publisher-based, profit-oriented, anonymous peer review, REF-driven practices of contemporary academic journals. Peter Osborne took it upon himself to design each issue and we often used our own photos to avoid copyright costs. We took it in turn to act as Issue Editor, which would start with making a grid for assigning reading responsibilities to members (we only occasionally sent things out for review). A number of people – maybe five – would be chosen to report on each submission and since there were invariably several experts for any given topic, our discussions about the merits of each piece would be long and profound. I remember those editorial sessions as a master class in continental philosophy. As a rule, everyone looked at all the submissions in advance so they could join in, but woe betide anyone who didn't have an arguable opinion on an article they'd been allocated.

It was not, in fact, uncommon for every submission to falter before our critical scrutiny and then we'd find ourselves without sufficient material for the next issue. Fortunately, the collective was well connected, so our default would either be to commission pieces or to translate some ourselves, usually from French. In any case, we only included three actual articles as such per issue, the rest comprising of (often in-house) book reviews, reports on special symposia or papers derived from *RP*'s annual conferences.

The conferences were an important part of our calendar, both for providing copy and for advertising the journal to wider audiences. We spent ages planning them and choosing the year's topic. They were always splendid events, well attended thanks to casts of illustrious speakers who generated lively discussions. I remember speaking on one such occasion, in 1996, when the conference was held at SOAS. I joined several leading members of the Women's Movement who reminisced about their roles in organising the second wave and reflected on its enduring challenges. My contribution, 'Feminism without Nostalgia', was published alongside the others the following year (*RP* 83).

I left the collective in 2002, partly in recognition of the importance for a collective to refresh itself periodically, but also, perhaps, as a result of feeling less attuned to the more cultural, aesthetic direction the journal was taking. My final piece in the journal, 'Thinking Politically with Merleau-Ponty', was published in 2001 (*RP* 108), and my name appeared on the content's page for the last time in issue 112.

I still read *RP* and I continued to attend the annual conferences for many years, gratified to find them often being housed at Birkbeck (where I'd moved in 2004, to a department also founded in 1972). It's exactly 20 years since I left the collective and I still feel incredibly privileged to have been involved with a journal that's played a unique role in framing essential debates over a turbulent half century. Nonetheless, those days back in the late '90s now feel like the tail end of an era, when meeting for hours in dingy rooms to discuss the most profound ideas of the day still felt as if it might help change the world.

Stella Sandford, 1996–2016

In what sense is radical philosophy feminist and feminist philosophy radical?

When I joined the *Radical Philosophy* editorial collective in 1996 it had a strong feminist identity. In my experience this had as much to do with the conduct of editorial meetings and the ethos of the collective as it did with support for feminist philosophy more specifically. When I joined I was a PhD student. There were still relatively few women employed in philosophy departments in universities in the UK at that time. At university, as an MA student, I had been part of a feminist reading group that was also effectively a consciousness-raising group – or at least it was for me. We talked about male dominance in the classroom, the subtle and more overt ways in which male students belittled and tried to silence the women in the classroom, and the marginalisation of feminist concerns in the classroom and on syllabuses. You had to constantly argue for feminist perspectives to be taken into account in institutional contexts. In the *RP* editorial meetings it was different. It was taken for granted that such perspectives must and should be taken into account. So I think *RP* was then and is now feminist in a quite general sense.

If you look at the *RP* 'Founding Statement' (*RP* 1), every aim aligns with the demands of feminist philosophy, although feminism isn't mentioned there. The statement is about changing the world, making philosophy more inclusive, challenging disciplinary divisions, connecting philosophy to classroom politics, challenging the then-prevailing (and perhaps still dominant) narrow conception of philosophy in the universities. Feminist philosophy has always made these same demands. The hostility towards feminist philosophy in the UK, in the 1970s and '80s in particular, can probably be explained by the fact that feminist philosophy made these criticisms of philosophy and demanded – and tried to enact – these changes in the discipline. Radical feminist philosophy wasn't demanding a seat at the table with the same menu and it wasn't just about how women were treated or whether the climate was hospitable (which it wasn't). It was about fundamental challenges to the very conception of the discipline. Radical feminist philosophy and feminist theory more generally is critical theory – Kate Soper was arguing that clearly in the late 1980s. Basically, you couldn't be a radical philosopher and exclude feminist philosophy – it just wouldn't make sense.

How would you characterise RP*'s conception of feminist philosophy?*

I don't know if *RP* has ever really had a particular conception of feminist philosophy – certainly not as a kind of subfield of philosophy. That idea – feminist philosophy as a subfield – contradicts the idea that the challenge of feminist philosophy goes to the heart of the discipline. But actually it is also the idea of 'the discipline' itself that is the problem. The problem is that philosophy is reduced to an *academic* discipline. To criticise this doesn't mean to say that everything is philosophy; it's not that philosophy is the intellectual night in which all cows are black. Feminist philosophy is philosophy done from a feminist standpoint or taking into account feminist concerns, not philosophy with a particular subject matter. Of course it is often going to be about gender oppression but it is striking how much of the early feminist philosophy in *RP* was also about ecology and the environment. But all radical philosophy must be feminist philosophy, or it is not radical. This is the basic point that socialist feminists and Marxist feminists were making from the beginning of the twentieth century – you don't get radical anything without feminism. And it isn't a point about inclusion. It's a point about the inadequacy of any radical or critical analysis that can't take feminism into account. Now we can see (which most white philosophers didn't see then and probably many don't see now) that there is also no radical theory that isn't alive to the legacies of imperial and colonial histories, and that can't take critical race theories into account. But looking back it has to be admitted that the feminist philosophy in *RP* has been overwhelmingly white feminist philosophy. It wasn't until the past few years that any attention has seriously been paid to addressing that. We should have done better in that regard.

Can you comment on the contribution feminist philosophers have made to the journal's output and ethos since it was founded? And do you think the journal has had an impact on feminist philosophy in the UK, and UK philosophy more generally?

I think it is fair to say that in the 1970s *RP* was the only philosophy journal in the UK committed to feminist philosophy. The UK Society for Women in Philosophy (SWIP) was formally founded in 1989 and based on informal networks in philosophy that had been around since the 1970s, but their journal – The Women's Philosophy Review – was first published in 1993 (succeeding the Women in Philosophy Newsletter, also begun in 1989). For a good while the memberships of the SWIP executive committee and the *RP* editorial collective overlapped, with different people (myself included) at different times part of both. Jean Grimshaw and Alison Assiter were founding members of SWIP while they were members of the *RP* collective. There were few articles by women in *RP* until the early 1980s, although Kate Soper's, Joanna Hodge's and Jean Grimshaw's names appeared regularly in commentary and reviews sections from the beginning. The first special issue (I think there have only ever been three special issues) was *RP* 34 (Summer 1983) called 'Women, Gender and Philosophy'. After that, from issues 35 to 70 (roughly 1983-1996) it is remarkable that there is almost always feminist content in every issue. There was no other general philosophy journal of which this was true, and even now it is only true of journals like *Hypatia* that are dedicated to feminist philosophy. From *RP* 61 (Summer 1992) *RP* bears the subtitle 'A Journal of Socialist and Feminist Philosophy'. So there was definitely a distinct feminist bulge in *RP* in this period, and given that there were very few places where people could publish feminist philosophy it did play a significant role in promoting feminist philosophy in the UK. This was also due to the influence of prominent feminists who were not part of the collective but were close to people (men) who were. Lynne Segal, for example, was never a member of *RP* but is an important part of its history and was influential in its increasing feminist orientation. Did this have an effect on philosophy more generally? That is difficult to say. Certainly some feminist philosophy is more accepted now. But what kind of feminist philosophy is acceptable to the mainstream? Is it the kind of radical feminist philosophy that we were talking about earlier? I fear not.

Was there a clear collective sense of the kind of work you wanted to publish during your involvement with the journal?

In the late 1990s and early 2000s there were often disputes – sometimes quite angry arguments – in editorial meetings about whether particular submissions ought to be published. To be honest, by the mid-2000s, I think a lot of the time we knew what kind of thing we wanted to publish but people weren't writing it. Or, if they were writing it, there was less and less connection with philosophical analysis, because there was less and less philosophical work engaged with the kind of political questions *RP* wanted to ask. I'm afraid this is true also of feminist philosophy.

By the time I left the collective most of the journal content was commissioned; we were publishing very few 'cold' submissions. This was partly due to the increasing conservatism of research in universities in the UK. I mean, the RAE (now called the REF) (which Sean Sayers criticised back in *RP* 83, 1997) seemed to be leading people to be pressured into publishing in the 'right' journals, and *RP* was very definitely the 'wrong' journal in this respect. Journals began to be 'ranked' more or less officially, and people were – they still are – pressured by their institutions to publish in the high-ranking journals.

The greatest irony is that *RP* has probably always had a far greater readership (by which I mean people actually reading the journal, not necessarily distribution) than any other contemporary philosophical journal. If you want people to actually read your work, publish in *RP*. If you want institutionally-approved kudos and mainstream legitimation, go elsewhere.

You were a member of the editorial collective from 1996 to 2016. Can you recall any particularly memorable situations from this period?

For me the 1998 conference on 'Philosophy and Race' is particularly memorable. Charles Mills was one of the speakers. I confess that at the time I didn't realise quite what a big deal that was, even though I invited him. I talked to him about the murder of Stephen Lawrence (in 1993) and he helped me to understand how and why it was so important that Doreen Lawrence had become a public figure in the UK. We published a special issue on 'Philosophy and Race' (*RP* 95, May/June 1999) with some papers from the conference. At the conference Isaac Julien called me out about the special issue. *Screen* had published what they called 'The Last Special Issue on Race' in 1988 (Vol. 29, no. 4) in which he and Kobena Mercer had described it 'as a rejoinder to critical discourses in which the subject of race and ethnicity is still placed on the margins conceptually, despite the acknowledgement of such issues indicated by the proliferation of "special issues" on race in film, media and literary journals'. I accept the point, but the fact was that, to my knowledge, there had been *no* special issues on *philosophy* and race in the UK up to that time. Philosophy was – still is – so very far behind in the humanities and the social sciences when it came to understanding its own implication in histories of colonialism and racism, and how its white-washed view of its own history perpetuates this.

But honestly, the whole period was absolutely formative for me. I saw what a collective intellectual project was for the first time which I had never previously seen in my university experience. Or perhaps it allowed me to recognise collective intellectual projects when I saw them, because many of the philosophy departments in the polytechnics had something of that about them in the 1980s and 1990s, and certainly that was how a bunch of my colleagues saw things at the Centre for Research in Modern European Philosophy at Middlesex University and now at Kingston University. *RP* was a fantastic mixture of intellectual work and sociality. We had meetings in a downstairs room of a pub in Bloomsbury and afterwards we went up to the pub and often continued there for hours. It was really very, very enjoyable, and that was not a peripheral aspect of it, it was part of the collectivity itself. I have to mention that I didn't have children then, because once childcare became an issue sociality suffered. This aspect of social reproduction is still one of the biggest issues for feminist politics. Crèches can be great but not all children are happy to be left for a day with adults they have never met before. Crèches are an ad hoc solution to a problem whose resolution requires far greater social change. One time I had to bring the children with me to a meeting, and afterwards we had dinner with members of the collective in an Italian restaurant. It was really good. If an intellectual organisation can't accommodate children when it needs to, it is not radical.

What do you consider RP*'s project to be, and to what extent do you consider it to have succeeded?*
RP's project has probably changed. When I joined I was fully on board with the project as I understood it then to be: to challenge narrow disciplinary conceptions of philosophy, to make explicit the political stakes in all philosophy, to render philosophy relevant and useful to radical political projects (especially for me, at that time, feminist political projects). It definitely succeeded in providing an alternative to the existing, mostly conservative philosophy journals. It definitely succeeded with its content – the archive is extraordinary. I think *RP* succeeded on its own terms. But it alone could not face down the institutional and national policy changes in the UK that have tended to render philosophy in the universities more homogenous (bye, bye continental philosophy…), more subject to market imperatives, and more abjectly in thrall to making a mark in ever more shallow, popular forms and to having 'impact' as it is defined by Tory governments (which doesn't stop Tory governments hating it more and more anyway). In this sense *la lutte continue*.

Philosophy as cultural form
The histories of *Radical Philosophy*
Interview with Peter Osborne

Peter Osborne is the longest serving editor in Radical Philosophy's *history. He joined the editorial collective in 1983 and was involved in the publication of 168 issues until he stood down as an editor in 2016. Over these four decades he undoubtedly did more than any other member of* RP *to define the journal's direction and identity. He is Director of the Centre for Research in Modern European Philosophy at Kingston University in London and is the author of* The Politics of Time *(1995),* Philosophy in Cultural Theory *(2000),* Anywhere or Not At All: Philosophy of Contemporary Art *(2013),* The Postconceptual Condition *(2018), and* Crisis as Form *(2022). Peter was interviewed for the fiftieth anniversary of* RP *by David Cunningham, a member of the editorial collective since 2003. The conversation took place in London in September 2022.*

David Cunningham: What was the intellectual context that *Radical Philosophy* sought to intervene in when you joined in the early 1980s, especially, but not only, with respect to philosophy? Had this changed in the period since the journal's founding in 1972?

Peter Osborne: It seemed to be changing around the time I joined. Looking over the earlier issues, one could see that in the first eight to ten years *RP* was largely oriented towards the politics of the student movement and the struggle to change – to expand – university curricula. By the early 1980s, it was becoming more focused on the details of theoretical debates and less immediately connected to student politics, which was on the wane. I first encountered *RP* when I was an undergraduate student at Bristol in the late 1970s. I remember going to a meeting of the local group there towards the end of my first year, in 1977. By 1983 what had begun as debates about the university – including getting Hegel, Sartre and Marx onto syllabuses in philosophy departments – had become more about issues internal to Marxism, and the Marxist critique of 1960s and '70s French philosophy in particular. There was also a fairly intense ongoing concern with the Marx-Hegel relation throughout the 1980s, in the work of people like Sean Sayers, Chris Arthur and Joe McCarney, and to a lesser extent myself. That fed into the discussions about 'science' and 'dialectics' that had begun earlier as an effect of Althusserianism. The first article I wrote for *RP*, just before I became an editor, was on Gillian Rose's *Hegel Contra Sociology*.

The other thing that *RP* was doing in the 1970s and early '80s was introducing the work of contemporary European thinkers. The translations of Goldmann (1972), Rancière (1974) and Foucault (1976), and the introductions to Althusser (1973), Derrida (1979) and Lacan (1982) were very early pieces of and on their work in English – especially in a philosophical context, where it took another thirty years for these figures to become recognised.

DC: What was the main readership for the journal in this period?

PO: It's hard to be sure, but if at the outset *RP* was principally read by graduate students and young left-wing academics in philosophy departments, by the early '80s it was increasingly being read by academics working in the social sciences – sociology, in particular, which was the still-growing radical discipline of the day, since it was the only one outside economics which taught Marx. *RP* was also beginning to become more concerned with what in the 1990s became called 'continental philosophy', which was then still primarily taught in English departments as a part of literary theory, although we didn't use the term 'continental philosophy' in *RP* back then.

DC: Was this also about a changing relationship of the journal to analytical philosophy? It's notable that in the first decade you've got quite a few critical engagements with, say, Popper and Russell, Austin and Searle. This gradually disappears. Indeed, there's an editorial from Jonathan Rée in issue 20 from 1978 that bemoans precisely this waning engagement with what he calls 'British philosophy'.

PO: Yes, Jonathan was very bound up with the idea of 'British philosophy' – which is actually a much wider (as well as a much more restricted) category than 'analytical philosophy' – all the way through to the eventual publication of his 2019 historical doorstopper, *Witcraft: The Invention of Philosophy in English*. I had a rather less respectful idea of it, as you can see in my *RP* 114 review of Baggini and Strangroom's *New British Philosophy* of 2002: 'The Erotics of Deference'.

Most of the earliest members of the *RP* collective were trained in analytical philosophy (as I was myself, slightly later on) whilst also being on the left politically. But they didn't see much of a tension between analytical philosophy per se, as a distinctive approach to philosophical argument (and an exclusionary attitude to other philosophical approaches), and socialist intellectual traditions. Keith Graham, for example, who was my first tutor at Bristol in 1976, wrote a critique of J. L. Austin's version of ordinary language philosophy, which remained almost wholly within the analytical idiom. In fact, at my very first tutorial at Bristol, in reaction to a reference to Sartre in my essay, he patiently explained to me that I would be very ill-advised to continue reading Sartre, since his work had nothing in common with what was thought of and practiced as 'philosophy' in Britain. He wasn't an editor of *RP*, but he was close to members of the collective and he appears in the 'Local Sellers' lists, for Bristol, in the early issues. Many of the early editors had done the BPhil at Oxford and were working at what were then the new universities of the 1960s, such as Kent, Sussex and Essex, or the new polytechnics of the early 1970s, such as Middlesex and North London, where there had been a mass of new jobs in philosophy.

This was well before the association of any of these philosophy departments with what became known as 'continental philosophy'. They taught individual figures from within that canon, but it wasn't coded as 'continental philosophy' until the late 1980s; and that was predominantly a US genre, associated with the reception of Husserlian phenomenology, Heideggerianism, Derrida and Levinas, and so on. With the exception of Derrida, that is a deeply conservative tradition in many ways. It was imported into Essex and Warwick in the UK. Marx, for example, was never part of the canon of continental philosophy, because Marx wasn't considered a philosopher at that time. Nor were the Frankfurt School. A lot of things got re-coded in the early 1990s, at the point at which continental philosophy was emerging as the anti-analytical genre. This was the period when Jonathan Rée and I established the Centre for Research in Modern European Philosophy (CRMEP) in 1995 at Middlesex University, which was so named precisely to distinguish it from the idea of continental philosophy. For Jonathan, this was in order to incorporate analytical positions viewed from the standpoint of their European beginnings. His idea was that someone like Wittgenstein was a modern European philosopher; analytical philosophy was an offshoot of modern European philosophy. That was connected to his desire to stay in touch with the mainstream but to be dissident within it. I was more concerned to use the broader inclusivity of the term to include figures like Marx and Benjamin in the philosophical field.

DC: Was this true of *Radical Philosophy* also?

PO: Well, at that point, the journal had already largely lost touch with analytical philosophy. The project of relating critically to British mainstream philosophy had ebbed away. And one should not underestimate the hostility of the analytical philosophical community. As I said, *RP* was initially based at the so-called new universities of the 1960s, and in some of the polytechnics. Then, in 1992 there was a second round of 'new universities', when the polytechnics became universities. The philosophy departments in those post-92 universities never really had much of a relation to the mainstream (they weren't generally staffed by people who had done the BPhil at Oxford with Ryle). The institutional culture of the polytechnics related more to adult education – there were still a lot of so-called 'mature' students there in those days. Those of my generation who were awarded PhDs in the 1980s, when there were almost no jobs in philosophy, had often worked in adult education colleges. I taught at Camden Working Men's College and Morley College, for example, before Middlesex Polytechnic. Interestingly, that connected

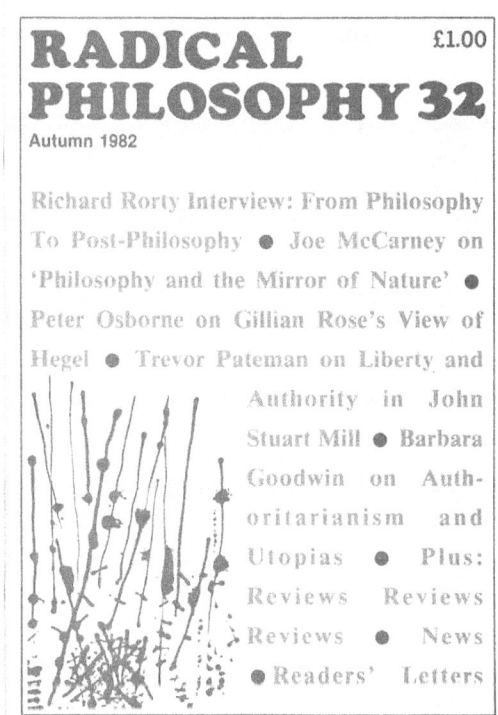

us, pedagogically, to the history of cultural studies in Britain: Raymond Williams and E. P. Thompson in the 1950s. This provided a kind of organic connection between the expanding polytechnics of the 1980s (soon to be the new universities of the 1990s) and organisations like History Workshop and the early cultural studies journals, as well as to *Feminist Review*, to which *RP* became more connected in the 1980s, through common membership of the Socialist Society.

DC: How was *RP* editorially organised and produced when you joined? Was there a clear collective sense of the kind of work that the editors wanted to publish?

PO: For the first 5 or 6 years that I was involved, and for the 10 years before that, there wasn't really an *editorial* project at all. Indeed, for the first 10 years there wasn't much actual editing. There was a sense that the author's text was sacrosanct. Nobody messed with other people's sentences. What the author submitted was what was published. Editing was opposed because of a view that it was in some sense anti-democratic. This was the libertarian side of the radical democratic aspect of the student movement. My view though was always that, if it's not a movement journal as such, you have to have a more critically intellectually-based editorial policy, you have to commission, and you have to make each issue make sense, structurally, as a cultural form.

You need to remember that, in its earliest years, *RP* had no fixed membership, no editorial collective that was continuous between issues. The idea was that the time and place of a meeting would be advertised and anyone who turned up would be part of the group that would edit the next issue and would decide what would go in that issue. Clearly, there was a continuity in the sense that various people continued to turn up regularly – founding members like Richard Norman, Tony Skillen, Sean Sayers (the Kent group), Chris Arthur and Jonathan Rée.

When I joined *RP* it didn't really have an editorial history; it just had a publishing history. And publishing histories are over-determined by production technologies (the forms of setting and printing) and by the modes of distribution (initially, primarily, sales via local groups). The real material history of *Radical Philosophy* is the history of the changes in the technologies of production, of which there have been four or five distinct ones during its lifetime, and in the modes of distribution of the journal. To begin with, the journal was sold on campuses by student groups. You bought your copy from the *RP* representative on campus. It didn't really have a commercial existence apart from one or two left-wing bookshops. There was no distributor other than a member of the collective driving up with their car to somewhere with a bunch of issues in the boot. That changed as *RP* became more subscription-based. And we started to sell in bookshops through Central Books. That also changed the economics of the journal, because the journal had no real distribution costs before then. Because distributors take 55% of your cover price, you have to become more expensive in order to be able to pay the printer. Until the mid-1990s, the journal only published three issues a year, which meant the collective only met as a whole about three, or exceptionally four, times annually. So, fundamental changes in the journal, like moving to six issues a year – which I proposed and which meant a much a bigger commitment on the part of editors – were driven partly by the need to increase subscription prices because bookshop distributors took 55%. We had to double the price because we had to get more income. So, we doubled the number of issues primarily in order that the subs price could double, while the price of each individual issue remained relatively cheap, because subs cost less than bookshop sales. It was also my view that we couldn't have an effective cultural impact if we didn't come out more often.

DC: How much is this about the changing nature, more generally, of the journal, or the magazine, as itself a cultural form?

PO: Well, *RP* began as a sort of Xerox-style magazine and became a kind of magazine-y journal. The magazine-y side – and especially the images and the occasional sardonic humour – stopped it from becoming too academic and maintained its 'para-academic' status. That was very self-conscious. The other thing was the *Radical Philosophy* conferences, because the conferences were never really philosophy conferences as such. Even when they were occasionally more explicitly philosophical in topic, they were always quite broadly politically and culturally defined, and the majority of speakers were generally not in philosophy departments. So, the conference represented the disciplinary plurality of the writers and readers more than it did 'philosophy', and certainly more than academic philosophy in the UK.

As the connection to the student movement and the activist side diminished, we became more professionalised in relation to production and distribution. The main things that kept *RP* more like a magazine, as opposed to an academic journal, was the way we used images. This was connected to the earlier history of the journal, the way that situationist-style *détournements* of cartoons were used in the first few years, for example. But in the 1990s and 2000s this became defined instead by amateuristic, photo-conceptualist forms of irony, so that both the placement of images and the titling of reviews became a kind of counter-discourse to the journal's own academicism. Again, I was very self-conscious about that, at the point of production, although it was never explicitly discussed by the collective.

The politics of radical philosophy

DC: How then did the content and readership of the journal change in the late '80s and '90s?

PO: It followed the larger political context. If you look at what was new in the journal in the late '80s and early '90s, in terms of content, it was the introduction of feminism into philosophy, and also ecology, as represented on the collective by people like Kate Soper, Ted Benton and Andrew Collier. There were various different moments in the course of the late '80s and early '90s, when there were proposals for editorial changes to the journal which were conflictual, and some people left after each of those, including Ted. This relates to the introduction of the subtitle of the journal. From the late '80s to around 1993 when it was introduced, there were debates about whether the journal should have a subtitle. These began in a slightly comical way, from my point of view, when Joe McCarney proposed (I assumed ironically but perhaps not) that *Radical Philosophy* should be subtitled 'The Journal of Left Hegelianism'. This seemed, auto-destructively, to restrict the range of interests represented by the journal to the point of annihilation! But it introduced a debate about subtitles. What then happened was that *History Workshop*, which had been subtitled 'A Journal of Socialist and Feminist Historians', removed their subtitle when they went from being self-published to becoming published by Routledge. So, I proposed that we become 'The Journal of Socialist and Feminist Philosophy', as a kind of ironic counter-move to what I took to be *History Workshop*'s concession to a growing anti-Marxism after 1989. But this led to inevitable debates. So, it was argued, for example, why weren't we a Journal of Socialist, Feminist *and* Ecological Philosophy? At which point the list of potential subtitles started to multiply, imaginarily, and it became clear that we couldn't do this multiplication: so we stuck with 'Socialist and Feminist Philosophy'. Another point here was to put pressure on ourselves to maintain a regular feminist content (and to encourage such submissions), as the initial wave of feminist material had begun to break.

DC: Were there any objections to it being 'socialist' rather than 'communist'?

PO: No. None of the collective had historical ties to the Communist Party of Great Britain. Socialism was understood as a strong position between organised Marxist parties, on the one hand, and the Labour Party, on the other. It's a position that has, unfortunately, largely disappeared. Once Communism no longer had an 'actually existing' variant and became an Idea, then philosophers started to like it, right? But that was a bit later. While it was an organisational practice, there wasn't so much connection.

DC: Did the broader relationship between intellectual work and political forms – institutional or otherwise – alter significantly during this period?

PO: The major change happened in the 1990s. In the mid-1980s, supported by municipal socialism and the trade unions, there were still independent political cultures in Britain, served by independent left bookshops. Collet's in Charing Cross Road, which went bankrupt and closed in 1993, for example, would take 100 copies of each issue of *Radical Philosophy* in the early eighties; and Compendium Books in Camden, which survived until 2000, would take a pile too. [See Philip Derbyshire's obituary for the Compendium Bookshop in *RP* 105 (2001).] Institutionally, too, in the 1980s, *Radical Philosophy* was one of the journals that was connected to the Socialist Society, which was founded by Raymond Williams. The Socialist Society was a non-Trostkyist, left of the Labour Party, extra-parliamentary organisational space. So, it was non-sectarian – it wasn't involved with the SWP or the IMG [International Marxist Group], or any of the Trotskyist groups, but it also wasn't affiliated with Labour, although it included some left-wing Labour MPs. It was where many of the Bennites went after Tony Benn lost the Labour Deputy Leadership contest in 1981. And it became more generally politically significant because it became a founder of the Chesterfield conferences – Chesterfield was Tony Benn's parliamentary constituency – and it was connected to the GLC under Ken Livingstone and to the Campaign Group of Labour left MPs. So, in the late 1980s we used to have our Socialist Society meetings in the GLC building, with *RP*, *Feminist Review*, *Capital and Class*, *History Workshop*, and so on – all these self-produced, self-published journals.

The first big Chesterfield conference, I think, was October '87, because it took place during so-called Black Monday, when the stock market crashed. It happened during the conference, and John Ross, who was economic advisor to Livingstone at the time, suddenly got up and made a preposterous speech about how it was the end of capitalism because of the collapse of the stock market. That was the point at which we realised that actually there were still some quite old-school Trotskyists involved in the Labour left.

DC: Were members of the collective participating in, and speaking at, these kinds of events?

PO: Well, some of us were – I was, Gregory Elliott was, Kate Soper was. Greg and I wrote for the Socialist Society journal, which later became *Red Pepper*. We didn't write about politics so much in *RP* at that time. There were a lot of debates around, for example, the neo-constitutionalism of the people around *New Left Review* who were hoping to base an alternative left politics of human rights on the Czech Charter 77 movement and on this idea that, for progressive politics to develop in Britain, you have to have a written constitution. Anthony Barnett was the main purveyor of this position. Greg and I were very much against that kind of institutional formalism, at the time, and we co-wrote some things about it.

More generally though, I should repeat: at that point *Radical Philosophy* was not a politically-defined space in an everyday political sense. It was a space in which people who shared a very broad left political position – left of the Labour Party – wrote intellectual and quasi-academic pieces. *RP* was not a place in which it was really considered appropriate to write directly political things, because the journal didn't want to have a political line on issues on which there were disagreements on the left. Later, in the 1990s, we introduced the Commentary section, which was coded as a different kind of writing – a kind of intellectual journalism or opinion piece – which didn't need to be so philosophical. But this also wasn't like an 'editorial', in the sense that it didn't have to represent anything like an editorial position of the collective. So, from the 1990s onwards, the journal evolved towards a structure which was made up of a Commentary, Articles, Interviews, Reviews, News, which were much more structurally differentiated, editorially, than in the early years of the journal.

Later, *RP* gradually became less philosophical. Being more political was a way of replacing the philosophy, but at the same time, as it became more directly political, it also became more academic. So, in a way, the journal was more political in later years, but also less political in the sense that it was actually more academic.

This is partly a history of the collapse of intellectual into academic work. That became a major problem for the journal. For the first maybe 20 years, nobody wrote in *Radical Philosophy* because it might further their career. Later, there was a period when people used to submit articles that they wanted to enter into the REF or whatever, and write them in such a way that they could do this. So, there was a pressure for academicisation. The other thing, of course, is that UK academia has completely changed in the last 20 years. It has become far harder to find people who will commit the necessary amount of free time to this enterprise in a way that is intellectually related to their academic work but also separate from it. People either wanted to see it as part of their academic work, and think of it more as an academic journal, or they didn't want to, or couldn't, spend the time, the free labour. Self-published journals consume a huge amount of free labour from their collectives; and it can also become very unequally distributed within these collectives, for all their formal 'collective' status. The demands made on staff time by academic jobs – the incredible increase in 'productivity', in a crude economic sense – has rocketed in the last two decades.

The changes in *RP* were also connected to the change in the institutional spaces available outside the university. Whereas there was first the student movement, and then cultural and intellectual left spaces like that of the Socialist Society, Blairite hegemony of Labour kind of closed down these left intellectual political spaces, which had often been generated by anti-Thatcherism, and energised by that opposition, which was then taken away. The character of the opposition to Blairism was different because it was more internal to a broad coding of the left. That's the point really, in the late 1990s, that *RP* started to relate more systematically to, for example, *art* institutions. There was a classical displacement from politics to art spaces. The ICA was really important in the late '80s and early '90s as an intellectual space for talks and conferences in London – focused mostly on French philosophy, but for non-philosophers – and *RP* took up the idea behind such programmes.

DC: How far was this connected to the disciplinary construction of the academy itself? I'm thinking of the ways in which, say, literature or art departments in universities increasingly became homes for people who wanted to write books about Foucault or Derrida, or indeed Marx, but who couldn't do so from institutional spaces coded as 'philosophy'. Because the other thing that changes in the 1990s – maybe already in the '80s – and which is partly connected to the emergence of continental philosophy as a genre, is the growing number of people trained or part-trained in philosophy, for whom there were increasingly no jobs in actual philosophy departments. So, these people ended up teaching in literature departments, or in art, sociology, cultural studies, politics departments, and so on. If you look at the changes in the make-up of the *RP* collective over time, at the beginning almost everybody is working in a philosophy department, but by the 2000s there's only a handful teaching philosophy as such.

PO: Well, literature has certainly become a lot less hospitable a place for that, with the removal of 'theory' from English departments – which began in America actually at the end of the '90s and took a little while to travel over to the UK – and a return to a combination of aesthetic discourse and literary history. The relation to the art world is a bit different, because in a way we were using their *spaces* in order to maintain a public-facing discourse that wasn't wholly academic – not their discourses. Theory in the art world largely became a belated version of the serial importation of French thinkers – with a ten-year time lag – beginning with Foucault, and then Derrida and Levinas, moving on to Deleuze and then Badiou, Rancière, and now to Latour. Maybe it's terminating in Latour … It's true that the way that French philosophers got into English was by being read in literature departments and then in the art world. But *RP* wanted to provide a more critical and philosophically nuanced counter to those readings; to perform a more serious educative function.

DC: Coming back to the loss of independent bookshops and of cultural and intellectual left spaces like the Socialist Society, how did *Radical Philosophy* continue to be independently published after the 1990s, when so many other self-produced journals set up in the same period either simply stopped or went to commercial publishers?

PO: In terms of bookshops, we did ok for a while through extending sales venues, to Waterstones in the UK and through selling in art spaces like Tate Modern, the Serpentine and the ICA. But then bookshop policies changed, so Waterstones stopped having interesting individual magazine sections in their stores, the ICA became a less political space, and the Tate Modern bookshop is now basically only for children. The subscriptions market was also increasingly difficult. We never really made much money from individual subscriptions –

certainly when we were shipping copies to the States, from which we made no money – but we made money from library subs. However, the peculiarity of library subs – and this takes us back to the history of the journal – is that university libraries tend to be departmentally organised, which means you have to get ordered by someone in the philosophy department. And philosophy departments generally weren't going to order *Radical Philosophy*, after the 1970s! So, it was hard to increase these. At the same time, once we had a website, we had the question of how are we going to relate the subs model to what appears online? The result was that we had to use the website for 'tasters' of new content and then only open up more of the website once a new issue was published. Otherwise, we couldn't sell the subs. At the end of series 1 with issue 200 in 2016, we were still, economically, wholly viable – in fact, more so than ever before – but solely through raising the price of the institutional library subs. The main problem was whether or not you want to have a paywall. The more things were made available on the web, the more it seemed hard not to make *RP* generally available, but doing so would have destroyed the economic model of the journal. This wasn't the reason Series 1 of the journal came to end in 2016, though; that was about the lack of collective commitment to the amount of free labour required at the time.

DC: How would you periodise the years during which you were involved with *RP*?

PO: There are three different ways of periodising the journal, which are formally unconnected, but which, in practice, are obscurely linked. First, you can periodise in terms of dominant themes in its content: from its early phase, through its 'left Hegelian' phase, to its broader cultural, feminist and ecological phases, and then to the more cultural theory-related period. So, you can do that and that would be true. But second, and more decisive for me, is a periodisation based on forms of production: the move from line drawing to photography, the move from laying out with rulers, scissors and paste to using computer design, the move from outsourced computer design, to in-house, at-home computer design. A history of self-publishing, in other words. A third way would be about the changing internal structure of the journal. So, there's the content of the journal, the forms of production and the editorial organisation of the journal space, in which it became increasingly structured into the discrete sections and increasingly editorially self-reflective. To understand the history of *RP*, you have to lay these three histories on top of one another to get a sense of the dynamic between them.

Philosophy beyond philosophy

DC: In a talk you gave at a conference to celebrate *RP*'s 30th anniversary in 2002, you wrote an interesting piece about the idea of a 'radical philosophy' itself. I wonder what you think of this now twenty years on: 'if philosophy wants to be true to the political dynamic of radicalism – with its split, disjunctive, contradictory, self-surpassing form – it will have to embrace the moment of realisation as the moment of its own supersession, qua philosophy. … It will have to destroy itself as "philosophy", in the strict sense, in order to be true to the political potential of its philosophical concepts: freedom, equality, and justice, but also truth. It will have to endow these concepts with determinate historical meanings'. How far is there still a space for this 'idea of a radical philosophy as one that is inherently ambivalent about its own philosophical character' in philosophy today?

PO: That is the *only* space, the only *philosophically serious* space: one that is inherently ambivalent about its own philosophical character. The point about *Radical Philosophy* is that it was initially ambiguously or ambivalently philosophical because it was politically overdetermined – but by a cultural, philosophical, institutional project. So, it always thought about institutions in a way that most philosophers themselves were not interested in. It always took institutions seriously. Jonathan Rée was very good, for example, in the early years, at thinking about philosophy as an institution. After the politics of this went away, it then became ambivalently philosophical in relation to other disciplines. So, my own thinking about *Radical Philosophy* – at least in the last decade that I was involved with it – was as a transdisciplinary space: not as multidisciplinary, or as a little bit interdisciplinary, but as a transdisciplinary space in which philosophy was double-coded, because it was one of the disciplines that was at play, but also the conceptual resource for thinking the relations between all the disciplines as being a kind of immanently conceptual one that nonetheless exceeded philosophical conceptuality.  So, it played this sort of double role: one of which was philosophy in its particularism and then a kind of metaphilosophical thinking of a relation between disciplines, one of which was philosophy. So, the statement about 'a radical philosophy as one that is inherently ambivalent about its own philosophical character' holds true, although the nature of the ambivalence has changed.

DC: In that same talk (published in *RP* 103), you situated *RP*'s foundation – and its wider contribution to left intellectual culture - in relation to the 'institutional establishment of what has become known as "cultural studies"', which you present as raising 'the question, not only of the contribution of philosophy to Left intellectual culture in Britain since the 1950s, but also, more specifically, of its relationship to the theorisation of culture'. It's a question you broach too in the interview that you and Lynne Segal did with Stuart Hall for *RP* in the late 1990s. Is this still an important framing for you of both the journal and of a radical philosophy more generally?

PO: This has perhaps more to do with my own intellectual interest because I was always struck by the lack of a philosophical dimension to cultural studies. This is partly what the interview with Stuart Hall is about, despite the fact that cultural studies drew on a lot of philosophical sources, particularly in the early days – think of the importance of someone like Althusser. That always struck me and I always felt that a radical philosophy should in part be a philosophical critique of cultural studies. That was the point of my book, *Philosophy in Cultural Theory* (2000): not 'and' but 'in'. It was also because I associated cultural studies in the UK, politically, with the thin gruel of the populist democracy of the *Marxism Today* of the late 1980s.

DC: Given what you said about Blairism and the loss of independent left spaces, it's notable that the interview with Stuart Hall was done a month after Blair's victory in the general election in 1997, which places its discussion of the relationship (or non-relationship) between philosophy and cultural studies at an interesting political and intellectual conjuncture.

PO: The thing about the politics of cultural studies in Britain was that because of the relationship between Stuart Hall and Martin Jacques, who was the editor of *Marxism Today*, cultural studies in Britain was framed partly in terms of the Eurocommunist project. In the late 1980s and early 90s, *Radical Philosophy* was very much constituted politically against and to the left of *Marxism Today*. So, the *RP* conferences of the late '80s and early '90s, for example, were always constituted against the big *Marxism Today* conferences, to which we considered ourselves to be a kind of alternative. So, the critique of cultural studies and the critique of *Marxism Today*, as the journal of a kind of weak liberal-democratic Eurocommunism, were, we could say, part of the same thing.

What my conception of *RP* took from cultural studies was the idea that the journal was a cultural form, one of the institutionalised cultural forms of philosophy. Jonathan [Rée] thought about philosophy and its institution, but by that he really meant universities and the history of the relation of the university to non-university philosophy, whereas I thought of the journal and our relationship to the amateurism of conceptual art uses of photography, for example, as part of its *philosophical* form. This was because the enemy increasingly became academicisation in general, which was associated with disciplinarisation, but in a complicated way because the disciplines became much broader and more sophisticated within themselves. So, it wasn't the fact that they were disciplined, it was the fact that they were academicised. Disciplines have become internally pluralised within humanities to become quite multi- and interdisciplinary disciplines, but they have also become more and more subjected to bureaucratic academic norms.

DC: Which, one could argue, is connected to what happens to cultural studies itself, which basically disappears and returns to its original sources in a more pluralised media studies, sociology, literary studies, etc.

PO: And, in doing so, it often loses its political project. Some of this work has moved back towards anthropology – which is ironic given the conservative anthropological origins of Raymond Williams' model of cultural studies – but to a supposedly 'reformed' anthropology. Current debates within anthropology set off by globalisation are the most interesting at the interface of the humanities and the social sciences, I think. Another side of cultural studies became a branch of policy studies. That is, to the extent that it survived, it did so by making a pragmatic (often theoretically pragmatist) policy-related move. It became the intellectual form of a certain kind of cultural managerialism – especially in Europe, in funding terms, and especially in relation to questions of diversity, which are taken more seriously by many EU states than in the decrepit and increasingly undemocratic political culture of the UK. On the other hand, the whole move away from antagonistic concepts of racialisation, and strong philosophical concepts of difference of whatever kind, towards bland notions of diversification and diversity, with this soft social democratic, conservative cultural management of difference is itself a depoliticisation.

DC: What about philosophy's own status as a discipline today?

PO: As an institutionalised discipline, philosophy still doesn't really relate intellectually or critically to other disciplines. The quiet desperation of its insistence on intellectual self-sufficiency makes much of it irrelevant and self-marginalising; hence its reactive investment in the narrow practicalities of the impact agenda, and the sad spectacle of 'experimental philosophy'. In that respect, it's become very much a part of the general post-neoliberal policy-based academic pragmatism. In this regard, it too is giving up education for training, which the main structural tendency of university life in the humanities in the UK.

DC: Is this a symptom of analytical philosophy's own constitution of philosophy as an autonomous discipline gradually collapsing in on itself?

PO: I'm not sure. My own view is that analytical philosophy's self-narration of a move from analytical to post-analytical philosophy is largely illusory and that actually so-called post-analytical philosophy is just analytical philosophy with a textually expanding base: narrowly analytical readings of so-called continental philosophers. Methodologically (and characterologically) they haven't really changed that much.

DC: A final question: what do you consider *Radical Philosophy*'s central project to have been over the course of your more than thirty-year involvement with the journal, and how far did it succeed?

PO: I think it was pretty successful in a number of ways. First, it helped introduce post-Kantian European philosophy into the UK philosophical space. Second, it contributed to the philosophical education of left intellectual cultures and people on the left with different disciplinary formations. And third, it did so with a certain level of criticality, irony, humour and visual literacy that wasn't to be found anywhere else in philosophy. So, I think it did alright.

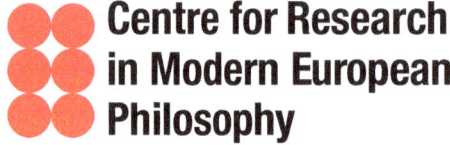

Centre for Research in Modern European Philosophy

3RD GILLIAN ROSE MEMORIAL LECTURE

'Solidarity: necessary fiction or metaphysical given?'

ROWAN WILLIAMS

THURSDAY 20 OCTOBER 2022 6.00 pm

Kingston University
Penrhyn Road campus
Kingston upon Thames KT1 2EE

followed by a reception in the Courtyard of the Town House

BOOKING www.kingston.ac.uk/grml3

Generously supported by the Tom Vaswani Family Trust

Anti-abortion feminism
How is this even a thing?
Victoria Browne

On 24th June 2022, anti-abortion activists across the US celebrated as the Supreme Court voted to overturn *Roe v. Wade*, among them some self-described 'feminists'. For a long time now, the anti-abortion movement has been declaring itself 'pro-woman' as much as pro-foetus, presenting abortion as a harm to women that they are coerced into or ultimately regret. Signs brandished at rallies and outside clinics declare 'We love them both' and 'We value them both', just as digital activists traffic in hashtags like 'BothLivesMatter'. But there is also a strand of anti-abortion politics that explicitly describes its position as 'feminist', claiming that an anti-abortion stance is the only 'true' feminist position. An amicus brief, for example, claiming that 'the judicially-created right of abortion disadvantages women' was submitted to the Supreme Court by '240 women scholars and professionals, and pro-life feminist organizations' including Feminists for Nonviolent Choices, New Wave Feminists and Feminists Choosing Life of New York.[1] Far fewer anti-abortion feminist groups and networks exist in the UK, though there are some worth noting, including the Pro-Life Feminist Society at Bristol University.

A common feminist response to anti-abortion feminism is to simply dismiss it as an oxymoron – to say that even if it is sincere, it is a contradiction in terms and hence there can be 'no such thing'. But unfortunately, it *is* a thing, however much we wish it wasn't, and however marginal it may be. Contradictory political positions, moreover, are hardly unique to anti-abortion feminists. So rather than denying the possibility of its existence, or being drawn into categorical battles over what counts as 'feminism' and what does not, the aim here is to try to get to grips with the logics, rhetorics and tactics of anti-abortion feminism so as to better resist its advances and prevent it gaining further traction. What do you have to think to think that state-mandated pregnancy is ethically preferable to elective abortion? How can the criminalisation of pregnancy and increased restrictions on reproductive freedom be taken as a sign of feminist progress?

To engage with US anti-abortion feminism, I acknowledge, is to risk boosting its visibility, and we must be careful not to treat it as a more significant or widespread phenomenon than it actually is. It is always worth emphasising that most Americans support some legal access to abortion, and that anti-abortion feminism is a small grouping under the anti-abortion umbrella. That said, having a better understanding of its different variations and ways of operating will enable more effective opposition. Particularly troubling is the left-leaning version of anti-abortion feminism because this is the strand most likely to catch us off guard. The usual pairing of an anti-abortion position with a right-wing political agenda produces a set of blatant inconsistencies which make it all too obvious that attacks on abortion are not really about matters of 'life' at all. In response to the overturning of *Roe*, for instance, Hazel Carby highlights the raft of recent 'anti-life legislation' coming out of the Supreme Court, such as the expansion of gun rights only weeks after the Ulvade shooting in Texas, and the stripping of power from the Environmental Protection Agency to limit carbon emissions.[2] As Amia Srinivasan has put it, right-wing anti-abortionism should be understood as essentially a 'symbolic' form of politics because a 'real movement' to abolish abortion would have to be premised upon a programme for serious structural change, including state-guaranteed parental leave, childcare provision and universal healthcare, as well as safe, free, accessible contraception and massive investment in sex education.[3] But what about when anti-abortion activists *do* support state-provided healthcare and childcare, gun control and environmental protections, and use the language of social justice, anti-capitalism and 'consistent life'? If this is the 'real' movement against abortion, what is it up to and how can it be confronted?

Origin stories

Anti-abortion feminists have been present in the US since the early 1970s. Feminists for Life, for example, was established in Ohio in 1973 by activists in the women's liberation movement, Pat Goltz and Catherine Callahan, who found no space for their anti-abortion views in the National Organization of Women.[4] In these early days, anti-abortion feminists like Goltz and Callahan sought a 'respected place' within the women's liberation movement. But as Laury Oaks demonstrates, their goal was soon reformulated to 'the task of rescuing it', constructing an 'oppositional position to the feminist movement from their pro-life stance'.[5] In their original declaration, for example, FFL stated that 'we pledge ourselves to help the feminist movement correct its failures' and 'purge itself of anti-life sentiments and practices'.[6] But rather than having any influence over mainstream feminism, anti-abortion feminists have instead found a home within the anti-abortion movement, playing a key role in developing the 'pro-woman' arguments that it has increasingly favoured. The complaint of being 'left out' of feminist organising, however, still periodically re-emerges. In 2017, for example, the *New York Times* published an opinion piece by a public relations manager for the anti-abortion charity Human Coalition, Lauren Enriquez, condemning the exclusion of anti-abortion groups from the official list of participants in the Women's March on Washington: 'To us', she writes, women's '"resistance" has to include opposition to the lie that freedom can be bought with the blood of our preborn children'.[7]

To secure the claim that 'true' feminism is opposed to abortion, contemporary US anti-abortion feminists trace their political lineage to feminists of the 'first wave' such as Susan B. Anthony and Elizabeth Cady Stanton, framing the 'second wave' demand for legal abortion access as a deviation from 'original' feminist principles. Erika Bachiochi – the Harvard-affiliated leading light of academic anti-abortion feminism, and co-author of the Supreme Court amicus brief – claims that these nineteenth century feminists 'were, without known exception, opposed to abortion'.[8] They believed, she tells us, that 'unborn children should be protected by the law' while also 'call[ing] for mercy for women whose unequal social status and difficult circumstances led them, out of desperation, to seek out abortions'. Their feminist goal, apparently, was to '[agitate] for improved social conditions so that women might responsibly carry out their duties to their children, born and unborn'. But the 'easy abortion access' sought by feminists in the 1970s betrayed this original mission, by devaluing motherhood and propping up a masculine ideal of equality that has 'stalled' the feminist revolution. Feminists today, then, must 'heed the wisdom of the early feminists' and work to realise their 'vision for justice' in our own lifetimes.[9]

This strategic 'return narrative'[10] has also been widely deployed by anti-abortion activist groups outside of academia, since FFL began perpetuating it in the 1990s. Feminists for Nonviolent Choices, for example, provide a 'herstory' of anti-abortion feminism on their website which claims that the 'first wave' of US feminism represented by Cady Stanton and Anthony unequivocally supported the 'right of the unborn' and considered abortion to be 'child murder'; but 'second wave' feminists like Betty Friedan and Gloria Steinem were wrongly persuaded by male 'abortionists' that 'women needed abortion if they expected to maintain positions in the workforce'. Fortunately, they write, the 'third wave' turned away from this masculinist form of feminism and paved the way for the current 'fourth wave': an 'emerging feminism that progresses beyond justice for women, the poor, ethnic groups, to also include justice for the unborn'. Feminism, therefore, 'has come full circle'.[11]

The views of the early US women's rights advocates were in fact more equivocal than the contemporary anti-abortion feminist narrative would have us believe. Various historians have now debunked it as a work of anachronistic invention evidenced by a handful of selectively assembled quotations. The widely circulated 'child murder' quote attributed to Anthony, for example, was extracted from an article written by an anonymous author in the magazine that Anthony edited whose identity remains unknown.[12] But this is not to try and rescue these nineteenth-century icons for our own side. It must not escape notice that the anti-abortion revival of white 'first wavers' like Anthony and Cady Stanton is occurring at a time when their investment and entanglement in white supremacy is becoming much more widely understood. While Bachiochi tries to straightforwardly align them with the cause of racial justice by glossing that the 'nineteenth-century women's rights advocates' had 'nearly all cut their teeth on slavery abolition work before turning their attention to women's unequal status in marriage and in society',[13] it has been amply demonstrated that these 'suffragist heroines' repeatedly betrayed the interests of Black women and traded on racist representations of Black men to elevate their own cause.[14] Cady Stanton, for instance, declared that it was better for a Black woman 'to be the slave of an educated white man, than of a degraded, ignorant black one'.[15] Her vision of 'enlightened motherhood', moreover, was eugenic through and through. She argued that women must be educated into the idea that 'to bear noble children to noble men with sound bodies and sound minds' is a 'worthy work and one that brings its own happiness and reward', while 'to fill the world with idiots, lunatics, criminals, the blind, the deaf, the dumb ... is not a work worth a Christian woman, but a sin against herself, the state, and a gross violation of the immutable laws of God'.[16] There may well be anti-abortion feminist groups and individuals that are unaware of this, but that is surely not the case for professional academics such as Bachiochi. So why is the association between Cady Stanton, Anthony and eugenic white supremacism being hidden from view?

This should be further considered in light of another omission from the 'return narrative' constructed by US anti-abortion feminists, which is the formation of the reproductive justice movement by women of colour in the 1990s. These activists were themselves deeply critical of how abortion rights became so centralised as a single issue within mainstream US feminism since the 1970s. They also rejected the dominant framework of 'choice': for its failure to foreground the grossly unequal social structures that enable or constrain individual choices in the first place; and to reckon with the numerous ways that the reproduction of women of colour, poor and disabled women has been controlled and precluded by the state, for example, through forced/coerced sterilisation.[17] The core point of the reproductive justice framework, however, is that 'the right to choose' is *not enough*. 'Even when abortion is legal', the founders of the movement emphasised, 'many women of colour cannot afford it, or cannot travel hundreds of miles to the nearest clinic. There is no choice where there is no access'. Their other central argument, moreover, is that while abortion access is essential, it is no more so than access to pregnancy and postnatal care, alternative birth options, safe homes and environments, and adequate childcare and education.[18] But the exclusion of the reproductive justice movement from the anti-abortion 'return narrative' enables anti-abortion feminists to present their own constructed tradition as the only one that has ever stood up for the women within oppressed social groups so unserved by the politics of choice, and for the material needs of pregnant people, parents and children.

The efficacy of the narrative also trades on a divisive generational dynamic, as contemporary anti-abortion feminists define themselves as the 'post-*Roe* generation' who are righting the wrongs of '1970s feminism'. Generational logics that imply younger women must turn on the previous generation to forge their own path have long been critiqued by feminist theorists like Judith Roof and Astrid Henry, for importing the 'full force of Oedipal rivalry, recrimination, and debt' into relations between feminists.[19] As Henry has argued, new iterations of feminism are so often steeped in the logic of 'disidentification', as assertions of a new political identity are achieved through evoking a maternalised figure – the 'bad mother' – to rebel and identify against. This is endemic within anti-abortion discourse, as 'second wave' feminists are demonised as grossly 'out of touch' with the views and needs of young women today who now see the 'tragedy of abortion' for what it is – a strategy that comes particularly to the fore in materials targeted at college students. FFL, for example, whose Campus Outreach Program has been operative since the 1990s, makes statements like 'Challenge the status quo. While members of the '70's women's movement continue to promote abortion, Feminists for Life is moving forward with woman-centred solutions in the workplace, home, and school'.[20] The strategic historiography of the 'post-*Roe* generation' is thus as much a matricidal enterprise as a mythic act of 'return'.

Though there may be a common origin story, however, anti-abortion feminism is not a singular political entity. Some groups sit fairly comfortably within the mainstream conservative anti-abortion movement, promoting a moral case against abortion as a 'tragic' form of 'violence against women' without questioning too deeply the basic socio-economic structures of US society. FFL, for example, may speak of 'systematically eliminating the root causes that drive women to abortion' and of 'working for low-income women' through backing a handful of national and state-level welfare reforms; but it focuses mainly on campaigning for better facilities for pregnant/parenting students on campus and producing breezy brochures like 'Raising Kids on a Shoestring', as well as supporting 'pregnancy crisis centres' that mask their anti-abortion intents.[21] Its politics can thus be characterised as Mama Grizzly-style 'compassionate conservatism' rebranded for college-age women, such that it can claim right-wing Republican politician Sarah Palin as one of its members without too much ideological tension.

But there are also versions of anti-abortion feminism in the US that are further to the left, or at least left-presenting and left-sounding. Rewriting anti-abortion ideology in the language of redistributive economics and social justice, they may be just as deceptive as any 'pregnancy crisis centre'. Though Bachiochi, for instance, is stationed firmly within the tradition of Catholic social conservatism, in economic terms she is a vocal critic of free market capitalism and a former supporter of Bernie Sanders. In response to the fall of *Roe*, she wrote that 'Red states should not be able to stand on their post-*Roe* abortion bans as evidence of pro-life accomplishment while their pregnant residents and children face poverty, substandard health care … and nonexistent workplace accommodations'[22] – a line which, in isolation, one might assume has been taken from an article supportive of reproductive rights rather than one praising their removal. To be sure, Bachiochi and others in her camp go no further than calling for curbs on capitalism and moderate welfarist measures within its terms. But there are also anti-abortion feminists that describe themselves as 'anti-capitalist' and co-opt the terminology of radical political projects like prison abolition, border abolition and Black Lives Matter. For instance, the mission statement of Progressive Anti-Abortion Uprising – a group whose leaders are currently under investigation for taking a box of foetal remains from a medical waste company truck and burying them at a secret location – claims they are out to 'educate the public about the exploitative influence of the Abortion Industrial Complex through an anti-capitalist lens, advocate for pregnant people and connect abortion vulnerable communities with life-saving resources'.[23] What is the political imaginary behind such statements? How is anti-abortion extremism being packaged as anti-capitalist feminist struggle?

Abortion as false solution

The primary weapon of the right-wing anti-abortion movement is the law, its mission being to expand state control over pregnancy through criminalisation. Though overturning *Roe* has been the ultimate prize (with their sights now set on a national ban), the passing of 'TRAP' laws – Targeted Regulation of Abortion Providers that requires excessively high standards of abortion providers – by Republican-controlled states has also been a major triumph, hugely restricting abortion access since the 1990s. The Texas Heartbeat Act of 2021, or SB8, further marked a high point of legal ingenuity with its unique enforcement mechanism, which authorised private indi-

Photo: Panda Mery, 'Communal Broadcasting in Flats'

viduals to bring a lawsuit against anyone who performed or facilitated a post-heartbeat abortion (after around six weeks: a point at which many people don't know they are pregnant), leaving abortion providers and advocates with no government officials to sue over the Texan law's constitutional illegality.

In contrast, leftist anti-abortion feminists are far less fixated on the legal arena, insisting that abortion prohibitions alone cannot bring an end to abortion because they do nothing to alter the socio-economic circumstances which cause 'desperate women' to abort. Strategic discussions on how to create 'a world without abortion' are thus concerned more with 'root causes' and 'abortion prevention' than developing legal tactics, with 'tearing down systems that aren't working' and agitating the 'oppressive status quo'.[24] Yet it must be emphasised that for all the effort to distance themselves from the right-wing anti-abortionists' devotion to criminal punishment, it is still common for leftist anti-abortion feminists to claim that anti-abortion laws are necessary, if not sufficient. For instance, though unable to bring herself to vote for the 'boorish' Trump, writes Bachiochi, she was 'grateful' to the anti-abortion right for enabling his presidency and to the man himself for his anti-*Roe* Supreme Court picks.[25] What is the reasoning here? Is the criminal justice system not one of those systems that clearly 'aren't working'? If the goal is 'prevention' rather than prohibition and punishment, why are anti-abortion laws deemed necessary at all?

The argument made – from academics like Bachiochi to grassroots groups like New Wave Feminists – is that legal abortion access must be eradicated because it has precluded much-needed social, economic and cultural change by providing a false solution to feminised poverty and the patriarchal structuring of our institutions and workplaces. We have come to rely on abortion, it is said, as the answer for women in a society organised around corporate profit and the masculine norm, and so legal abortion is 'stalling' progressive politics.[26] According to this view of abortion's role in society, if the workplace does not accommodate pregnant people and those with caring responsibilities, and the state does not provide healthcare and material support, they can just get an abortion and business continues as usual. Legal abortion access thus reassures us, apparently, that there is no great need for paid maternity and parental leave, for improved healthcare and welfare provision, or for decent wages, and so it is the 'false' or 'privileged' solution to gender inequality.

The more conspiracy-oriented anti-capitalist activists, like Progressive Anti-Abortion Uprising, see US abortion providers as being in league with big money and the capitalist state, pushing abortion as a 'product expediently sold' to turn a profit, while providing an 'easy solution' for a state unwilling to support parents and children, and enabling the continued workplace exploitation of women whose maternity must be denied for the sake of their productivity.[27] This is what they mean by the 'Abortion Industrial Complex'. The more moderate, in contrast, present abortion advocates and providers as unwittingly propping up the status quo. But they are united in the claim that abortion buttresses patriarchal capitalism and stands in the way of either reform or revolution. As Bachiochi explains it, 'relatively easy abortion access has made it unnecessary for businesses and other institutions in the United States to acknowledge an essential cultural reality: Most working persons are (or ought to be) deeply encumbered by their obligations to their families. In the end, it may just be that an unmitigated right to abortion serves a profit-driven market above all else'.[28] It is also contended that the legal option of abortion perpetuates the social and cultural devaluation of pregnancy and parenting because it makes having a child seem like an 'unwelcome, inconvenient, and expensive "choice"' that must be subjected, 'like other "trade-offs" in the marketplace', to a '"cost-benefit" analysis'.[29] Legal abortion access, claim the anti-abortion feminists, thus perpetuates a male-dominated, market-driven society, and rather than being a lynchpin of women's reproductive freedom is the ultimate sign of women's oppression.

Mainstream feminism too is castigated for working much harder for abortion rights than for improved conditions for pregnant people and parents – a critique made also by reproductive justice theorists and activists. But while the latter group insist we need both, anti-abortion feminists propose that the demand for abortion necessarily works *against* the demand for better support for pregnant/parenting people. The argument is that legal abortion access 'undermines efforts to enact and implement crucial policies necessary for pregnant women and mothers to participate in society on equal footing with men', because it promotes a model of equality which sets up 'the wombless male body as normative, thereby promoting cultural hostility toward pregnancy and motherhood'. The feminist demand for abortion, it is claimed, 'is a sell-out to male values and a capitulation to male lifestyles'.[30] But once legal access to abortion is removed, all of us will finally realise that gender inequality and feminised poverty must be addressed through socio-economic and cultural change. Once the 'abortion regime' has been ended and society properly values reproductive care work, pregnancy will 'no longer hold the subordinate status it seems to have in the eyes of elite academic feminist scholars.'[31]

Totalitarian tendencies

The first thing to ask, of course, is since when did forcing people to do a thing make that thing more socially valued? But let us accept for a moment this mind-bending argument that state-mandated pregnancy is the way to boost the socio-cultural value of pregnancy and parenting and overturn patriarchal capitalism. What do anti-abortion feminists have to say to those they would deny abortion access? Is the idea that unwillingly pregnant people must take the hit in order to make things better for the pregnant people and parents of the future? Because if they had a legal abortion this would send a signal to the wider society that pregnancy is not to be valued and nothing needs to change? And then, after a period of time has passed, and enough people have endured unwanted pregnancies and births, pregnancy and motherhood will have become so highly valued and economically supported that no one will want abortions anymore?

This kind of sacrificial logic surfaces with disturbing regularity within anti-abortion feminist discourse. Feminists Choosing Life of New York, for example, write that 'the feminists who want abortion because they "don't want to be pregnant" are hurting the women who are forced to resort to abortion' because they are standing in the way of those women getting the support they need to have the babies they actually want.[32] The trope of the aborting woman as selfish and overprivileged is thus recycled here with a 'feminist' twist, as a strict divide between the 'good' aborter (oppressed with no choice) and the 'bad' aborter (pampered with too many choices) is firmly established. 'Not wanting to be pregnant' is presented as a petulant and superficial whim that warrants no moral consideration, and indeed actively does harm. So those who experience their pregnancies that way must simply put up with it and give birth against their will.

Yet at the same time, leftist anti-abortion feminist discourse is characterised as much by a saviour complex as a sacrificial bent, which stems from the notion that under the right socio-economic and cultural conditions there would be no unwanted pregnancy. This view that an equitable and just society would be abortion-free implies that no woman ever *really* wants an abortion deep down, even the 'bad' aborter, because if we lived in a culture that truly valued pregnancy and motherhood, abortion would be simply 'unthinkable'. The argument against abortion then appears less about forcing unwillingly pregnant people to gestate and give birth in order to bring about the pregnancy-supporting society of the future, and more about saving them now for their own sake. 'Not wanting to be pregnant', from this angle, is not so much dismissed for being morally decadent as rendered discountable by anti-abortion activists prescribing what abortion-seekers would want if they were differently pregnant in a different reality.

State-mandated pregnancy and birth, then, is not only justified by leftist anti-abortion feminists in instrumental terms for the sake of the future – because it will bring down patriarchal capitalism! – but also for the good of the unwillingly pregnant in the present. This may be inconveniently contradicted by many women's own accounts of their experiences and decisions, but any personal account of abortion as a positive or straightforward experience is dismissed as evidence of patriarchal or pro-choice brainwashing, condemned as morally degraded, or simply ignored. The stories that anti-abortion feminist groups are interested and invested in, rather, are those which describe an experience of having no real alternative to abortion, alongside stories that speak of post-abortion regret, and those of people who went through with a pregnancy that was unwanted at the time, but are now glad they did (which they use as evidence that your future self will always want the baby, regardless of how you feel as pregnant). Once again, then, 'not wanting to be pregnant' gets negated as a lived state of being, this time by fiat of projected retrospect.

To call out this selectivity is not to diminish the fact that many people do feel they have no choice but to have an abortion, or are directly coerced into having one: for example, when threatened by an abusive partner, or as when a number of pregnant Black women in the 1980s and 90s were given the 'choice' of abortion or prison by the state after testing positive for drugs.[33] Anti-abortion feminists are right to be outraged that so many people make decisions they don't want to make because of economic hardship, employment requirements and gender-based violence, and by the long, scandalous, ongoing history of state control of impoverished, disabled and racialised women's reproduction. But why does this outrage not extend any further? Why is it harnessed to support reproductive coercion, control and cruelty of another kind? As reproductive justice activists have demonstrated in all kinds of contexts, the right to be pregnant and have a child, and to raise the children we have in healthy and safe environments, necessarily goes hand in hand with the right *not to*. One right cannot exist without the other, because without both, there are no reproductive rights and freedoms at all. So even in a society entirely liberated from economic injustice, patriarchal domination and sexual violence, with all the support that pregnant and child-raising people could ever need, abortion access too will always be needed. For how could pregnancy ever be undertaken freely without the freedom to opt out?

For all its progressive packaging, then, leftist anti-abortion feminism is not so far from the Mama-Grizzly Sarah Palin variety after all, because it reduces down to the usual patriarchal formulas: either a woman who does not want to be pregnant is no real woman at all, and hence forcing her to gestate and give birth against her will can still be deemed 'pro-woman'; or all women really do want to be pregnant and become mothers deep down – even if they may think, feel and know they don't – and so reproductive control is really reproductive kindness. This is a feminism that claims to stand up for the poorest and most oppressed women, but rhetorically constructs those women as victims in need of 'abortion rescue' and uses them as pawns in its anti-abortion argument. It calls for 'solidarity' yet promotes a divisive populist message that pro-abortion rights activists are 'elite' feminists packing off 'desperate' women to the abortion clinic because it is easier than fighting for economic and social justice. And though it prefers not to speak of criminal punishment (even posturing in some cases as being against mass incarceration and the prison industrial complex), making abortion illegal is nevertheless a fundamental objective for many leftist anti-abortion feminist groups and individuals. While trying to set themselves apart from the anti-abortion right, their relationship is actually more of the 'good cop/bad cop' type: the left side lets the right side do the dirty work of making abortion a crime, while they usher in the bottles and nappies and maternity pay. They claim that 'we simply want to work to make the world a better and safer place for women and children',[34] but remain rather silent on the fact that it is overwhelmingly poor women and disproportionately women of colour – the very women they are claiming to represent – that get arrested, prosecuted and incarcerated in the US for 'fetal homicide' or 'child endangerment'. And now the court has overturned *Roe*, the state power exercised in the name of 'foetal protection' or 'the unborn' will be greatly increased.[35]

It should also be emphasised that while leftist anti-abortion feminists may call for vital economic transformations like universal healthcare, childcare and wealth redistribution – and so it may seem that there is much common ground with reproductive justice feminists – the two groups are ultimately working to and from contradictory aims. Undoubtedly there are anti-abortion feminist grassroots initiatives that have made a serious difference to pregnant and parenting individuals in need of shelter, sympathy and basic items like food and formula. But we must not forget that the overarching goal of anti-abortion feminist activism is the ending of abortion, rather than enabling all people with the capacity for pregnancy to be self-determining agents with real options and multiple life possibilities before them. When anti-abortion feminist groups reach out to 'abortion-vulnerable' women and try to improve their material well-being, it is with the intention of keeping them pregnant; and when they call for revolution, it is with the aim of making abortion not just illegal and inaccessible but 'unthinkable' – a totalitarian ambition, as Susan Pedersen points out, if ever there was one.[36]

'Protecting the most vulnerable'

Another way in which anti-abortion feminists try to turn the tables is by claiming that only anti-abortion feminism holds true to the 'core feminist principle' of 'protecting the most vulnerable' – one of the most ubiquitous phrases in the discourse. Here the saviour complex is directed not so much toward the would-be aborter who doesn't realise her own interests, but toward the foetus as abortion's ultimate victim. While the right side of the anti-abortion movement seeks to promote the idea of 'foetal personhood' in the public sphere and have it recognised in law, leftist anti-abortion feminist groups tend to speak in secular terms and generally appeal instead to the 'humanity' of the foetus, co-opting human rights discourse in an effort to break the association of 'pro-life' values with Christian belief systems and political-economic power. The idea is that focusing on the 'humanness' of foetuses bypasses theological and philosophical debates over the 'personhood' category, because it is simply self-evident that a 'human being' is a human organism, and that the development of a human organism begins at fertilisation. This is just 'science'. So a foetus, even a blastocyst, counts as a 'human being': 'You do not have to be religious to value human life. You do not have to be religious to see the humanity of the fetus'.[37] It is also treated as self-evident that foetuses are the most vulnerable of all human beings, and that to be on the side of 'life' is to be against all forms of violence and killing (though no clarity is provided on whether this includes self-defence against misogynist violence or the uprisings of the colonised and enslaved).

Leftist anti-abortion feminist groups thus claim to be founded upon a 'consistent life ethic' of nonviolence 'from womb to tomb' and align anti-abortionism with other causes that 'protect human life'. Feminists Choosing Life of New York, for example, include abortion on their list of 'publicly sanctioned lethal violence' alongside war, euthanasia and capital punishment; and New Wave Feminists also align the anti-abortion cause with struggles against capital punishment and family separation at US borders. 'Our human dignity', they contend, 'doesn't begin at birth and it doesn't end at the border.'[38]

From this perspective, feminists on the left who stand up against police brutality and killings while supporting foetal killing by elective abortion are deemed as guilty of hypocrisy as anti-abortionists on the right, who oppose gun control measures to protect children from school shootings while supporting laws that 'protect the unborn'.

Bachiochi also charges that feminists on the left contradict ourselves when we demand abortion rights because we reject the ideology of property rights as applied to the economy, yet 'embrace it as applied to a pregnant woman and her unborn child'.[39] Caricaturing the pro-abortion rights image of pregnancy as the invasion of a sovereign individual's body-property by a trespasser, Bachiochi argues that feminism must give up the 'Lockean' commitment to bodily autonomy and self-ownership, and instead ground itself in a philosophy of interdependence and care premised on our shared vulnerability:

> A post-*Roe* America will need to move beyond its wrong-headed obsession with autonomy. It will need to align both its rhetoric and its policies better with the realities of human existence and so should work to bring forth a renewed solidarity instead. We humans are not best understood as rights-bearing bundles of desires who progress through life by the sheer force of our autonomous wills. We are beings who are deeply dependent on one another for every good in life – first and foremost for our very existence, as we did not come to be by an act of our own will.[40]

But as Bachiochi well knows, plenty of feminists on the left have articulated arguments supporting abortion that are in no way premised upon concepts of the body as 'property'.[41] It is not to John Locke that we turn, but feminist philosophers like Simone de Beauvoir, Iris Marion Young or Kathryn Sophia Belle, for whom the body is our mode of being in the world and not an object owned; or Judith Butler and Lisa Guenther, who for decades have worked to elaborate a bodily politics of vulnerability and interdependence as an alternative to liberal individualism. These latter philosophers reject the masculinist notion of vulnerability as an affliction or affront to the individual which must be vanquished, promoting instead an ambiguous model of vulnerability as an 'openness to being affected': a shared and inescapable condition of existence which makes possible not only violence, harm and exploitation, but also collectivity, care and love.[42] Yet this existential fact of vulnerability and interdependence, as Erinn Gilson insists, does not in itself come with a set of normative principles.[43] So while Bachiochi contends that the vulnerability of the foetus automatically bestows an 'affirmative duty of care' upon the pregnant person (and the rest of us) to keep it alive, Gilson, Butler and others argue that the supposition of vulnerability can only be 'a starting point rather than a concluding one: it does not have ameliorative normative force but rather is the supposition from which we can begin to reckon with political and ethical difficulties'.[44] How do specific discursive systems and operations of power transform our 'openness to being affected' into unequal and unjust social relations? What political and ethical responses are necessitated by different forms of vulnerability? Are keeping alive and 'protecting' the only forms that care can take? Are they always acts of care?

The politics of vulnerability

When we take this critical approach, we must indeed consider how foetuses are made vulnerable by their dependence upon a living pregnant body, and on the decision-making of the pregnant person so embodied, shaped by the circumstances in which they live. But we also need to examine how the foetus is framed and produced as vulnerable through particular discursive and visual techniques. The anti-abortion narrative of the foetus's vulnerability implies that the foetus just *is* vulnerable, as if its vulnerability somehow exists outside historically shifting sociopolitical contexts. This gives 'the vulnerability of the foetus', as Katie Oliviero argues, a commonsense, instinctive appeal, promising 'an irrefutability where bodily harm is obvious and outside the manipulative forces of ideology'. Yet the 'emotional and moral clarity' promised by the notion of vulnerability 'conceals the discursive production of meaning'.[45] At no other time in American history have embryos and foetuses been so represented as 'beautiful, precious, vulnerable creatures that require the utmost levels of protection'.[46] It is through highly emotive and sensationalist rhetoric that the foetus comes to be understood as the most vulnerable, most helpless, most defenceless of all 'human beings', and through cartoon sketches and highly mediated sonogram imagery that it is rendered as a baby-in-waiting, 'who only requires further incubation in a maternal body in order to emerge as the autonomous subject that it already "is" in nascent form'.[47]

What also must be questioned is the quantitative presumption that the foetus is the *most* vulnerable in the situation that is pregnancy. It is true that the relation between the foetal body and pregnant body is asymmetric and uneven: the foetus is passively dependent upon the pregnant body for its continuing existence, while the pregnant person does not, in most cases, similarly depend upon the continuing existence of the foetus for their own life. Yet a pregnant person is not simply an incubator *in which* a pregnancy takes place and *on which* a foetus depends. Pregnancy is a transformative state of being that brings multiple experiential possibilities and multiple forms of burden, pressure and risk. Miscarriage and particularly stillbirth, for instance, can put a pregnant person in significant physical peril, especially when medical care is absent or withheld for political reasons; and pregnancies that continue to term can also cause extreme illness, pain, injury (both temporary and permanent) and sometimes death – a risk that in the US is highest for low-income women, women of colour and Indigenous women.[48] Pregnant people from disadvantaged social groups are made disproportionately vulnerable by insufficient material, social and emotional support, the stresses of everyday racism, sexism, classism, ableism and xenophobia, and by laws controlling pregnancy that remove their rights to bodily integrity and may see them arrested, prosecuted and imprisoned.

Anti-abortion feminists, however, refrain from grappling with the physically, psychologically, ethically and politically complex varieties of entangled vulnerability that pregnancy entails (and which pregnant people themselves negotiate on an everyday basis). As we have seen, the 'pro-woman' case against abortion rests on the claim that it is not chosen by, but forced upon, women. In relation to abortion, then, women are only vulnerable, and never at the same time self-determining agents. But when the argument shifts to the pro-foetus tack, the pregnant person is figured as the very source of the foetus's vulnerability who must be placed under state control or social imperative to enforce their 'duty of care' to it. As Lauren Berlant described it, the pregnant person is expected to 'act like a mother' to the foetus whist effectively being made a 'child to the fetus', through the de-legitimation of their agency and identity as they become 'more minor and less politically represented than the fetus'.[49] The humanism that claims to consistently 'recognize the full humanity of both people groups, women and the unborn', thus reveals itself to be a strictly hierarchical humanism in which the actual lived lives of pregnant people are subordinated to the very form of 'life' that would not exist without them. Insofar as the foetus is rendered as 'vulnerable' or 'precarious life', as Penelope Deutscher argues, the vulnerability and precarity of the pregnant person is redoubled: 'The making of fetal precariousness is a making of maternal precariousness'.[50]

The anti-abortion feminist claim that they are 'protecting the most vulnerable' is therefore a perfect illustration of what Oliviero describes as a 'reactive vulnerability claim': an invocation of 'vulnerability' which licenses forms of paternalist control that exacerbate the actual everyday vulnerabilities and precarities experienced by oppressed social groups. A particularly egregious example is the way that some contemporary US anti-abortion feminists seek to align themselves with Black Lives Matter – a movement founded by Black women which has been extremely clear that 'full access to abortion care is necessary for all Black people'[51] – by claiming that removing abortion access is essential for racial justice because it will protect and save 'Black lives'. In a report entitled 'ALL Black Lives Matter', for instance, Feminists Choosing Life of New York cite the comparatively higher rate of abortions had by Black women as evidence that abortion is a tool of eugenic white supremacy and one of the foremost threats to 'Black lives'. It suggests that 'if Planned Parenthood tends to set up camp where large populations of people of colour are, it may be evidence of racial targeting and a continuation of their eugenic policies from the past'; and approvingly cites the 'abortion is Black genocide' myth that has been pushed by both Black and white anti-abortion activists on the right for years.[52] Including rates of abortion within overall rates of 'death', the FCLNY report states that 'the abortion rate in the black community exceeds the top ten causes of death among blacks combined', treating a Black woman having an abortion as equivalent to the killing of George Floyd by Derek Chauvin.

Once again, there are very real issues being invoked here. Planned Parenthood, under Margaret Sanger's direction and beyond, has indeed been complicit with white supremacist eugenics; and the higher incidence of abortion among Black communities must of course be understood within contexts of structural racism that leave Black women as a group with fewer resources to raise children, inadequate housing and healthcare, and less access to reproductive services including quality contraception. These factors also produce higher rates of miscarriage and stillbirth. But in this 73-page report by FCLNY, there is not one single mention of the reproductive justice movement, which has led the way in exposing and opposing the racist past and present of abortion provision in the US while also working to secure equal abortion access for all. Nor does it mention the robust response of Black feminists to the 'Black genocide' myth which, in the words of Loretta Ross, 're-enslaves Black women by making us breeders for someone else's cause'.[53] Instead, in the name of protecting 'unborn Black lives', anti-abortion feminist groups like FCLNY present Black women as simply falling victim to Planned Parenthood and the racist state.[54] Yet while being treated as victims and dupes with no agency to decide for themselves, they are simultaneously designated as dangerous subjects who 'wield the power to kill and let live' over the 'most vulnerable'[55]. The chilling logic is that Black women's reproductive lives cannot be left up to them, in case they inadvertently abort their own people out of existence.

Sex and consequences

The final core argument made by anti-abortion feminists relates directly to sex. It is said that abortion is harmful to women not only because it forces them to end the lives of their 'unborn children', but also because it leads to their sexual exploitation. As abortion enables 'consequence-free' sex, the argument goes, it perpetuates a 'casual sex ethic' that is to the benefit of men and the detriment of women, because 'the kind of sex that women want' is committed and reproductive.[56] Indeed, the claim is sometimes made that women simply are not *designed* for 'consequence-free' sex because of their presumed capacity to become pregnant.[57]

This line of argument is much more prominent in the more socially conservative strands of anti-abortion feminism, like the Catholic version Bachioci has constructed which makes common cause with the new essentialism promoted by 'gender-critical' feminism:

> The modern-day feminist movement on the whole has difficulty condemning epidemic pornography, the sexual mutilation of children at the behest of a cultish gender ideology and other forms of sexual exploitation (from "sex work" to now normative casual sex) ... and as increasing numbers of ordinary women lament today's male-oriented sexual norms ... easy abortion access in the United States has allowed *women to be taken advantage of* more fully in the workplace and in the bedroom.[58]

The more progressive-presenting strands of anti-abortion feminism, in contrast, tend to refrain from such overt transphobia and austere sexual moralising. Progressive Anti-Abortion Uprising, for instance, recognise 'that there are many people who are sexually active and are not prepared for or do not desire children', and proclaim their commitment to 'radical inclusivity' and 'amplifying LGBTQ+ voices'.[59] But they also say explicitly that bodily integrity is not an absolute value and that 'it is unjust to deny a pre-born child's right to life in favour of a bodily autonomy right that could have been vindicated earlier, and without violence, through the practice of abstinence or contraception'.[60] Unmarried sex for pleasure is just about allowed, then, but spontaneity, mistakes or mind-changing are not, at least if you have the capacity to get pregnant.

Contraception itself, moreover, is a matter of debate in anti-abortion feminist circles. If a form of contraception is deemed to be an 'abortifacient', including contraception that prevents implantation like the morning-after pill, there is general agreement that it cannot be permitted. But there is also intense suspicion of all forms of 'techno-pharmacological' contraception, including condoms and the pill, such that even the more apparently 'progressive' groups like PAAU admit to being divided on the issue. A common notion perpetuated by anti-abortion feminists, for instance, is that contraception actually increases the likelihood of unplanned and unwanted pregnancy, and therefore rates of abortion, because it encourages 'risky' and 'irresponsible' sexual behaviour by uncoupling sex from reproduction, allowing men to behave simply as 'coital animals'.[61] A related argument is that the widespread availability and use of contraception means that women feel they can no longer use fear of pregnancy as a reason to say no to sex. And thus denied their role as gatekeepers, they end up consenting to sex they don't want. Indeed, this argument may even be given a #MeToo spin: for instance, when Bachiochi writes that 'As the #MeToo movement has revealed in spades, the new "coital animal" – lacking the formative schooling of desire expected of an aspiring gentleman – will not so readily heed the word "no"'.[62]

The issue of consent, however, opens up a line of questioning that anti-abortion feminists may well prefer to shut down again. Consent plays an important role in their argument that pregnant people have to take responsibility for the reproductive consequences of sex, not only because of the 'sexual asymmetry' of 'biological design' (which means they are the ones who get pregnant and so have an in-built 'duty' to gestate), but also because they chose to have sex in the first place. FCLNY, for instance, write that 'in the overwhelming majority of cases, pregnancy is the result of consensual sex, meaning two people freely engage in the act that is known to potentially make new, completely dependent human children'.[63] Essentially, then, if you have the capacity for pregnancy, to consensually engage in sex is to forfeit your right to bodily integrity and self-determination in matters of reproduction. But if we accept the concurrent argument made by anti-abortion feminists like Bachiochi that the availability of abortion and contraception creates a 'casual sex culture' in which women feel they have to consent to sex they don't really want, this makes the '*you had sex so now you must face the consequences*' stance seem both weaker and harsher.

Further, once the question of consent has been raised, we must also ask what anti-abortion feminists have to say about non-consensual sex, and on this issue they can be harsh indeed. Some, like Bachiochi, do concede that abortion should be legally permitted when there has been an 'entire lack of consent', but this exception usually comes with many caveats: for instance, that it must occur very early in the pregnancy and must take place in a hospital setting.[64] Others say that all foetal lives are precious and so must not be ended no matter the circumstances of their conception. Feminists for Life, for example, say it would be 'discriminatory' to allow foetuses conceived through rape to be aborted while those conceived through consensual sex were allowed to live: 'People used to value a woman based on who her father or husband was. It is similarly medieval to value a child by the actions of her father. That way of thinking is patriarchal and antifeminist, and it should have gone out with the Dark Ages.'[65] They also make the case that abortion after rape is not in the interest of the survivor herself because it is 'a second act of violence against a woman who is raped'. Though 'it is normal to wish we could erase a painful memory such as rape', writes the FFL President Serrin Foster, 'the hard truth is that as much as we want to, we can't. Abortion doesn't erase a memory'. And so the pregnancy must be endured, because 'a child is never a punishment'.[66] A survivor of sexual violence, exploitation or coercion must not 'pass on' the violence to an 'innocent unborn child'. Indeed, in light of the anti-abortion feminist claim that state-mandated pregnancy is the route to bringing down the patriarchy, are we to infer that forcing rape survivors to gestate and give birth to their rapists' children is the way to bring an end to sexual violence once and for all?

Regrouping after *Roe*

When encountering statements like those cited above, it is very difficult to understand how anti-abortion feminism has any adherents at all. And it is worth emphasising again that it doesn't have many. But contemporary anti-abortion feminists in the US have become increasingly adept at crafting affective rhetorical strategies and co-opting contemporary political movements like #MeToo or Black Lives Matter to advance their own cause. And the leftist strand may well be effective where right-wing anti-abortionism fails, precisely because of the ways in which mainstream US pro-choice politics tends to operate, and the kinds of alliances that emerge as a result. Though most people, for example, would not view the offers made by Google, Apple and JP Morgan to cover employees' travel costs to out-of-state abortion clinics as evidence of a patriarchal plot to force their pregnant employees into abortion, plenty will be feeling uncomfortable as the fall of *Roe* gets converted into a PR opportunity by corporate power.

There is surely little doubt now that what is required of all pro-abortion rights advocates and activists is a full commitment to the reproductive justice framework, which entails putting the most disadvantaged at the centre and fighting for proper socio-economic support for all kinds of pregnancies, whether they end in abortion, miscarriage, stillbirth or live birth. It also means 'connect[ing] the dots' between social issues that seem unrelated to traditional views of reproductive politics, from decarceration and prison abolition to environmental justice.[67] But there are still vital strategic questions to consider, including questions about coalition-building. Coalitions for reproductive justice clearly cannot include anti-abortion feminists like those discussed above who support the criminalisation of abortion, and therefore the criminalisation of pregnancy more generally, however progressive and feminist they may present themselves to be. We might as well, as Sarah Jones writes, set the tent on fire.[68] But what about those feminists who identify as 'pro-life' but do not seek to criminalise other people's reproductive decisions and so could be categorised simultaneously as 'pro-choice'? Or those who aim at 'abortion reduction' rather than elimination, and claim to be guided by the principles of reproductive justice?

There are various reproductive justice thinker-activists who argue for greater flexibility as we reconsider who our allies might be. As Andrea Smith argued in her 2005 'Beyond Pro-Life and Pro-Choice' article, for example, 'we often lose opportunities to work with people with whom we may have sharp disagreements but who may, with different political framings and organizing strategies, shift their positions'.[69] She cites as an example the North Baton Rouge Women's Help Center in Louisiana – a 'crisis pregnancy centre' that 'articulates its pro-life position from an anti-racist perspective'. Why, Smith, asks, would we automatically assume that Planned Parenthood is an ally and the Women's Help Center is not, when both organisations 'support some positions that are beneficial to women of colour' while 'equally support[ing] positions that are detrimental to them'? Instead, Smith argues, we must 'think more creatively about who we could work in coalition' with, while simultaneously 'hold[ing] those who claim to be our allies more accountable for the positions they take'.[70] To take another example, in the 2017 collection *Radical Reproductive Justice,* Loretta Ross and fellow editors include an essay by 'pro-life feminist' Mary Krane Derr which argues that the reproductive justice movement 'is less than it could be if it is not for all unborn and already born humans', while at the same time denouncing the criminalisation of pregnant and aborting women.[71] The idea behind this inclusion, Ross states, was to show that the reproductive justice framework is 'broad enough to include a lot of different perspectives', including those the editors disagree with, and 'to show how we could use the framework in some inventive and creative ways to build a forward-looking movement'.[72]

Arguably, though, there is a tension between this flexible approach to coalition-building and the growing feminist conviction that wrangling over the ethics of abortion has so far done us more harm than good. Mainstream abortion-rights advocacy has for decades adopted a reactive discursive strategy which has allowed the anti-abortion movement to set the terms of debate and curtail the sayable. 'Members of the general public who support abortion rights', writes Charlotte Shane, have thus 'been abandoned to the unforgivably self-defeating slogan of "safe, legal, and rare" and the polite-company taboo – accommodated by "my body, my choice" – against even uttering the word "abortion"'.[73] So, as the failure of this strategy is so painfully felt in this post-*Roe* moment, more and more feminists are going on the offensive, refusing to concede anything to 'pro-life' ideologies, and redefining the right to elective abortion in unequivocal terms as a positive right, which is not just to be defended but championed – wholeheartedly, unapologetically, absolutely: 'From now on, we who fight for reproductive freedom must announce our cause in the clearest terms: every impregnatable person has the right to not be pregnant'.[74] And it is difficult to see a place in this project for dialogue with those, such as Derr, who do not support criminalisation but do not support abortion either, reluctantly acknowledging that some kind of legal abortion access may be needed yet casting doubt on its morality.

To highlight this potential tension is not to present the capacious coalition-building approach taken by reproductive justice pioneers like Ross or Smith as concessionary, nor to presume that engaging opposing views is necessarily a 'gateway ... to a de-radicalised politics'.[75] The process of working through tensions and disagreements can indeed be generative, just as trying alternative framings and strategies can bring new people in. But there are nonetheless issues to address, because even if the most left-leaning 'pro-life' feminists on the fringe insist that they do not support legal restrictions and criminal punishment, or that they follow Loretta Ross rather than Serrin Foster, any kind of anti-abortion argument (however complex and caveated it might be) can bolster the principles under which the mainstream anti-abortion movement claims to operate – a movement which is entirely invested in the criminalisation and stigmatisation of abortion and which is going after further controls. Indeed, as argued above, the 'softer', leftist, secular versions can actually serve to broaden its appeal. So questions of strategic alliance are paramount as the terms on which feminists conduct our reproductive politics are re-set. How might calls to renew or expand our coalitions be squared with calls to consolidate our position, double down on our principles and 'meet the absolutism' of the right with an absolutism of our own?[76]

Victoria Browne is a member of the editorial collective of Radical Philosophy. *Her new book* Pregnancy Without Birth: A Feminist Philosophy of Miscarriage *is out now.*

Notes

1. The brief was authored by Teresa Stanton Collett (Professor of Law at the University of St. Thomas and Director of its 'Prolife Centre'), Erika Bachiochi (Fellow of the Ethics and Public Policy Center and Senior Fellow at the Harvard-affiliated Abigail Adams Institute) and Helen M. Alvaré (Chair in Law and Liberty at Antonin Scalia Law School, George Mason University). It can be viewed here, accessed 5 October 2022: supremecourt.gov/DocketPDF/19/19-1392/185366/20210804180314919_19-1392 Brief of 240 Women Scholars et al In Support of Petitioners.pdf.
2. Hazel V. Carby, 'Prejudice Rules: *LRB* Contributors on the Overturning of *Roe v. Wade*', *London Review of Books* 44:14 (21 July 2022). The Supreme Court rejected New York State's restrictions on carrying a concealed gun in public and ruled that the constitutional 'right to keep and bear arms', affirmed for self-defence within the home in 2008, can now be applied outside it.
3. Amia Srinivasan, *The Right to Sex: Feminism in the Twenty-first Century* (London: Bloomsbury, 2021), 155.
4. The Ohio chapter of NOW went on to expel Goltz in 1974, though her membership of NOW at the national level was not revoked. See Laury Oaks, 'What Are Pro-Life Feminists Doing on Campus?', *NWSA Journal* 21:1 (Spring 2009), 178–203; or Mary Ziegler, 'Women's Rights on the Right: The History and Stakes of Modern Pro-Life Feminism, 1968 to the Present', *Berkeley Journal of Gender Law & Justice* 232 (2013), 232–268.
5. Laury Oaks, 'What Are Pro-Life Feminists Doing on Campus?', 181–182.
6. Ibid.
7. Lauren Enriquez, 'How the New Feminist Resistance Leaves Out American Women', *New York Times*, 27 February 2017, nytimes.com/2017/02/27/opinion/how-the-new-feminist-resistance-leaves-out-american-women.html.
8. Erika Bachiochi, 'After Roe v. Wade and Dobbs v. Jackson', *Plough*, 25 June 2022, https://www.plough.com/en/topics/justice/culture-of-life/after-roe-v-wade-and-dobbs-v-jackson.
9. Ibid. See also 'The Feminist Revolution Has Stalled: Blame *Roe v Wade*', *America: The Jesuit Review*, 1 November 2021, https://www.americamagazine.org/politics-society/2021/11/01/roe-wade-casey-texas-heartbeat-law-241725.
10. In her critical analysis of 'feminist storytelling' in the 1990s and 2000s, Clare Hemmings identifies three main narrative structures that are deployed: 1. the history of feminist thought and practice is constructed as a 'progress narrative' whereby feminism becomes ever more enlightened and inclusive; 2. a 'loss narrative' whereby feminism gradually loses its political efficacy and theoretical punch; 3. a 'return narrative' whereby feminism loses its way but recovers itself by looping back through the past. While Hemmings highlights feminist 'new materialism' as the core example of a feminism that constructs its identity through a 'return narrative', it is interesting to observe how anti-abortion feminism also deploys this historiographical structure. See Clare Hemmings, 'Telling Feminist Stories', *Feminist Theory* 6: 2 (2005), 115–139.
11. Feminists For Nonviolent Choices, 'What We Believe', accessed 5 October 2022, https://www.ffnvc.org/what-we-believe. As another example, Feminists Choosing Life of New York write: 'The founders of the feminist movement all opposed abortion in the strongest terms. Pro-life feminism actually preceded pro-choice feminisms and has been here ever since. It was only in the 1960's that the National Organization of Women (NOW) incorporated abortion into their version of feminist goals and intertwined the idea of abortion and feminism in the minds of the public'. 'FAQs', accessed 5 October 2022, fclny.org/faqs.

12. See, for example, Tracy A. Thomas, 'Misappropriating Women's History in the Law and Politics of Abortion', *Seattle University Law Review* 36:1 (2012); Ann D. Gordon and Lynn Sherr, 'No, Susan B. Anthony and Elizabeth Cady Stanton Were Not Antiabortionists', *Time*, 10 November 2015; or Ann D. Gordon, 'Knowing Susan B. Anthony: The Stories We Tell of a Life', in *Susan B. Anthony and the Struggle for Equal Rights*, eds. Christine Ridarsky and Mary Huth (Rochester NY: University of Rochester Press, 2012).

13. Bachiochi, 'After *Roe v. Wade*'. A fuller exposition of her views can be found in *The Rights of Women: Reclaiming a Lost Vision* (Notre Dame, IN: Notre Dame University Press, 2021), which draws particularly on the work of Mary Wollstonecraft who she appropriates here for the anti-abortion cause.

14. Cady Stanton and Anthony, for example, did support abolition but opposed the 14th and 15th Amendments which enshrined Black voting rights in the constitution due to the use of the phrase 'male citizens' in the text of the 14th, arguing that the cause of white women would be set back and humiliated if Black men were granted suffrage rights ahead of them. See, for example, Lori D. Ginzberg, *Elizabeth Cady Stanton: An American Life* (New York: Hill & Wang, 2009); Rosalyn Terborg-Penn, *African American Women in the Struggle for the Vote, 1850-1920* (Bloomington and Indianapolis: Indiana University Press, 1998).

15. Ginzberg, *Elizabeth Cady Stanton*, 122. This is a widely quoted line that appears, for example, in Angela Davis, *Women, Race and Class* (New York: Random House, 1981).

16. Tracy A. Thomas, *Elizabeth Cady Stanton and the Feminist Foundations of Family Law* (New York: NYU Press, 2020).

17. See, for instance, Dorothy E. Roberts, *Killing the Black Body: Race, Reproduction, and the Meaning of Liberty* (New York: Pantheon, 1997); or Loretta J. Ross and Rickie Solinger, *Reproductive Justice: An Introduction* (Oakland, CA: University of California Press: 2017).

18. SisterSong, Women of Color Reproductive Justice Collective, accessed 5 October 2022, https://www.sistersong.net/reproductive-justice.

19. Judith Roof, 'Generational Difficulties, or The Fear of a Barren History', *Generations: Academic Feminists in Dialogue*, eds. Devoney Looser and E. Ann Kaplan (Minneapolis: University of Minnesota Press, 1997), 71; Astrid Henry, *Not My Mother's Sister: Generational Conflict and Third Wave Feminism* (Bloomington and Indianapolis: Indiana University Press, 2004). Elsewhere I have emphasised that to dismiss generational paradigms as wholly or exclusively patriarchal and Oedipal is to miss the multiple meanings and temporalities that they can express and establish within feminist discourse. See Victoria Browne, *Feminism, Time and Nonlinear History* (London and New York: Palgrave, 2014). For example, we should consider the particular resonance and meaning of matrilineal metaphors within the context of Black US feminism/womanism, as writers like Alice Walker have deployed the metaphor of matrilineage to overcome a brutal history of dislocation and disinheritance (see, for example, *In Search of our Mothers' Gardens: Womanist Prose* (New York: Harcourt, 1983)).

20. Quoted in Oaks, 'What Are Pro-Life Feminists Doing on Campus?', 186–187.

21. Feminists for Life, 'Accomplishments', accessed 5 October 2022, https://www.feministsforlife.org/accomplishments/.

22. Bachiochi, 'After *Roe v. Wade*'.

23. Progressive Anti-Abortion Uprising, accessed 5 October 2022, https://paaunow.org/.

24. New Wave Feminists, 'About', accessed 5 October 2022, https://www.newwavefeminists.com/aboutnewwavefeminists.com/about; and Progressive Anti-Abortion Uprising.

25. Bachiochi, 'I Couldn't Vote for Trump but I'm Grateful for his Supreme Court Picks', *New York Times*, 7 December 2021, https://www.nytimes.com/2021/12/07/opinion/trump-supreme-court-abortion-dobbs-roe.html.

26. Bachiochi, 'The Feminist Revolution has Stalled'.

27. Progressive Anti-Abortion Uprising, 'Stances: Capitalism', accessed 5 October 2022, https://paaunow.org/stances-capitalism.

28. Bachiochi, 'The feminist revolution has stalled'.

29. Bachiochi, '*After Roe v. Wade*'; 'Reclaiming Feminism from the Logic of the Market', *Newsweek*, 15 July 2021, newsweek.com/reclaiming-feminism-logic-market-opinion-1607303.

30. New Wave Feminists, 'Dobbs Amicus Brief – Press Release', accessed 5 October 2022, https://www.fclny.org/_files/ugd/689b6c_08441c88202f493a8c1b104f0fbfd7a1.pdf.

31. Ibid.

32. FCLNY, 'FAQs', accessed 5 October 2022, fclny.org/faqs.

33. Roberts, *Killing the Black Body*, 181.

34. New Wave Feminists, 'The Bomb Shelter', accessed 5 October 2022, newwavefeminists.com/thebombshelter.

35. National Advocates for Pregnant Women, 'National Advocates for Pregnant Women Files Brief with U.S. Supreme Court Focusing on the Impact of Mississippi's Abortion Ban on All Pregnant People, Not Only Those Seeking to End a Pregnancy', 20 September 2021, accessed 5 October 2022, nationaladvocatesforpregnantwomen.org/dobbs-brief-release-9-2021.

36. Susan Pedersen, 'Prejudice Rules: *LRB* Contributors on the Overturning of *Roe v. Wade*', London Review of Books 44:14, 21 July 2022.

37. PAAU, 'Stances: Abortion', accessed 5 October 2022, paaunow.org/stances.

38. FCLNY, 'Mission and Purpose', accessed 5 October 2022, https://www.fclny.org/mission-and-purpose-staff-and-board; NWF, 'The Bomb Shelter', accessed 5 October 2022, https://www.newwavefeminists.com/thebombshelter.

39. Bachioci, 'What Makes a Fetus a Person'?, *New York Times*, 1 July 2022, https://www.nytimes.com/2022/07/01/opinion/fetal-personhood-constitution.html.

40. Bachiochi, 'I Couldn't Vote for Trump'.

41. See, for example, Margaret Olivia Little, 'Abortion, Intimacy, and the Duty to Gestate', *Ethical Theory and Moral Practice* 2:3 (1999), 295–312; or Catriona Mackenzie 'Abortion and Embodiment', *Australasian Journal of Philosophy* 70:2 (1992), 136–55.

42. See, for example, Victoria Browne, Jason Danely and Doerthe Rosenow, eds., *Vulnerability and the Politics of Care: Transdisciplinary Dialogues* (Oxford: Oxford University Press, 2021); or Judith Butler, Zeynep Gambetti and Leticia Sabsay, eds., *Vulnerability in Resistance* (Durham NC: Duke University Press, 2016).

43. Erinn Gilson, 'The Problems and Potentials of Vulnerability', in *Vulnerability and the Politics of Care*, 85–6.
44. Ibid., 92.
45. Katie E. Oliviero, 'Vulnerability's Ambivalent Political Life: Trayvon Martin and the Racialized and Gendered Politics of Protection', *Feminist Formations* 28:1 (2016), 19.
46. Deborah Lupton, 'Introduction: Conceptualising and Configuring the Unborn Human', in *The Unborn Human*, ed. Lupton (Open Humanities Press, 2013), 1.
47. Lisa Guenther, *The Gift of the Other: Levinas and the Politics of Reproduction* (Albany, NY: State University of New York Press, 2006), 146.
48. See, for example, the CDC data on maternal mortality, accessed 5 October, cdc.gov/reproductivehealth/maternal-mortality/pregnancy-mortality-surveillance-system.htm); or cdc.gov/mmwr/volumes/68/wr/mm6835a3.htm?s_cid=mm6835-a3_w#T1_down.
49. Lauren Berlant, 'America, "Fat", the Fetus', *boundary 2* 21:3 (1994), 147.
50. Penelope Deutscher, *Foucault's Futures: A Critique of Reproductive Reason* (New York: Columbia University Press: 2016), 155.
51. Black Lives Matter, 'Black Lives Matter Global Network Foundation Statement on Supreme Court Ruling Overturning *Roe*', 24 June 2022, blacklivesmatter.com/black-lives-matter-global-network-foundation-statement-on-supreme-court-ruling-overturning-roe.
52. FCLNY, 'ALL Black Lives Matter' by Caroline Bennett, 27 July 2020, https://www.fclny.org/_files/ugd/689b6c_b47b68a609fd4f789e690dd3cce30893.pdf. Cf., for example, Shyrissa Dobbins-Harris, 'The Myth of Abortion as Black Genocide: Reclaiming our Reproductive Cycle', *National Black Law Journal* 26:1 (2018), 86–125.
53. Loretta J. Ross, 'Re-enslaving African American Women', *On the Issues*, 24 November 2008, ontheissuesmagazine.com/cafe2.php?id=22.
54. Shyrissa Dobbins-Harris, 'The Myth of Abortion as Black Genocide'.
55. Lisa Guenther, 'The Most Dangerous Place: Pro-Life Politics and the Rhetoric of Slavery', *Postmodern Culture* 22:2, (2013).
56. 'Transcript: Ezra Klein interviews Erika Bachiochi', *New York Times*, 31 May 2022, nytimes.com/2022/05/31/podcasts/-transcript-ezra-klein-interviews-erika-bachiochi.html.
57. See, for example, Bachiochi, 'Embodied Equality'.
58. Bachiochi, 'Reclaiming Feminism from the Logic of the Market', *Newsweek* 15 July 2021, https://www.newsweek.com/reclaiming-feminism-logic-market-opinion-1607303.
59. PAAU, 'Our Commitments', accessed 5 October 2022, paaunow.org/about.
60. PAAU, 'Stances: Contraception', accessed 5 October 2022, paaunow.org/stances-contraception.
61. Bachiochi, 'After *Roe v. Wade*'.
62. Bachiochi, 'The feminist revolution has stalled'.
63. FCLNY, 'FAQs', accessed 5 October 2022, fclny.org/faqs.
64. Ezra Klein interviews Erika Bachiochi, *New York Times*, 31 May 2022, https://www.nytimes.com/2022/05/31/podcasts/transcript-ezra-klein-interviews-erika-bachiochi.html
65. FFL, 'What About Rape?', accessed 5 October 2022, https://www.feministsforlife.org/what-about-rape/.
66. Ibid.
67. Loretta J. Ross and Rickie Solinger, *Reproductive Justice: An Introduction* (Oakland, CA: Uni of California Press, 2017), 69.
68. Sarah Jones, 'There's No Such Thing As a Pro-Life Feminist', *Intelligencer*, 31 November 2021, nymag.com/intelligencer/2021/11/theres-no-such-thing-as-a-pro-life-feminist.html.
69. Andrea Smith, 'Beyond Pro-Choice versus Pro-Life: Women of Colour and Reproductive Justice', *NWSA Journal* 17:1 (2005), 119–40.
70. Ibid., 133–134.
71. Loretta J. Ross, Lynn Roberts, Erika Derkas, Whitney Peoples and Pamela Bridgewater Toure, eds., *Radical Reproductive Justice: Foundations, Theory, Practice, Critique* (New York: Feminist Press, 2017).
72. Quoted in Regina Mahone, 'The Future is "Radical Reproductive Justice"', *Rewire*, 28 November 2017, rewirenewsgroup.com/2017/11/28/future-radical-reproductive-justice/.
73. Charlotte Shane, 'The Right Not to be Pregnant: Asserting an Essential Freedom', *Harper's*, October 2022, https://harpers.org/archive/2022/10/the-right-to-not-be-pregnant-asserting-an-essential-right/; see also Erica Millar, *Happy Abortions: Our Bodies in the Era of Choice* (London: Zed Books, 2018), and Sophie Lewis, 'Abortion Involves Killing – and That's OK! To Be Prochoice is to be Against Forced Life', *The Nation*, 22 June 2022, thenation.com/article/society/abortion-ethics-gestation-reproduction.
74. Shane, 'The Right Not to be Pregnant'.
75. Amia Srinivasan, 'What Should Feminist Theory Be?', *Radical Philosophy* 212 (Spring 2022), 49.
76. Shane, 'The Right Not to be Pregnant'.

Tutelage or assimilation?
Kant on the educability of the human races
Marie Louise Krogh

Der Mensch kann nur Mensch werden durch Erziehung.
Immanuel Kant, *Lectures on Pedagogy*, 1803.[1]

Few topics have in recent years caused more controversy in studies in the history of philosophy than the issue of Immanuel Kant's conception of race and its significance for the universalism of his moral and political philosophy. In this article, I turn to these debates to make the case that it matters not simply *that* we recognise the centrality of Kant's conceptual work in natural history to his critical philosophy, but also *how* we subsequently conceive of the importance of such a realisation to the universalisms of later works in the Kantian tradition of philosophy and critical theory. I do so in three steps. First, I introduce Kant's natural historical conception of race and present an abridged history of the reception of Kant's works on race that has taken place since Emmanuel C. Eze's seminal 'The Color of Reason: The Idea of "Race" in Kant's Anthropology' was first published in 1995. I do this in order to discuss some of the different interpretative strategies that have been leveraged to deal with the perceived divide between Kant's racism and his moral universalism. Second, I will make the case that what I call the 'Schillerian' reading of how to bridge this divide presents the standpoint from which we can refuse a false choice between what Pauline Kleingeld famously termed Kant the 'inconsistent moral universalist' and Kant the 'consistent inegalitarian'.[2] Third, I will show that this Schillerian reading can be grounded in Kant's own reflections on pedagogy, which thus far have been absent from discussions of how to understand the function and significance of Kant's concept of race. By recovering Kant's reflections on pedagogy and demonstrating their links to the theory of race, I wish to emphasise how the nexus between Kant's racism and his concept of race might be expressed not only in relation to the brute domination of slavery and colonial exploitation but also in the ideological conception of an educative function attributed to the white race: a function which can be fulfilled by softer powers but which fundamentally assumes a relation of inequality up until the point where those who are to be educated can be said to assume their own maturity (*Mündigkeit*). From this perspective, Kant's writing on race leaves us with a somewhat starker choice when it comes to his universalism: we can view it either as a false universalism for the white race only, or as a universalism that also implies an assimilationist regime. To conclude, I will make the case that though the former scenario – that of a false universalism – may be more obviously offensive, the latter – that of an implied assimilationist regime – is the more insidious of the two, because it presents itself as no racism at all.

(Re)placing race in the history of philosophy

Every so often, an interventionist reading in the history of philosophy is produced, such that the field in which it intervenes is forced to reassess, discard or defend its basic tenets. For Kant studies broadly conceived, Eze's 1995 essay 'The Color of Reason: The Idea of "Race" in Kant's Anthropology' can be said to have constituted such a reading, as it forced a reckoning with Kant's conception of race, and in particular with its place and function within his critical system.[3] What Eze brought back to public memory was the fact that Kant had been an eager participant in eighteenth-century debates on the possibility of a systematic knowledge of organised living beings, as the second part of *The Critique of the Power of Judgement,* 'The Critique of Teleological Judgement' (1790), so amply testifies. However, Eze focused not on the *Critique,* but rather on Kant's writings on physical geography and anthropology, alongside three then lesser-known essays: 'On the Different Races of Human Beings' (1775), 'Determination of the Concept of a Human Race' (1785) and 'On the Use of Teleological Principles in Philosophy' (1788). If, as Robert Bernasconi has since argued, the invention of a concept coincides with that articulation and demarcation of said concept which made it possible for others to subsequently debate and question its scientific status, then Kant might, in these three texts, hold the very dubious honour of having 'invented' the modern and 'scientific' concept of race.[4]

What Kant proposed was that the already prevalent classificatory division of the human species into four different races – 'the whites, the yellow Indians, the Blacks and the copper-red Americans'[5] – could be grounded in a natural historical *concept* of race. This concept was articulated by Kant within a natural history of humankind, encompassed within a physical and generative system of nature as opposed to a merely synchronic classificatory system.[6] In all three of the essays, Kant followed what he called 'Buffon's rule', arguing that all humans, despite synchronically notable and classifiable differences in their appearances, belong to one and the same line of descent [*phylum*] since even members belonging to different classes of physical appearance can produce fertile offspring.[7] Races, in turn, name those classes defined by *unfailingly* hereditary characteristics that have developed over the course of generations, under the prolonged influence of different climatic conditions upon the original predispositions [*Anlage*] and germs [*Keime*] in the human *phylum*.[8] Kant's theory is that four basic climatic environments (cold and humid, cold and dry, hot and humid, hot and dry) would, as humans migrated to populate all of the Earth, have activated a determinate 'unfolding' of germs and predispositions that, once developed, settled each race into a form suited for the conditions of life corresponding to the region of the world dominated by this climate.[9] In the course of Kant's works on physical geography, what at first seems to have been a merely mechanist account of this activation, gradually develops into the conceptualisation of purposive nature, which can be seen to have unfolded as if it was 'willed' 'that human beings should populate the entire Earth. All animals have their special climates, but human beings are to be found everywhere. Human beings are not to stay in a small region, but to spread out across the entire Earth.'[10]

Where the first humans would have held the potential for all later developed racial characteristics, once a certain set of germs settled into their form this form would subsequently have rendered dormant all other potentials. Unlike mere *varieties* in the species (say, the synchronically notable and also classifiable differences in eye colour or hair colour), Kant therefore considered racial characteristics to persistently preserve themselves *and* to invariably 'beget half-breed young in the mixing'.[11] What is important to note here is that as much as the concept of race refers to a process of differentiation from a common origin, what it truly names is the final result, that is, the arrestation of this process and the fixing of the species into four different races.[12] On Kant's understanding, racial characteristics, in these essays primarily skin colour, entailed a permanent fixture within each race. We might therefore ask if it is only physiological and anatomical differences that are fixed in this manner? Since Kant's proposal for a division of the human species into four races was paired with a number of assertions about an innate lack of industriousness in some non-white races and a general inferiority in the areas of art and science in all non-white races, his conception of race, as Eze pointed out, seemed to stand in unbearable tension with his moral and political universalism.[13]

Consequently, one of the central questions following the reassessment of Kant's texts on race has been whether we are better off regarding him today as, in Pauline Kleingeld's words, an 'inconsistent moral universalist' or as a 'consistent inegalitarian'?[14] Perhaps predictably, this formulation both diagnosed and enforced a structural divide between accusers and defenders of Kant within the field of interpretation, a divide which was then largely carried over into ensuing stages of these debates, in which the possibility of a connection between changes within Kant's views on the legitimacy of colonisation and imperialism and a change within his conception of racial difference were placed at the forefront.[15] In short, debates concerning whether or not Kant changed his mind about the importance and indeed existence of a racial hierarchy have, at least within the disciplinary bounds

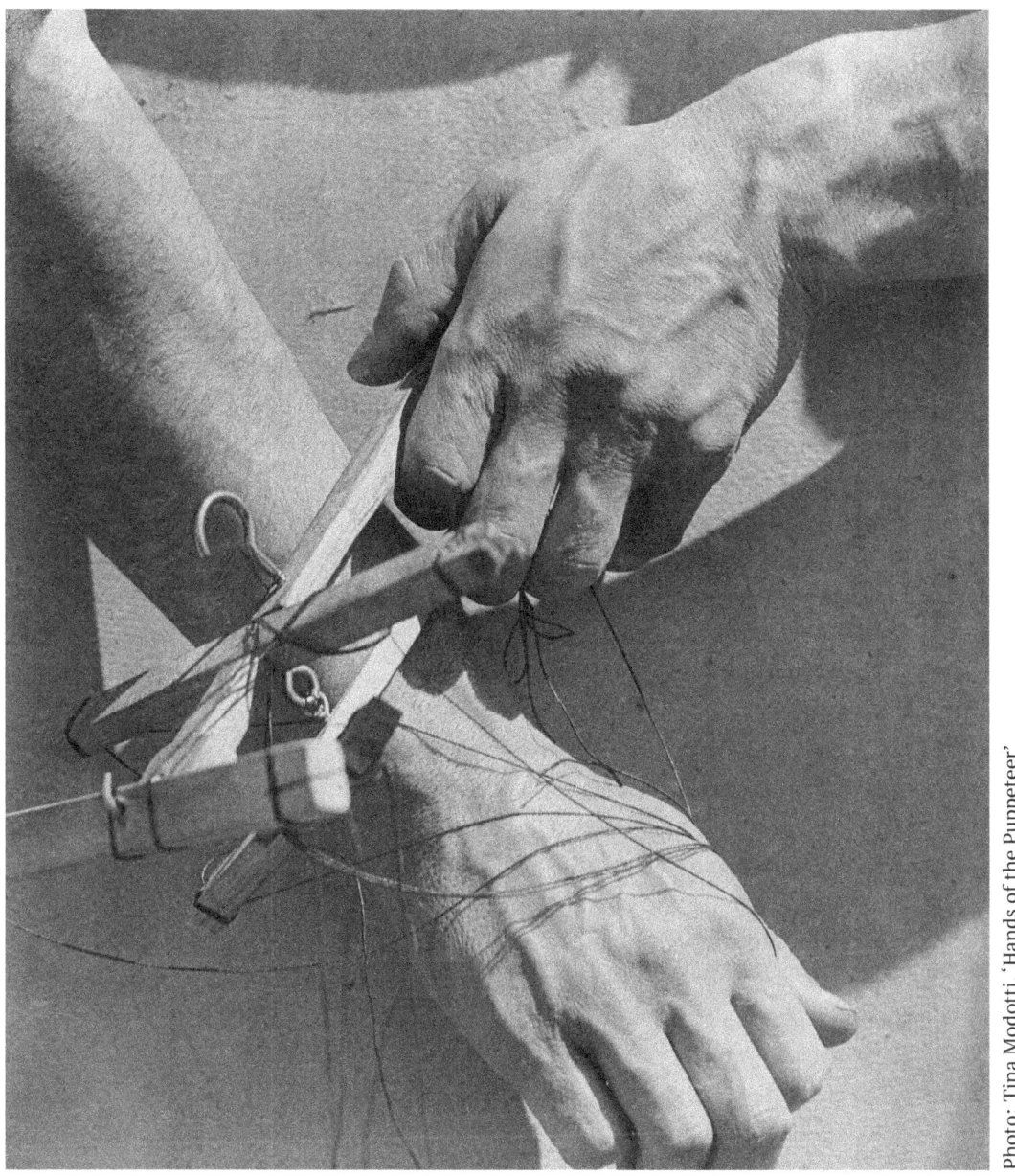

Photo: Tina Modotti, 'Hands of the Puppeteer'

of philosophy, come to dominate the work done on questions concerning Kant's theory of race.[16]

Another interpretative strategy, one that to my mind is more critically fruitful than that of attempting to exonerate the later Kant from the faults of the younger, follows Eze's initial insight and seeks to eschew the premise of a straightforward divide between an inconsistent moral universalism and a consistent non-egalitarianism. Instead, this strategy takes the form of an enquiry into the construction of Kant's universalism itself, in order to pose the question of whether the perceived depth of a contradiction between universalism and racism might in fact cover over a racist universalism, which thus calls for us to rethink the very concept of universality.[17] I'm thinking here of the different ways in which the works of Gayatri C. Spivak, Denise Ferreira da Silva, David Lloyd and Etienne Balibar each engage the Kantian corpus and its afterlife in critical and aesthetic theory and thereby take part in a both more subtle and more difficult attempt to rethink modern political epistemologies and the conceptual conditions for emancipatory thought on a global scale.

An aesthetic education: the Schillerian reading

From the standpoint of these critical engagements with Kant, the problem is not that he was inconsistent in his universalism nor really that he was personally racist. It is that racial hierarchies and processes of racialisation can be reinforced even by a consistent Kantian universalism. In the case of Lloyd's *Under Representation: The Racial Regime of Aesthetics* and Spivak's *A Critique of Postcolonial Reason*, this diagnosis is made through essentially Schillerian readings of Kant's third *Critique*. What broadly prompts the qualification of these readings as 'Schillerian' is that their objects are processes of subjectivation and subject formation rather than the transcendental conditions of possibility for theoretical, practical or, in this case, aesthetic and teleological judgments.[18] It was this displacement which famously caused Paul de Man to characterise Schiller's translation of critical philosophy into a *Bildungsphilosophie* as 'a regression, an attempt to account for, to domesticate the critical incisiveness of the original' in that it took the aesthetic itself 'as an exemplary category, as a unifying category, as a model for education, as a model even for the state.'[19] In short, Schiller re-anthropomorphised transcendental aesthetic philosophy within an educative programme in the service of good citizenship within a model state. In this sense, Schiller's *Letters on the Aesthetic Education of Man* appeared as 'the ideology of Kant's critical philosophy'.[20] But rather than take Schiller's anthropomorphic moment as a regrettable regression, Spivak and Lloyd each critically appropriate it as a lever through which a truth about Kant's universalism can be revealed, namely that the constitution of the subject of this universalism rests on a fundamental but unavowed geopolitical differentiation. As Balibar has commented in regard to Spivak's reading, the central problem of the empirical/transcendental split within the Kantian subject when considered at a global level is that as different humans seek to become adequate to subjecthood, 'empirical differences are converted into unequal capacities to realise the proper human, and [this] even leaves the possibility that some racially inferior humans will never be educated, i.e., will never prove able to recognise the idea of the community [of human beings] to which they should belong'.[21]

When both Spivak and Lloyd establish this insight through readings of *The Critique of the Power of Judgement*, it is in close reference to a passage from the analytic of the dynamic sublime, in which Kant hints at an empirical difference in the capacity for an experience of the sublime (that is, in the capacity to enact the displacement of an intuition of the boundlessness of reason into natural awe). 'Without the development of moral ideas', writes Kant, 'that which we, prepared by culture, call sublime presents itself to man in the raw [*dem rohen Menchen*] merely as terrible'.[22] And although the notion of 'man in the raw' within this argument structurally translates as 'uneducated man' (or so I will argue), the signification can be stretched, as it is by both Spivak and Lloyd, to include the 'savage' or the 'primitive'. From this standpoint, Spivak and Lloyd respectively emphasise two different orchestrations of racial inequality within the *Third Critique*. In her 'affirmative sabotage' of Kant's critique, Spivak uses the impossible inscription of an anthropological and ethnological figure of the 'native informant' in the *Critique,* to foreground a scenario in which the racialised not-quite-subject that is the 'other' of the subject of aesthetic judgement is constitutively excluded in an indefinite foreclosure.[23] Lloyd instead emphasises how the idea of a freely judging aesthetic subject implies a developmental trajectory and an intimated project for the assimilation of the racialised 'other' of this subject.[24] That is to say, it is the mark of an assimilationist universalism, since those standards held by a dominant group to be universal are translated into a demand for all others to assimilate to these standards and to leave their particularities behind while the dominant group can retain its now universalised particularity.

It is Spivak who explicitly admits to having purposefully committed the Schillerian 'mistake' of mixing the empirical and the transcendental in the 'interest of producing a counter narrative that will make visible the foreclosure of the subject whose lack of access to the position of narrator is the condition of possibility of the consolidation of Kant's position'.[25] Yet it is Lloyd's critique which most closely follows Schiller's focus on progress through pedagogical formation, to disclose its proximity to the developmental narrative that subtends the idea of a European colonial civilising mission.[26] In Lloyd's words, Schiller's *Aesthetic Education* reveals the 'necessarily pedagogical infrastructure of the *Critique of Judgement*. By the same token, Schiller draws most clearly out of Kant's aesthetic theory the intertwining of its pedagogically developmental ends with its corresponding racial formation.'[27]

What neither Lloyd nor Spivak do, however, is explicitly to connect Kant's writing on race to their respective assessments of racialisation in the *Third Critique*. This leaves the systematic links between the writings on race and the moral, political and aesthetic philosophy hinted at, but seldom explicated. It is in this regard that Robert Bernasconi has been a particularly significant critical reader of Kant. The questions that have propelled Bernasconi's readings are by now well known: how does Kant's concept of race affect his universalism? And more speculatively, how might his very cosmopolitanism quell or intensify the systemically racist implications of his theory of race? In Bernasconi's answers to these questions, he has tended to focus on the issue of race-mixing, arguing that Kant had conjectured that a continuous intermixing of the races would result in an undesirable homogenisation of the human species (and a 'degradation' of the white race). In view of a one posthumously published note, in which Kant wrote that 'All races will go extinct ... except the white one',[28] Bernasconi has raised the sinister question of whether a segregationist cosmopolitanism could, ultimately, have genocidal implications?[29]

Since Kant did not himself explicitly draw these conclusions anywhere, a certain amount of interpretative speculation is inevitably involved in their formulation. What I would like to do here is to propose a different trajectory and a different set of possible conclusions concerning race-relations in Kant's political and moral philosophy, ones that correspond, respectively, to the idea of indefinite guardianship remarked on by Spivak and to the assimilationist universalism implied by Lloyd.

To demonstrate how infinite guardianship and assimilationist universalism might operate in Kant's case, I will introduce Kant's own writings on pedagogy as the mediating factor between, on the one hand, his works on psychical geography and physical anthropology (among which the texts on the concept of race belong) and, on the other hand, his works on pragmatic anthropology, cosmopolitanism and universal history. Whereas Kant studies seem to have accepted that there is an unbridgeable divide between the different perspectives offered on the human being by physical geography, pragmatic anthropology and moral philosophy, it is my contention that questions of moral development in the philosophy of history bind these bodies of work together. If there is, in Kant's words, a marked difference between 'what nature makes of man' and what humans as freely acting beings 'make, can make, and ought to make of themselves',[30] I will argue that Kant's many reflections on pedagogy construct a bridge between these two, in their focus on how to best make use of what nature makes of humans, so that humans in turn can learn to follow reason and assume their rational nature. In regard to the concept of race, what I will emphasise is that, to Kant, the very capacity for such a learning is premised on a preliminary disciplining of one's natural inclinations. And since the racialised others in Kant's physical anthropology are characterised precisely by degrees of deficiency in an inner capacity to enact such restraints – as pathological or affectable subjects in the words of da Silvia and Lloyd – 'race' comes to matter socially and politically as a schematism for a hierarchical order in the capacity to assume reason and moral agency. To demonstrate this, I will first emphasise the centrality of the 'educability' of humankind to the idea of moral development in Kant's philosophy of history and then show how this educability appears, in Kant's own framework, to be racially differentiated.

Kant on education and progress in history

Like the writings on race, Kant's *Lectures on Pedagogy* form a highly contested part of the Kantian corpus, if for different reasons. Kant never actually published a book on pedagogy but was, in the 1770s, charged with delivering a course on this topic which, by Prussian decree, had been made mandatory at all universities. It was Friedrich Theodor Rink, the one-time student of Kant also responsible for the publication of his materials on geography, who in 1803 collected, edited and published the manuscripts for these lectures as the immensely popular book *Immanuel Kant on Pedagogy*.[31] Though Kant does not mention the contents of the lectures on which this book was based in any of his outlines of the two parts that make up 'pragmatic knowledge of the world' – physical geography and anthropology – some of the questions raised by them overlap significantly with both of these fields. Where the physical geography of human beings, as mentioned, had as its object field 'what nature makes of man', anthropology instead illuminated how and to what extent humans shape their own characters. Observations regarding the specifically human need for a proper moral upbringing (*Erziehung*) are scattered across the transcripts and notes for the anthropology lectures, and the 1775–76 transcripts of the *Anthropology Friedländer* even includes the concluding section 'On Education' or 'On Upbringing', which most explicitly connects the problematic of how to provide a determinate concept of the character of the human species with a number of observations as to the importance of pedagogy for 'the improvement of humanity toward its perfection'.[32] Nowhere among Kant's many lectures on anthropology is the Enlightenment goal of human perfectibility through education more apparent than here. This is hardly surprising, given that Kant's first set of mandated lectures on pedagogy stem from this same period, as does his written and published support of the *Philanthropinum Dessau*, an experimental school whose founder, Johann Bernhard Basedow, authored the *Methodenbuch* (1773) on which Kant's lectures on pedagogy were based.[33] Much like the end of the *Anthropology* and the essay 'Idea for a Universal History with a Cosmopolitan Aim', these lectures contain several extended discussions of Rousseau's critique of the distorting effects of culture upon human nature and circle around the questions of how natural predispositions might best be either restrained or put to use for civil and civic purposes. In other words, they consider how humans, as beings with a natural potential for reason, can be given the best possible education to allow them to assume the task of becoming actual rational acting and thinking beings and contribute to the formation of the species as a whole. These reflections, much like the *Lectures on Pedagogy* as a whole, therefore touch on one of the central aspects of Kant's philosophy of history, namely the idea that those natural predispositions whose end is the use of reason, and which among terrestrial animals are particular to humans, do not develop instinctively within a closed circuit (as Kant considers mere animal predispositions to do) but are both ungrounded and open-ended.[34] Two primary consequences can be drawn from this assumption, one which Kant very openly pursues in 'Idea for a Universal History' and one which is more implicitly at stake but which is nonetheless crucial for grasping the schematising function of the concept of race in Kant's philosophy of history. First, when measured against the immense space of possibility which this open-ended development entails, each individual human existence is dwarfed in its own finitude. An absolutely central aspect of Kant's philosophy of history is therefore the idea that whereas each individual animal may realise its species determination and fully develop its natural predispositions, no individual human being can do so. It is only at the level of the species as a whole that the full development of the natural predispositions of terrestrial reasoned beings can be accomplished.[35] Second, the non-instinctive character of the development of these predispositions renders crucial the different modalities of inter-generational (and, as argued below, potentially inter-racial as well as inter-national) transmissions in the relay of the perfection of the human species. Each generation (and potentially each race, each nation) must learn, develop and teach, form and be formed, such that in a long sequence of generations, humans may overall become continuously better able to fulfil the vocation [*Bestimmung*] of their species: to live in accordance with their rational nature.

Nowhere does Kant assume that this process is unwavering, fully continuous or grounded in the ultimate goodness of human nature. The fabric of history, he writes, seems 'woven together out of folly, childish vanity, and often also out of childish malice and the rage to destruction'.[36] What is more, since one generation might lose what had been gained by previous ones and leave only a 'seed of enlightenment' to be recovered at a later point, the progress toward the perfection of the species is 'only fragmentary (according to time) and offers no guarantee against regression'.[37] But this does not render education and formation as such any less crucial to Kant's conception of universal history. What it does is rather to heighten the importance of what is best understood as a notion of 'educability': the very capacity to *learn*, to take form and to shape a so-called 'second nature' for oneself. To Kant, as Manfred Kuehn has noted, educability is not just *an* important human characteristic, but 'the most important one of all'.[38]

Educability is not a term used by Kant himself, but it is implied by those numerous formation processes that are central to both Kant's anthropology and his philosophy of history. Caught in a difficult-to-translate German terminological matrix, *Erziehung*, *Ausbildung* and *Bildung* refer back to educability as their joint condition of possibility. The possible conceptual distinctions implied by these terms within Kant's writings are difficult to track, both in the original, since the meaning of each is not entirely consistent, and even more so in English translations, wherein a tendency to treat them as relatively interchangeable makes it almost impossible to identify subtle differences which partake in conceptual distinctions. Where *Erziehung* and *Ausbildung* respectively imply different forms of child rearing and concrete education[39] – being taught either customs, manners, skills or knowledge – *Bildung* is most often used in a broader sense, to imply either different individual processes of formation or numerous processes of formation taken together as a whole. In their focus on the different levels of formation and educative instruction, the lectures on pedagogy can therefore be seen as a set of practical experimental meditations on the principles for making the best use of what 'nature makes of humans'. They are what allow us to see that educability forms the unnamed condition of possibility for moral formation within Kantian practical philosophy and, in this sense, they form a bridge between the two parts of pragmatic knowledge of the world: between physical geography and pragmatic anthropology. As I have already indicated, it is this bridge we can follow to see how the concept of race elaborated in the context of physical geography comes to matter to pragmatic anthropology and the philosophy of history it implies.

The educability of the human races

The question of pedagogy is linked to the writings on race through the necessity of discipline to all other forms of learning. In the *Lectures on Pedagogy* and in *Anthropology*, Kant distinguishes between three predispositions whose end is the use of reason, each of which corresponds to three different forms of educative requirements and, correspondingly, three endpoints for their development: a technical predisposition whose telos is skill [*Geschicklichkeit*]; a pragmatic predisposition whose telos is prudence [*Klugheit*]; and a moral predisposition whose telos is morality. The process of the development of each of these predispositions is in turn called 'cultivation' [*Kultivierung*], 'civilisation' [*Civilisirung*] and 'moral formation' [*moralische Bildung*] or simply 'moralisation' [*Moralisierung*].[40] This threefold division is also the refrain according to which, in 'Idea for a Universal History', it is emphasised that while the age of Enlightenment may be both cultivated and civilised, it is far from moralised.[41] To this threefold division of predispositions, however, a crucial fourth is added when we look to the *Lectures on Pedagogy*. What we might call a theory of the educability of human beings as such is here revealed: that one must learn first of all to become disciplined enough to restrict one's animal nature and learn to learn. This is clear from the fourfold differentiation of the levels of education found in the *Lectures,* which spell out how one must first learn:

1) How to become self-disciplined, so as to 'prevent animality from doing damage to humanity, both in the individual and in society.' Discipline is here considered 'merely the taming of savagery [*Wildheit*]'.[42]

2) To become *cultivated*. This is the process of learning different skills and thereby becoming *skilful*, the shaping of a faculty for *carrying out* a purpose one has set oneself. It does not dictate what concrete ends are worth pursuing but fundamentally concerns the procurement of the means for carrying out ends. Because there are a multitude of ends, there is likewise a multitude of skills and the determination of *which* skills are to be learned largely depends on ones future rank in society and on what one has a natural predisposition for.

3) To become *civilised* or acquire the capacity to act *prudently*. This is the acquisition of the prerequisite knowledge for navigating human societies in accordance with established manners. It is this form of knowledge which the anthropology in part is meant to convey in its focus on 'national character', such that students might be better placed when faced with manners different from their own. This is the realm of what we might call 'cultural differences' in Kant.

4) To nurture the predisposition to become moralised. This last step differs in character from the others, in that one cannot on Kant's view, properly speaking, be *taught* to be moralised. It is something a moral agent does *freely*. The function of education here is rather to foster a good *disposition* toward moralisation, such that the human being will 'choose nothing but good ends', which is to say ends that 'are necessarily approved by everyone and which can be the simultaneous ends of everyone'.[43]

The starkest of the racial hierarchies mapped out on the basis of Kant's anthropology lectures, found in the so-called *Menschenkunde*, is articulated precisely in this vocabulary of *Bildung* as a formative process that breaks with mere natural inclination. What is at stake in this is the differentiated capacities of the different races to enter into such formative processes on their own incentive, and the different levels overtly repeat the different levels of education outlined above. The 'Americans' are said to 'acquire no culture [*Bildung*]', the Black race 'acquire culture, but only a culture of slaves; that is, they allow themselves to be trained' and while the yellow Indians 'acquire culture in the highest degree', it is only in the 'arts and not in the sciences. They never raise it up to abstract concepts'. By contrast, 'the white race' 'contains all incentives and talents in itself' and '[w]henever any revolutions have occurred, they have always been brought about by the whites'.[44]

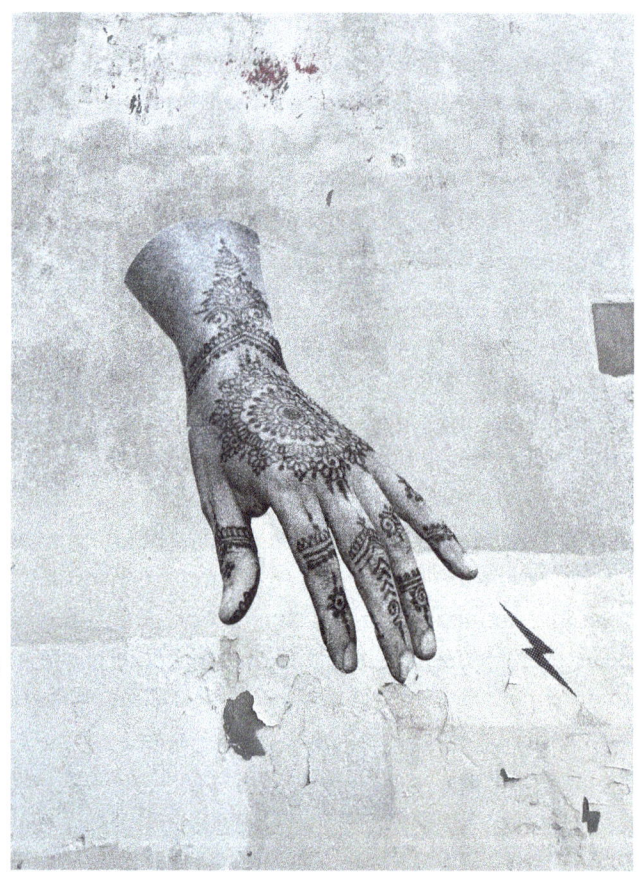

Photo: Panda Mery, 'Electric hand'

My argument, then, is that the hierarchy which divides those who do not acquire *Bildung*, those who can be formed but only into slaves, those who shape themselves according to highly refined forms but who stagnate there, and those who shape themselves according to all the natural predispositions for reason, reflects a conceptual differentiation, on Kant's part, in the educability of the different human races. The centrality of capacities, limitations and stagnations within different strata of *Bildung* is therefore crucial for any attempt to situate Kant's natural historical characterisations of races in relation to his universal world history of peoples. That some for Kant are *incapable* of *Bildung* – as a result of the development of their germs and predispositions – essentially entails that they have not been able to develop the means for restraining and reshaping their natural inclinations.

It is not, then, that Kant considered there to be different forms of transcendental frameworks for different races, nor that he considered other races to be devoid of reason as such. But what he did maintain was that there was something in the *natural historical* determination of each of these groups of humans that either aggravated or tamed those 'deficiencies' which cause *all* humans, as animals with rationality, to fall short of the demands of reason. In the published *Anthropology*, Kant explicitly ties such a deficiency – not in reason or the understanding as such but in the way in which it is exercised or executed – to questions that concern civil and therefore political maturity:

> An understanding that is in itself sound (without mental deficiencies) can still be accompanied by deficiencies with regard to its exercise, deficiencies that necessitate either a *postponement* until the growth to proper maturity, or even the *representation* [*Stellvertretung*] of one's person through that of another in regard to matters of civil nature. The (natural or legal) incapacity of otherwise sound human beings to use his *own* understanding in civil affairs is called *immaturity* [*Unmündigkeit*].[45]

This is the reason educability forms the prism through which we should be reading the essays on race, and why we have to carry that consideration through to the philosophy of history – because this is where race comes to matter and has consequences in a conception of a restricted capacity, within some humans, to impose the constraints necessary to educate *oneself*.

This perspective also sheds light on a striking feature of the *Anthropology*, namely that while it only briefly addresses the pragmatic significance of race, it extensively treats the subdivision of the national character of European nations that sit under the category of white racial lineage. One possible explanation of this exclusionary focus is found in the extended citation from the *Menschenkunde* discussed above, wherein the transition from a discussion of race to a discussion of nationality is effected through the already quoted conclusion that since 'the white race possesses all incentives and talents in itself ... we must examine it somewhat more closely.'[46] Another possible explanation is that while national characteristics specifically are said to be derived primarily from cultural distinctness, this is the case *only* for those nations in which a certain level of cultural development has been reached – in this sense Kant writes that it is only to the French and the English that national character proper can be attributed. For all others, a mixture of natural and cultural determinations, of national and racial limitations and potentials, will guide what such a people can make of themselves. In other words, their non-inclusion in the *Anthropology* reflects a highly normative set of assumptions inscribed within the idea of what a true national character is composed of, with only a fraction of the world's population truly qualifying as such.[47] And yet, Kant does specify, again and again, that what is special about humankind as opposed to other living species is that the entire species progresses in perfection. Despite serious consideration of the racism and race theory enveloped within this teleological conception of history, this is what causes scholars like Louden to conclude that the

> ideal of a truly universal moral community where all people count remains the most important single legacy of Kant's ethics ... Kant's writings in anthropology and empirical ethics do not tarnish this legacy. On the contrary they show us what we need to do to make it real. At the same time the underlying vision of gradual moral universality in these texts also reveals that the true intent of Kantian anthropology lies somewhere between transcendental and merely empirical concerns. In his lectures on anthropology Kant is not trying to make good on the ambitious claim that all philosophical questions are at bottom anthropological questions concerning the human subject but neither is he simply engaged in a descriptive account of human cultures. Rather his aim is to offer the species a moral map that they can use to move toward their collective destiny.[48]

Insofar as this describes a conception of what *Kant* considered the function of his *Anthropology* to be, this is a both perceptive and apt description. But, by downplaying how a racial dimension co-determines the questions of moral development, with which both Kant and Louden are wrestling, questions concerning the politics of race are ignored rather than addressed. The view that 'only some' will progress to perfection and others remain behind or forever stuck (women, other races than whites) is said to contradict Kant's continuous insistence upon the progress of the entire human species. But assertions to that effect do not so much *contradict* as they *introduce* the pedagogical question of education into the relation between races and genders (whites become the educators of non-whites, men the educators of women). Indeed, since the *whole* of the species is at issue while a part is particularised, the idea that an educative relation might, across the species, be what binds whole and part together, forcefully imposes itself. Summarising the characterisation of humankind in the *Anthropology*, we find the following statement:

> The sum total of pragmatic anthropology, in respect to the vocation of the human being and the characteristic of his formation [*Charakteristik seiner Ausbildung*] is as follows. The human being is destined by his reason to live in a society with human beings and in it to cultivate himself, to civilize himself, and to moralize himself by means of the arts and the sciences. No matter how great his animal tendency may be to give himself over passively to the impulses of ease and good living, which he calls happiness, he is still destined to make himself worthy of humanity by actively struggling with the obstacles that cling to him because of the crudity of his nature. *The human being must therefore be educated to the good*; but he who is to educate him is on the other hand a human being who still lies in the crudity of nature and who is now supposed to bring about what he himself needs. Hence the continuous deviation from his destiny with the always repeated returns to it.[49]

From this passage, we see that education, as already noted, has a crucial, but not straightforward, role to play in the philosophy of history, since at least two operative ideas of an educative journey are to be found therein: that of the immanent education of humankind and that of an 'education [*Erziehung*] from above'. Kant had, in *The Critique of the Power of Judgement,* also described the latter as an 'education by nature', and he here goes on to specify that this education is 'salutary but harsh and stern in the cultivation [*Bearbeitung*] of nature' and 'extends through great hardship and almost to the extinction of the entire species [*Geschlechts*]'.[50] It is the first, most straightforwardly recognisable educational relation between different generations *and* different peoples that I have primarily focused on here, since it concerns the transmission of models for thinking and for learning to orient oneself within the world. It is in this context that Kant encounters, restates and recognises the problem of the education of educators as one of the greatest challenges faced by humankind. As he noted in the *Lectures on Pedagogy*, 'two human inventions can probably be regarded as the most difficult, namely the arts of government and education'.[51] That humans are fallible means that no educator could ever teach perfectly according to the ends of reason:

> the problem of moral education for our *species* remains unsolved even in the quality of the principle, not merely in degree, because an evil tendency in our species may be censured by common human reason and perhaps also restrained, but it will thereby still not have been eradicated.[52]

In effect, what amounts to any form of progress here is the process of the improvement of the conditions for an education, aiming at generational moral improvement. As such, moral improvement is in no way secured and progress by no means certain, but it is more likely that if good education is in place, better citizens and more moral human beings will develop.

This is also clear in *The Conflict of the Faculties*, where the problems of a philosophy of history capable of predicting the progression of the human species are refracted through the problem of education.[53] The immanent idea of education is here divided into two models: one in which education comes from below (from individuals that improve themselves and then go on to improve the social and political whole), and one in which the form and principles of education are imposed by the state in a top-down model. Kant is unequivocal in his support of this latter model, writing that the general education of a people – a condition for their becoming not only good citizens but also good human beings who can improve and take care of themselves – depends on a training which is not the prerogative of families alone but should be carried out at state-level policy:

> The whole mechanism of this education has no coherence if it is not designed in agreement with a well-weighed plan of the sovereign power, put into play according to the purpose of this plan, and steadily maintained therein; to this end it might well behove the state likewise to reform itself from time to time and, attempting evolution instead of revolution, progress perpetually toward the better.[54]

When compared to the early texts on Basedow's *Philanthropinum* and on Enlightenment experiments in educational methods, it seems clear from these passages that Kant actually became increasingly agnostic as to the extent to which national improvements of education could be the key to the uninterrupted progression of the human species toward the better. But this does not dispel the problem of the possible means of *spreading* progress across the globe, to all the populations of the Earth, such that, eventually, a move from 'international barbarism' to a 'lawful cosmopolitan whole' can be effectuated. Among the mechanisms of distribution discussed by Kant, war and commerce, the 'unsocial sociability' of humankind, are central as the dynamic and conflictual forces in a universal world history toward cosmopolitanism. Though Kant seems to have wavered about the degree to which commercial sociability might either quell or incite conflict,[55] he remained unwavering on the view that war – though it may in the short term impede progress by the way in which it funnels funds away from the task of educating each population, and is in this and other regards to be considered, unquestionably, one of the greatest evils – served a purpose from the projected standpoint of the whole of universal world history, insofar as it drives nations toward the formation of a cosmopolitan whole.[56] It is, in other words, a part of that 'harsh and salutary' education through which purposive nature pushes humankind to continuously shape itself and develop its predisposition to reason. Though Kant may not sanction colonisation from the standpoint of his moral or political philosophy, in the philosophy of history it appears as a part of this very same history of the 'harsh education' of humankind. In this history, one part of humanity seems retrospectively to have been entrusted with the immanent education of those who have not of themselves been able to progress. The explanation for why this is the case is grounded in the concept of race that implies a conception of the restricted capacity within some humans to impose the constraints necessary to educate *themselves*. Since Kant considered the teleological end of history to be the transformation of a 'crude natural capacity for moral discrimination' into an actual moral regard for duties and rights and, with it, the transformation of a 'pathologically compelled agreement to form a society finally into a moral whole',[57] the question then seems to be whether such transformations are predicated on postponing the self-legislation of peoples considered dependent on an educational process of assimilation, or whether they are predicated on a perpetual state of representation in which guardianship of the cosmopolitan whole is entrusted to a select population, or indeed a select race? In short, what is entailed by that differentiation of educability seems inevitably to be either indefinite guardianship (Spivak's assessment) or a postponement of self-representation upon the point of maturity, premised upon a process of assimilation (Lloyd's assessment). Both appear to be possible: they represent the two primary interpretational options for understanding civic consequences of the fourfold difference in the educability of the human races – between those who acquire no culture; those who can be trained; those who acquire culture to the highest degree; and those who acquire both culture to the highest degree *and* the capacity to abstractly conceptualise it.

Conclusion

Two slightly different sets of questions can at this point be asked. First, in terms of a systematic assessment of Kant's writings, are there grounds for thinking that either of these two scenarios – that of indefinite guardianship or that of assimilation – was envisaged by Kant? And second, in terms of the afterlife of Kantian philosophy, what do they respectively mean for universalism today? In conclusion, I will briefly consider each of these sets of questions.

Through the first of these interpretational prisms, the fixation at a certain moment of the development of some germs and predispositions over and above others entails that for *some* races, no process of cultivation or education is at all possible in Kant's view. This would seem to entail the idea of a permanent social and political organisation of the world under white supremacy.[58] This racist idea of tutelage most obviously thrives in some formations of far-right ideology, and is in many ways easily recognisable as such. It makes no claim to true universality and inscribes permanent inequality within its very constitution. Through the second interpretational prism, the limitation in educability is not to be understood as permanent *tout court* but as a limitation of what, within each race, those who belong to such a race can *make of themselves*; that is, as something which, through the proper training and education from those who have already acquired a certain base level of cultivation, might be imparted to them. Where some of Kant's statements seem to hint at the first option, a note concerning the *global* prospect of a historical progression of the human species toward perfection, found among the loose sheets of teaching notes for Kant's anthropology lectures, hints at the latter:

> We must seek the continuous progress of humankind toward perfection in the occident, and from there its dissemination around the Earth [*Verbreitung auf der Erde suchen*].[59]

The passage is ambiguous with respect to the concluding reference to the *dissemination* of progress toward perfection – most notably with respect to the *means* of dissemination. When we inquire into the function of geography within Kant's philosophy of history, we should take our cues from such ambiguities. Though Kant may have changed his position on the permissibility of conquest and of the slave-trade, the question of the dissemination of the continuous progress of humankind toward perfection 'around the Earth' persists in the stability of a racialised differentiation between educators and educated. What can be said to have changed might then merely be Kant's view on the legitimate means for the promulgation of such an education. As I mentioned above, this means that the nexus between Kant's racism and his concept of race is expressed not only in relation to the brute domination of slavery and colonial exploitation but also in the ideological conception of an educative role – a civilising mission – that fundamentally assumes a relation of inequality up until the point where those who are to be educated can be said to assume their own maturity (*Mündigkeit*). This goes to the core of Kant's philosophy of history in which the institution of cosmopolitanism is premised on a passage through the state-form, and in which white Western European nations, as the generators of the socio-political models appropriate to the full realisation of the predispositions of the human species, form the privileged locus for historical dynamism. The education of the 'rest' of humanity that follows might employ a variety of means but the aim remains that of learning to adopt the 'appropriate' model. In other words, learning to assimilate. This position can still be upheld as a universalism, yet it is one where self-determination on the part of those always-already excluded never comes into the picture. Can we think and enact an emancipatory universalism that is not assimilationist? That is the question Kant's view of the differential educability of the human races seems to leave us with.[60]

Marie Louise Krogh is University Lecturer in Continental Philosophy at Leiden University. She holds a PhD from CRMEP, Kingston University, London.

Notes

1. Immanuel Kant, *Pädagogik* in *Kants gesammelte Schriften*, Akademie Ausgabe Vol. IX (Berlin: Walter de Gruyter, 1923), 443. Henceforth all references to the *Akademie Ausgabe* of Kant's works are abbreviated as AA followed by the volume number.
2. Pauline Kleingeld, 'Kant's Second Thoughts on Race', *The Philosophical Quarterly* 57:229 (October 2007), 576.
3. As Robert Bernasconi notes, that Kant was a recognised theorist of race seems to have been common knowledge in the nineteenth and even early twentieth century. See Robert Bernasconi, 'Kant as an Unfamiliar Source of Racism', in *Philosophers on Race*, eds. Julie K. Ward and Tommy L. Lott (Malden, MA: Blackwell, 2002), 162n6.
4. Robert Bernasconi, 'Who Invented the Concept of Race? Kant's Role in the Enlightenment Construction of Race', in *Race*, ed. Robert Bernasconi (Oxford: Blackwell, 2001), 11–36.
5. Immanuel Kant, 'Determination of the Concept of a Human Race', trans. Holly Wilson and Günter Zöller, in *Anthropology, History and Education*, eds. Günter Zöller and Robert B. Louden (Cambridge: Cambridge University Press, 2007), 147.
6. Immanuel Kant, 'On the Use of Teleological Principles in Philosophy', trans. Günter Zöller, in *Anthropology, History and Education*, 200.
7. Kant, 'Of The Different Races of Human Beings', trans. Holly Wilson and Günter Zöller, in *Anthropology, History and Education*, 84.
8. Kant, 'Determination of the Concept of a Human Race', 155. In the first iterations of this theory, there is an operative distinction between germs [*Keime*] as the ground of a determinate 'unfolding' that effects the particular parts of an organism and natural predispositions [*natürliche Anlage*] as the ground of a determinate 'unfolding' of the relations between parts and their size. However, as Phillip R. Sloan has shown, when the question concerning the purposive development of organisms is taken up in the *Critique of the Power of Judgement*, Kant, likely influenced by Blumenbach, no longer uses the term *Keime* and instead appears to have reconfigured his theory of race to centre on *natürliche Anlage*, which, in turn, takes on a more dynamic role within this theory. See Phillip R. Sloan, 'Performing the Categories: Eighteenth-Century Generation Theory and the Biological Roots of Kant's A Priori', *Journal of the History of Philosophy* 40:2 (April 2002), 229–53.
9. Extensive work has been done on the extent to which Kant relied on preformationist or epigenetic theories of organismic development and on the possible changes in his view – that is, if the full potential for development was inherent in the original predisposition or if the very potentiality for development may have changed over the course of several generations. See Immanuel Kant, *Kant and The Concept Race: Late Eighteenth-Century Writings*, ed. Jon M. Mikkelsen (New York: SUNY Press, 2013). On the shifts in Kant's own position on preformation and epigenesis, see John H. Zammito, 'Kant's Persistent Ambivalence Towards Epigenesis, 1764–1790', in *Understanding Purpose: Kant and the Philosophy of Biology*, ed. Philippe Huneman (Rochester: University of Rochester Press, 2007), 51–74.
10. Immanuel Kant, 'Antropologie Friedländer', trans. G. Felicitas Munzel, in *Lectures on Anthropology*, eds. Allan W. Wood and Robert B. Louden (Cambridge: Cambridge University Press, 2012), 215.
11. Kant, 'Of the Different Races of Human Beings', 85, and 'Determination of the Concept of a Human Race', 149.
12. While Kant does not exclude the possibility that there are other races, these are the four for which he considers there to have been indisputable proof that their characteristics are 'unfailingly hereditary'. Kant, 'Determination of the Concept of a Human Race', 153.
13. A good account of this tension can also be found in Thomas A. McCarthy, *Race, Empire, and the Idea of Human Development* (New York: Cambridge University Press, 2009), 42–68.
14. Pauline Kleingeld, 'Kant's Second Thoughts on Race', 576. When the field is split in this manner, Charles W. Mills (along with Eze and Bernasconi) has typically been considered representative of the view of Kant as a 'consistent inegalitarian', arguing to the effect that Kant did not count all humans as fully human and that therefore not all humans would have been either subject to or included within the moral demands of the categorial imperative. For his most recent defence of this position, see Charles W. Mills, 'Kant and Race, Redux', *Graduate Faculty Philosophy Journal* 35:1-2 (2014), 125–57. In a more recent piece, Mills however also made it clear that his critique of Kant was never *against* Kantianism in any straightforward manner. See Mills, 'Radical Black Kantianism', *Res Philosophica* 95:1 (January 2018), 1–33. For the view that Kant is best understood to have been an inconsistent moral universalist, Kleingeld, Louden, Thomas E. Hill and Bernard Boxill have all argued that while Kant in his pre-critical works expressed racist beliefs and while his theory of race might be regrettable, his moral philosophy also contains the universalist tenets necessary to counter these. See Thomas E. Hill and Bernard Boxill, 'Kant and Race', in *Race and Racism*, ed. Bernard Boxill (Oxford and New York: Oxford University Press, 2001), 448–71; Robert B. Louden, *Kant's Impure Ethics* (Oxford and New York: Oxford University Press, 2000), 93–106.
15. See Kleingeld, 'Kant's Second Thoughts on Colonialism' and Lea Ypi, 'Commerce and Colonialism in Kant's Philosophy of History', both in *Kant and Colonialism: Historical and Critical Perspectives*, eds. Katrin Flikschuh and Lea Ypi (Oxford: Oxford University Press, 2014), 43–67, 99–126; and Ian Storey, 'Empire and Natural Order in Kant's "Second Thoughts" on Race', *History of Political Thought* 36:4 (Winter 2015), 670–700.
16. I've focused almost exclusively on the English language literature on this topic. A book-length study of Kant's conception of the human races, and its connection to the anthropology, can also be found in Raphaël Lagier, *Les races humaines selon Kant* (Paris: PUF, 2004).

17. While this approach has had, unsurprisingly, hardly any traction within Kant studies, its history predates many of the debates that have unfolded in the latter. For a broad outline of this argument see Étienne Balibar, 'Racism as Universalism' in *Masses, Classes, Ideas*, trans. James Swenson (New York and London: Routledge, 1994) 191–204; and, later, 'Ontological Difference, Anthropological Difference, and Equal Liberty', *European Journal of Philosophy* 28:1 (March 2020), 1–12. For two discussions which situate Balibar's argument in relation to Kant's conception of cosmopolitanism, see James Ingram, *Radical Cosmopolitics: The Ethics and Politics of Democratic Universalism* (New York: Columbia University Press, 2013), 68–76, and Todd Hedrick, 'Race, Difference, and Anthropology in Kant's Cosmopolitanism', *Journal of the History of Philosophy* 46:2 (April 2008), 245–68.

18. For the emphasis on the 'Schillerian lens' through which Lloyd reads Kant, see Lucie Kim-Chi Mercier, 'The racial regime of aesthetics: On David Lloyd's *Under Representation*', *Radical Philosophy* 2:06 (Winter 2019), 58.

19. Paul de Man, 'Kant and Schiller' in *Aesthetic Ideology* (Minneapolis: University of Minnesota Press, 1996), 130.

20. De Man, 'Kant and Schiller', 147.

21. Etienne Balibar, 'Human species as biopolitical concept', *Radical Philosophy* 2.11 (2021), 10.

22. I quote here from Gayatri C. Spivak's translation in *A Critique of Postcolonial Reason* (Cambridge, MA: Harvard University Press, 1999), 13. Werner S. Pluhar's translation reads: 'What is called sublime by us, having been prepared through culture, comes across as merely repellent to a person who is uncultured and lacking in the development of moral ideas'. See Immanuel Kant, *Critique of the Power of Judgement* (Indianapolis: Hackett, 1987), 124 [AA:V, 265].

23. I discuss Spivak's critical strategy of affirmative sabotage in Marie Louise Krogh, 'General Predicament, Specific Negotiations: Spivak's Persistent Critique', in *Afterlives*, ed. Peter Osborne (London: CRMEP Books, 2022), 58–71.

24. See, in particular, Spivak, *A Critique of Postcolonial Reason*, 26, and David Lloyd, *Under Representation: The Racial Regime of Aesthetics* (New York: Fordham University Press, 2019), 51.

25. Spivak, *A Critique of Postcolonial Reason*, 9.

26. When, at a later point, Spivak did undertake an 'affirmative sabotage' of Schiller's notion of an aesthetic education, it was to salvage the field of imaginative figuration for transnational cultural studies within a generalised critique of (post)colonial ideology. See Gayatri C. Spivak, *An Aesthetic Education in the Era of Globalization* (Cambridge, MA: Harvard University Press, 2013).

27. Lloyd, *Under Representation*, 73.

28. Immanuel Kant, note 1520, AA:XV/2, 878. Translation mine.

29. Bernasconi, 'Kant as an Unfamiliar Source of Racism', 156–59. See also Mark Larrimore, 'Sublime Waste: Kant on the Destiny of the Races', *Canadian Journal of Philosophy*, Supplementary Volume 25 (1999), 113–15.

30. Immanuel Kant, *Anthropology from a Pragmatic Point of View*, trans. Robert B. Louden, in *Anthropology, History and Education*, 231.

31. There exist no extant copies of the original manuscripts out of which Rink gathered the *Lectures on Pedagogy* (as his edition is titled in the translation by Robert B. Louden in *Anthropology, History and Education*). For an account of the content and context of the lectures, see Robert B. Loudon, 'Becoming Human: Kant and the Philosophy of Education' in *Kant's Human Being: Essays on His Theory of Human Nature* (Oxford: Oxford University Press, 2011), 136–148. See also Werner Stark, 'Immanuel Kant's *On Pedagogy*: A Lecture Like Any Other?', trans. Robert R. Lewis, in *Reading Kant's Lectures*, ed. Robert R. Lewis (Berlin: De Gruyter, 2015), 259–276.

32. Kant, 'Antropologie Friedländer', 250–55.

33. In the summer of 1780 Kant would be forced to instead use his colleague Friedrich Samuel Bock's *Lehrbuch der Erziehungskunst für christliche Eltern und künftige Jugendlehrer*, published that same year, as the textbook for this course. See Manfred Kuehn, 'Kant on Education, Anthropology, Ethics', in *Kant and Education: Interpretation and Commentary*, eds. Klas Roth and Chris W. Surprenant (New York: Routledge, 2012), 56.

34. Immanuel Kant, 'Idea for a Universal History with a Cosmopolitan Aim' in *Anthropology, History, Education*, 109–10; and *Anthropology*, 424.

35. This is a point of dispute in Kant's famous critique of Herder and in Herder's reply to Kant's critique. Where Herder finds ridiculous the idea that perfection happens in the species and not out of the individual's relation to the species-concept, Kant, contrary to this, emphasises that in that case, 'species' would be a merely logical category whereas 'if "the human species" signifies the *whole* of a series [*Reihe*] of generations going (indeterminably) into the infinite (as this meaning is entirely customary), and it is assumed that this series ceaselessly approximates the line of its destiny [*Bestimmung*] running alongside it, then it is not to utter a contradiction to say that in all its parts it is asymptotic to this line and yet on the whole that it will coincide with it, in other words, that no member of all the generations of humankind, but only the species will fully reach its destiny. The mathematician can give elucidation here; the philosopher would say: "The destiny of humankind is on the whole a *ceaseless progress*, and its completion is a mere idea, but very useful in all respects – the idea of a goal to which we have to direct our endeavours in accordance with the aim of providence"'. Immanuel Kant, 'Review of J.G. Herder's Ideas for the philosophy of history of humanity. Parts 1 and 2', in *Anthropology, History, and Education*, 142.

36. Kant, 'Idea for a Universal History', 108.

37. Kant, *Anthropology*, 421 [AA:VII, 326] (translation modified).

38. Kuehn, 'Kant on Education, Anthropology, and Ethics', 66. Kuehn alludes to the transcendental function of 'educability' but does not develop the conceptual distinction between the formation and the education of the species.

39. In the 'Essays regarding the Philanthropinum', Kant uses the term *Ausbildung* practically analogously with his use of *Erziehung* in *Lectures on Pedagogy*: as the unifying term which implies a number of different modalities of an educative process, including ''discipline', training', 'instruction', 'schooling'. See Immanuel Kant, 'Essays regarding the Philanthropinum' in *Anthropology, History, and Education*, 102, and *Lectures on Pedagogy*, 437.

40. Kant, *Anthropology*, 418–419 [AA:VII, 322-333] and *Lectures*

on *Pedagogy*, 444 [AA:IX, 449-450].

41. 'We are *cultivated* in a high degree by art and science. We are *civilized*, perhaps to the point of being overburdened, by all sorts of social decorum and propriety. But very much is still lacking before we can be held to be already *moralized*.' Kant, 'Idea for a Universal History', 116.

42. Kant, *Lectures on Pedagogy*, 444 [AA:IX, 449].

43. Kant, *Lectures on Pedagogy*, 444 [AA:IX, 450].

44. Immanuel Kant, *Menschenkunde*, in *Lectures on Anthropology*, 320–21.

45. Kant, *Anthropology*, 315 [AA:VII, 208].

46. Kant, *Menschenkunde*, 32, translation modified, [AA:XXV/2, 1187].

47. Louden, *Kant's Impure Ethics*, 90.

48. Louden, *Kant's Impure Ethics*, 106

49. Kant, *Anthropology*, 420 (my emphasis).

50. Kant, *Anthropology*, 423 [AA:VII, 328]. This sentence is a reworking of one found in *The Critique of the Power of Judgement*, where Kant writes that in regard to the discipline of our inclinations, 'we find nature acting purposively, for it strives to give us an education [*Ausbildung*] that makes us receptive to purposes higher than those that nature itself can provide.' Kant, *Critique of Judgement*, 321 [AA:V, 433].

51. Kant, *Lectures on Pedagogy*, 441.

52. Kant, *Anthropology*, 422.

53. Immanuel Kant, 'The Conflict of the Faculties', trans. Mary J. Gregor and Robert Anchor, in *Religion and Rational Theology*, eds. Allen W. Wood and George di Giovanni (Cambridge: Cambridge University Press, 1996), 308.

54. Kant, 'The Conflict of the Faculties', 308

55. Ypi, 'Commerce and Colonialism', 99–126.

56. Immanuel Kant, 'Toward Perpetual Peace', in *Practical Philosophy*, trans. and ed. Mary J. Gregor (Cambridge: Cambridge University Press, 1996), 319, and *Anthropology*, 427.

57. Kant, 'Idea for a Universal History', 111.

58. This is largely the interpretation which ensues from the argument presented in Tsenay Serequeberhan, 'Eurocentrism in Philosophy: The Case of Immanuel Kant', *The Philosophical Forum* 27:4 (1996), 333–56.

59. Immanuel Kant, Refl.1501, [AA:XV, 788-89]. Erich Adickes, the editor of this part of Kant's *Nachlass*, dates this reflection to a period between 1775-83. A similar diagnosis of the stasis of 'Oriental peoples' is found in the lecture transcripts from the anthropology Friedländer (1775/76), the anthropology Pillau (1777/78) and in *Menschenkunde* (c.1781/82). The first sentence is ambiguous and it is unclear if it is poorly formulated, unfinished, or both. In his comments on this passage, Bernasconi translates '*Die orientalischen Nationen würden sich aus sich selbst niemals*' as: 'The oriental nations would never improve themselves on their own'. Bernasconi, 'Will the Real Kant Please Stand Up: The Challenge of Enlightenment Racism to the Study of the History of Philosophy', *Radical Philosophy* 117 (January/February 2003), 18.

60. Parts of this article originated as a chapter in my PhD thesis *Temporalities and Territories: The Geopolitical Imaginary of German Philosophies of History* (Kingston University London, 2020). An early draft of the article itself was presented at the Art as Forum Research Symposium: 'The Subject of Art Criticism's Universalism' at Copenhagen University 2021. I am grateful to the organisers for the invitation and the many insightful points the discussion generated. Thank you also to Miri Davidson and the editors at *Radical Philosophy*, whose comments and questions made all the difference.

The Red Pill
Breaking out of The Class Matrix
William Clare Roberts

Rare is the book that provokes in me both frequent agreement and teeth-clenching, head-shaking, wincing frustration. But such is Vivek Chibber's *The Class Matrix*.* Chibber is his generation's foremost advocate of analytical Marxism, a program of articulating and defending socialist politics using the tools of contemporary social science. The journal he helms, *Catalyst*, has quickly become a premier outlet for socialist research, something of an Old Left Review. He has supervised a raft of young researchers from his position in the NYU Department of Sociology. His previous book, *Postcolonial Theory and the Specter of Capital*, elicited both rave reviews and real anger for its sustained attack on Subaltern Studies, the school of postcolonial research that emerged from the work of Ranajit Guha and his students.

In *The Class Matrix*, Chibber argues for a stripped-down Marxist theory of capitalism, structured by the class relation between wage-workers and capitalist employers. His goal is to vindicate both the explanatory priority of the class structure and the political priority of class interests. Both have been eclipsed, according to Chibber, by the turn to culture and ideology initiated by mid-century Marxist academics, but is now fundamentally antithetical to both Marxist research and socialist politics.

Chibber never fully explains what he means by the titular 'class matrix'. Is it supposed to refer to 'the deep structural facts about capitalism', or to the more mutable form in which this structure is reflected in modes of reproduction and struggle? Is it supposed to be the two-by-two matrix (Figure 3.1, on page 109) schematising possible outcomes of economic growth and working class political organisation? Or, in keeping with the red and blue cover, is it a nod to the Wachowskis' movie and its contemporary afterlife in online political discourse? Perhaps, *The Class Matrix* is also meant to name the false, superficial world of academic culturalism from which Chibber offers you a 'red pill' exit into real class struggle?

I argue that *The Class Matrix* is itself what must be escaped. It is superficially rigorous but built upon critical ambiguities, equivocations and contradictions. Like much online and podcast commentary, it hovers indefinitely between angst and trolling. Like a bad legacy sequel, it can match neither the scope nor the insight of the original work of Erik Olin Wright or Adam Przeworski, to which it hearkens nostalgically. If this is what analytical Marxism is today, it is time to cancel the franchise.

But first the good news ...

In Chibber's story, classical Marxism as a theory and practice of class politics had two basic premises. First, it presupposed that the capitalist economy established the parameters for politics by imposing real constraints on what people could reasonably be expected to do. This economic base defined the class positions of individuals, established their fundamental interests and limited their avenues for action. Second, classical Marxism assumed that the capitalist organisation of production was simultaneously the organisation of the proletariat as a revolutionary force. The common interests and common experiences of wage-workers would forge them into a self-conscious political agent, capable of and willing to transform the economic structure itself. Thus, capitalism,

---

* Vivek Chibber, *The Class Matrix: Social Theory After the Cultural Turn* (Cambridge: Harvard University Press, 2022). 224pp., £28.95 hb., 978 0 67424 5 136

above all, produces its own gravediggers.

Chibber wants to rescue the first premise by revising the second. He wants to analyse the economic base of capitalist society, and its fundamental division into classes, while jettisoning the sense of historical destiny that marked the period of classical Marxism. There is no guarantee that the workers will win. In fact, the economic structure of capitalism militates against the workers of the world uniting. The class structure incentivises 'go it alone' strategies. Individual workers are constantly tempted to pursue their own narrowly-conceived interests by working harder, applying for promotions, kissing up to the boss, saving money for their kids' educations, and so forth, rather than to undertake the hard and risky work of collective action.

But in order to focus on the real problem of building institutions of horizontal solidarity, and a solidaristic culture to support those institutions, Chibber also thinks we must upend the received way of thinking about culture on the Left. Cultural Studies and the New Left more broadly have bequeathed to the contemporary Left the notion that cultural hegemony or the culture industry has fully incorporated the working class into capitalism. The workers consent to be ruled in exchange for Marvel movies, the wages of whiteness and other vehicles of vicarious pleasure and ersatz emancipation.

There is quite a lot to agree with, and be grateful for, in Chibber's intervention. The model of the capitalist economic structure he advances is parsimonious – cartoonishly so, even – but it gets the job done, pedagogically speaking. In contrast to the buzzing blooming confusion and niche specialisations of much academic scholarship, there is something refreshing about Chibber's anti-nuance. This is not to say that his model – there are two classes, one owns the means of production and the other owns only their labour-power, the relationship between the two is exhausted by the wage contract and the exploitation of wage labour at the point of production – explains everything about class in the modern world. It doesn't. But it does effectively accomplish two tasks.

First, it is a proof of concept for the idea that economic structures are real and effective, and that we can specify them as stable background conditions that give rise to predictable strategies and interactions among those who participate in them. 'Structure' is a word frequently invoked but rarely elucidated in academic and para-academic writing, so it's welcome to encounter such a straightforward and explicit articulation of a social structure, even if the simplicity of the model masks some deep ambiguities (I'll come to this in a bit).

Additionally, Chibber demonstrates that the sixty-year-old 'structure/agency debate' has been a colossal waste of time. The economic structure of capitalist society does not override conscious human agency, but relies upon it. As Chibber points out, 'there is nothing automatic or passive about seeking out and finding a job, or holding onto one in competitive conditions, or marketing a product and winning out in the warlike domain of the product market'. These are also the very activities that predictably reproduce the class structure of society year in and year out.

Finally, Chibber is persuasive with regard to two of his central theses. Class formation is hard, uncertain work, and it is backwards to think that what needs to be explained is the *absence* of a successful revolutionary movement among the global proletariat, or even among the working classes of the most developed capitalist nations. The surprising and explanation-worthy phenomenon is that there has *ever* been large-scale collective action carried out by people operating 'in a condition of generalised insecurity'. Why don't people get together and rebel against the social order that oppresses them and renders them systematically vulnerable? This is a question that answers itself.

Consequently, Chibber's thesis that resignation rather than consent is the basis of capitalist stability is well-founded and valuable. Workers – in Ohio or Kinshasa – submit to the economic structure of capitalist employment, with its exploitation and subjection, not because they think it legitimate or the freest and fairest system, but because they don't know what else to do or how to change the world for the better. It reasonably seems that there is no feasible alternative.

These are important lessons for any socialist project today. I am glad that someone is arguing them forcefully. It is unfortunate, however, that they come as part of a package-deal with the rest of Chibber's book: a collection of threadbare assertions that evince more conviction than thought. As in his previous book, Chibber is often more concerned to hit the right people than to accurately reconstruct intellectual and political history, and more concerned to draw stark lines between himself and his opponents than to figure out exactly what it is he is defending. Indeed, it seems crucial to the argument of the book that Chibber avoid reflecting on and clarifying his own position. If he did, he would face the discomfiting realisation that many things he criticises are, in fact, at work in or implied by his own argument.

Chibber accuses the New Left, for example, of forsaking materialist explanation. However, his model of the economic structure replaces the material analysis of social power with a generic rational choice framework applied arbitrarily to only a subset of market relations. The result is an explanatory framework that applies to only one structure in all of human history and a declaration that everything else is sheer contingency. Similarly, Chibber accuses 'culturalists' and 'social constructionists' of obscuring the reality of material interests. However, he never defines material interests, and his constant and equivocal invocations of the term militate against nailing it down. Chibber's house is not built upon rock, but upon sand.

In the greatest irony of all, a book that loudly and repeatedly proclaims its opposition to all notions of cultural hegemony and ideological false consciousness ends up concluding that only the formation of *just the right kind* of working class cultural identity can make class conscious collective action by workers possible.

In what follows, I will substantiate each of these judgments. If you believe Chibber's words, the story is simple: people act on their interests as given by their position in the class structure. But if you follow the implications of his argument, you find that the rabbit hole of culture goes deep.

Structure (well, ... *a* structure)

Things quickly go awry. Chapter One is dedicated to Chibber's effort to differentiate the capitalist class structure from all of those culturally contingent norms, institutions and power relations that social constructionists and interpretivists are interested in. However, defending his overly-tidy model just embroils Chibber in more difficulties. Every time he expels a form of cultural contingency he implicitly admits another, which must be expelled in turn, allowing yet another to slip in. In the end, keeping the structure free of culturally contingent mediations looks like a fool's errand.

The social constructionist challenge to structuralist materialism was that, in the words of William Sewell, 'social and economic structures ... were themselves the products of the interpretive work of human actors'. Chibber's strategy in the first chapter is to give the constructionists every social structure but one: materialists get to keep the class structure. Yes, Chibber admits, the structure of a church is 'undoubtedly' constituted and activated by the construction of meaning. The sign that this is so is that this construction is highly contingent. People can fail to understand the norms and roles that constitute the church, or they can consciously reject them. Individuals or groups can fall away from the church, or the congregation as a whole can collapse. As Chibber puts it, 'culture's importance as the decisive link in the chain is elevated if it happens that the needed socialisation might not materialise'.

This emphasis upon contingency is the knife that allows Chibber to pare away the one structure that constructionism cannot comprehend: the class structure. Wage workers and capitalists have to internalise certain norms in order to participate in and successfully reproduce the class structure, but we can be *assured* that they will internalise those norms. Why? Because their livelihood depends on it. A worker who doesn't 'internalise the appropriate codes' – timeliness, appropriate dress, acceptance of managers' and employers' authority, etc. – will lose their access to wages, and hence to food and shelter. A capitalist who doesn't make the cultural adjustment necessary to profitably employ wage labour will cease to be a capitalist and will have to adjust, instead, to the norms and meanings required of a wage worker. In other words, 'economic compulsion' makes failure or refusal to play a role into 'extremely rare deviations'. Therefore, culture and interpretive work just don't have the same explanatory prominence with regard to class roles and structures that they do with regard to more contingent social roles and structures.

Economic compulsion is not the only sort of compulsion, however, and performing class roles is not the only action that economic compulsion compels. Chibber notices the first difficulty, and he tries to turn it to his advantage by aligning the class structure with compulsion by 'economic vulnerability' and aligning contingent, socio-culturally constructed structures with compulsion by 'agent-imposed sanctions'. If you reject your church, your community 'might impose sanctions', such as ostracism or even 'physical intimidation'. But, Chibber insists, economic compulsion is not like this: 'no one has to monitor' or 'use social pressure' on recalcitrant workers, who don't need 'a socially imposed punishment' in order to be driven back to work.

This won't work, though. First of all, unemployed proletarians are subject to all manner of coercion and social pressure to get them to return to work. If you walk off your steady job today, what are you going to do? Access to land is conditional on having the money to pay for it. You can try moving in with relatives or friends, but you might find that ostracism, the denial of certain social privileges, and other agent-imposed sanctions coming to you. If you turn to panhandling or crime, you'll discover that this is recognised as a transgression, a breaking of convention. Monitoring and coercion imposed by other parties – even by specially uniformed and armed parties specifically employed for this purpose – will likely follow.

Yes, the mute compulsion of economic relations is a real thing, but everyone – including, presumably, Chibber – knows that the state is back there somewhere, maybe out of sight for now, but ready to step in with 'agent-imposed sanctions' if people get too far out of line. In the biggest working class rebellions that the US has seen in decades – the Ferguson and George Floyd uprisings of 2014-15 and 2020 – the state was not out of sight at all. In Joshua Clover's phrase, the state was near and the economy far.

Moreover, Chibber's whole discussion turns on an equivocation regarding the predictability or reliability of certain behaviours. In the first step of Chibber's argument, social structures were contingent cultural constructs to the extent that the agent's socialisation into and participation in them were themselves contingent. To the extent that people face 'a powerful incentive' to 'achieve competency' in norms and meanings, we can assume they will do so. Therefore, Chibber insists, 'the peculiarity of class resides in the fact that it is the only social relation that directly governs the material well-being of its participants. Because it has a direct bearing on their welfare, it motivates them to learn and internalise the meanings required to participate in their structural location'.

The discussion of interpersonal coercion has silently shifted the locus of predictability, however. Non-class structures are contingent not because they do not have a direct bearing on people's welfare, but because the sanctions enforcing participation and compliance, whatever the incentive they provide, are the actions *of other people* – contingent, 'wilful interventions by other members of the community'. But this is confusing, since market forces are themselves the aggregate effects of wilful buying and selling by other members of the community. The market is just people, after all.

Chibber, therefore, is caught in a trilemma. If what matters for sorting social institutions into 'culturally contingent' and 'materially structural' is the *predictability* of an agent's participation given existing material incentives, then lots of institutions besides the wage-labour/capital relation have to be admitted into a materialist analysis. If what matters for sorting is whether the incentives for participation emerge from *non-agential sanctions* or agent-imposed ones, then markets for labour-power and other commodities – and hence capitalist labour relations – are going to be appropriate for a culturalist reading. If what matters is the difference between direct coercion and *economic incentives*, then the fact that economic incentives compel all sorts of behaviour besides the performance of class roles becomes unavoidable.

Regardless of which path Chibber takes, he would have to admit that his simple model, in which materialist analysis, class analysis and economic analysis all line up very neatly – and happen to portray a perfect and homogeneous model of capitalist production as the only class-based, interest-driven social system to have ever existed – is too tidy to do any real analytical work. He might have to admit, as well, that the turn to culture, and the turn to other relations besides the wage-worker/capitalist relation, cannot be pinned on the heretical New Left, but were always already part of the Marxist analysis of modern society.

Marx strove to understand what it meant for a society to be dominated by this mode of production. Two consequences he highlighted are the production of a relative surplus population of wage-dependent but productively redundant people and the rise of a powerful centralised state wielding heretofore unprecedented levels of coercive force. The poverty of Chibber's theory is revealed by the fact that it cannot incorporate these two phenomena – a mass of wageless workers and workless wage-dependents and a coercive and interested state – into its conception of the economic structure of society. Chibber's simplified model is easy to grasp, and to wield as a weapon against those who would flatten society into intertextuality and meaning-making practices, but it is also incapable of articulating different levels and types of social power. This is a fatal drawback for what is supposed to be a materialist theory.

Interests (well, ... *some* interests)

The connection between the class structure and action is supposed to be interests. 'The entire premise of class analysis', Chibber tells us, 'was that it was possible to predict actors' economic strategies on the basis of their location in the structure'. Interests, determined by one's class position and motivating one's economic strategies, lend causal force to the structure by translating one's structural location into a reason for acting this way or that.

Remarkably, though, Chibber never defines 'interests', and never discusses the scope and specificity of interests. How are interests related to desires or preferences? How are they identified? How are trade-offs among interests articulated and decided? What is the temporal horizon of interests? How are individual interests integrated into collective action? Chibber does not raise any of these questions. In the absence of an explicit theory of interests, he uses the word opportunistically, treating contradictory phenomena as if they were equally interest-driven, as suits his present purpose.

As best as I can discern, Chibber uses 'economic interests', 'material interests' and 'class interests' interchangeably as terms denoting well-being or basic welfare. He claims that the strategies pursued by workers – whether individual or collective, conciliatory or militant – are constrained by their material interests in the sense that they are motivated and limited by a regard for their own well-being. This explains too little by explaining too much.

The crucial point to understand about any discussion of interests was well put by Göran Therborn. 'Interests by themselves do not *explain* anything', Therborn rightly noted. This is because '"interest" is a normative concept indicating the most rational course of action in a pre-defined game, that is, a situation in which gain and loss have already been defined'. In other words, to say that x is in your interest is to say that you have a good reason to want x, or that x is what you *should rationally* want, given your aims. Thus, you can't say what people's interests are unless and until you figure out what they are trying or otherwise aiming to do or be. Generally speaking, Chibber assumes that workers are trying to keep on living. This assumption is what gives economic interests their trump value when it comes to predicting worker behaviour. This is a fair assumption. There are certainly exceptions, but, given a choice between living and dying, most of us, most of the time, will choose life. Thus, anything that helps us to accomplish this modest goal is in our interest.

However, the vast majority of wage workers worldwide are not motivated to get out of bed and go to work each day by their desire for 'physical survival'. If survival were the *only* reason we had to do anything, our economic interests would be meagre indeed. Moreover, capitalism might well be the best possible system for satisfying *those* interests. Yes, it's exploitative, but if all we care about is 'maintain[ing] body and soul', then capitalist production would do the trick. (Our grandchildren might want a word, of course, but they aren't able to act on their interests yet.)

One of the things capitalist production does, though, is it produces new needs and allows us to play new games, giving rise to new interests: social and spatial mobility, social and political standing, investments in children, etc. Trade-offs among these interests are not straightforward. Is it in your interest to accept a decrease in spatial mobility for the sake of higher political status? Is it in your interest to accept a decrease in your own material well-being in order to invest in the security of your children's future welfare? 'It depends' is the only general answer to such questions, and any instance in which such questions arise is going to provoke reasonable disagreement among equally rational and well-informed people.

Chibber's appeal to interests, therefore, is equivocal. He uses it to indicate that workers are rational actors – sensitive to the likely costs and benefits of different courses of action – but also to imply that workers all want more or less the same things, by which he means mostly the really basic things, as if there were only one set of costs and benefits that workers had to weigh. There are only two paragraphs in the whole book that raise issues related to the heterogeneity of interests *among* workers, and even these focus on directly work-related interests, the sorts of issues that are subject to collective bargaining with an employer: 'the intensity of work, the length of the workday, the level of the wage, health benefits, pensions, and so on'. This leaves out of view both the political interests of workers and the struggles of and among workers to define a broader workers' movement, not to mention the intrapersonal conflicts we all experience among our multiple interests.

Anyone tempted to embrace Chibber's mantra that socialist and working class politics is the politics of interests should read Gabriel Winant's *The Next Shift*, which beautifully traces the intertwined collapse of the steel industry and rise of the healthcare industry in America. Winant doesn't doubt that needs and interests are real and vitally important, or that workers are rational agents in pursuit of their own welfare. But what emerges from his account – and is invisible in Chibber's – is the reality of conflicting priorities, partial and competing communities of interest, institutional constraints and path dependencies, the outsized role of the state in shaping the context of choice, and the uneven and sometimes openly exclusive webs of community support and solidarity that insulate some workers from harm by exposing others to those same harms. If you want a class politics based in material interests, then study Winant's book.

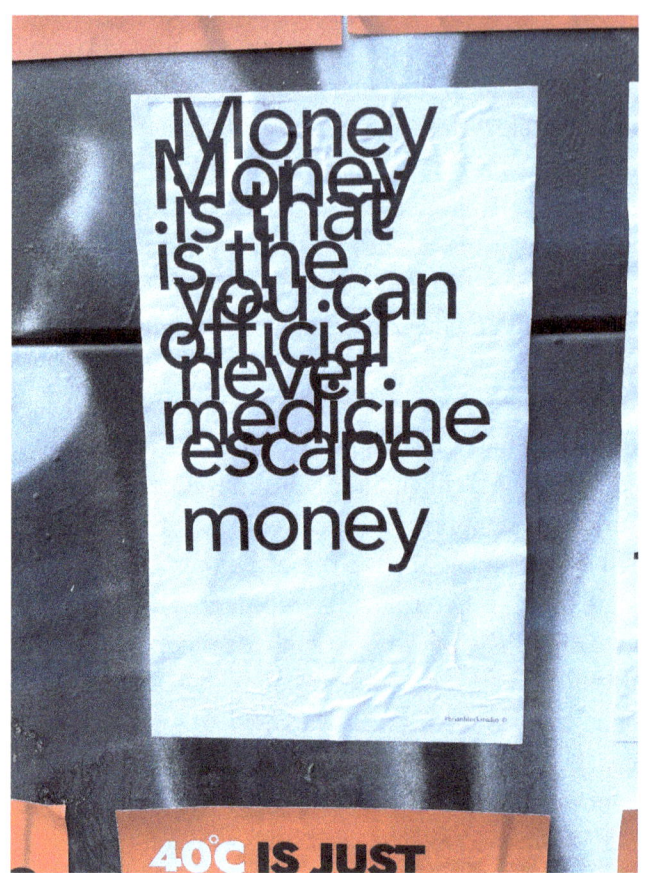

Culture (well, ... just *one* culture)

We have seen that Chibber's construal of the capitalist class structure disintegrates under pressure because it relies upon predictable behaviour and market incentives coalescing in opposition to agent-imposed sanctions when, in fact, the relations among the three are much more variable and messy. We have also seen that Chibber's invocations of interests won't stand up to scrutiny, since wage workers confront conflicts among multiple interests, and the most basic and widely-shared interest – in life itself – is not the motivating interest in most situations.

But all of this was scaffolding. The real thrust of the argument is supposed to be that, because the class structure places the burden of collective action entirely on the working class while simultaneously incentivising workers to pursue opportunistic strategies of individualised striving, class formation is not automatic, but must be driven by a conscious strategy of fostering a culture and institutions of solidarity among workers. Therefore, theories of ideological incorporation and false consciousness have got the wrong end of the stick. Workers are not kept in chains by culture but by the structure of capitalist power; their emancipation depends upon overcoming that structure by creating the right culture. Perhaps Chibber's structural model needs a lot of work, and perhaps interests are not as straightforward as Chibber claims, but those reservations need not impeach the conclusion that ideology and culture are not the lock but the key.

This gets to the real matrix of *The Class Matrix*, the contradiction that gives motion to its limbs. Chibber insists, repeatedly, that culture does not explain the absence of revolutionary working class collective action. Nonetheless, his argument clearly implies the contrary, that culture – 'ideology, discourse, normative codes, and so on' – *entirely explains* the absence of revolutionary working class collective action. Chibber tells us this while denying that this is what he is saying.

If the robust presence of the right kind of solidaristic culture and ideology is the decisive factor in bringing about class formation, despite the class structure – this is Chibber's thesis – then it must also be true that the absence or weakness of that culture explains the lack of class formation. The class structure is a constant. It militates against class formation among workers, and, in the absence of a strong working class culture and identity, it is sufficient to prevent class formation. The absence of one particular culture, however, is not the absence of culture *tout court*. If class formation is not happening, there are still cultures and ideologies abroad in the world, and the working class participates in those cultures and ideologies. They are simply *the wrong sorts of culture or ideology* to foster class formation. But this is the ideology theory Chibber denies.

Cultures are socially constructed and contingent. This is why Chibber argues that we must separate out the class structure. The codes and norms of cultures are invented, and our compliance with them is promoted by 'wilful interventions by other members of the community'. Therefore, if we don't have the right kind of culture to promote class formation, that is because we are creating and enforcing other cultures, the wrong kinds of cultures.

This reasoning is actually at work in Chibber's book, despite the fact that it contradicts Chibber's thesis. It shows up as a glitch in *The Class Matrix*, a point where Chibber suddenly and briefly claims that workers are prevented from engaging in solidaristic collective action as workers because they pursue their interests in the wrong way by creating and enforcing the wrong kinds of cultures.

The class structure is supposed to channel class conflict into individualised strategies by workers. That is Chibber's explicit claim. However, when he focuses in on these strategies, he briefly reveals that 'individualised' strategies need not be individualised at all. Rather than building unions, Chibber tells us, it is often easier for workers to rely on 'networks of kin, caste, ethnicity, race, and so on', into which they were born. Such 'ready-made' connections are 'a natural source of support'. Chibber also refers to these 'extramarket ties' as 'a means of exerting control over the labour market ... to hoard job opportunities'. Such a tactic, he concludes, 'only intensifies a class orientation in which one's welfare is secured by forms of association unrelated to class'. Using 'such ties' to organise the labour market 'runs directly against the principle of class organisation'. Then it is as if this interlude never happened. Chibber returns to the simple opposition between collective and individualised forms of resistance, writing that 'class formation occurs when workers seek out collective strategies to defend their wellbeing, as opposed to individualised ones'. He never mentions 'forms of association unrelated to class' again.

Culture plays a critical role in class formation, therefore – except when it plays a critical role in creating forms of association unrelated to class. Culture fosters a common identity among workers – except when it fosters a common identity among Black people, or kin networks, or trans women, or some other non-class – and hence cross-class – identity. Culture instils a sense of common goals and commitments, and helps to overcome the tendency to free ride – but it does this sometimes in the service of class consciousness and sometimes in the service of Indigenous communities, racial groups or age cohorts.

Chibber's argument, therefore, can be condensed as follows. The absence of proletarian revolution is not explained by the workers being integrated into ideology or fooled by culture, but by the capitalists' power and the difficulties of collective action. Collective action is possible only when there is *the right sort* of culture, a culture of solidarity among workers *qua* workers, and a workers' identity formed by that culture. Workers participate in many cultures, however, and many of them can help to secure workers' welfare. But any culture that helps workers secure their well-being *not as workers, but on the basis of 'extramarket ties'*, 'runs directly contrary to the principle of class organisation'.

Chibber might deny that this is a theory of *false* consciousness. The workers who go in for MAGA or BLM or LGBTQI+ are rational actors pursuing their material interests as best they can in the circumstances. They are not the passive receptacles of culture made by others or the dupes of ideology. They construct, interpret and enforce the terms of their identities. Nonetheless, Chibber's argument implies that all of these other identifications, ties and ideologies are, *for workers*, mistaken identities and obstacles to *class* consciousness.

The Class Matrix aspires, therefore, to be *What Is to Be Done?* with rational choice characteristics. Chibber tries to show that the spontaneous movement of the workers cannot even produce trade-union consciousness, much less socialist consciousness. Only purposive ideological struggle – appealing to workers *as* workers, telling them that their true interests lie in banding together *as* workers – can hope to break through the reliance on 'ready-made' cultures of kin, caste and colour. The foes to be overcome in this struggle are the stereotypical purple-haired, academic Leftists who talk about white supremacy, mysogyny, rape culture and so forth, and who think the workers are idiots and dupes, and who have to be told that the earth is round (that is, that interests, derived from class position, rule all).

In fact, *The Class Matrix* is not so much an updated version of Lenin's pamphlet as it is Lukács' *History and Class Consciousness* stripped of the Hegel. Lukács claimed that only the modern proletariat was capable of pursuing a consistently rational strategy, due to their position as the makers of both every use-value and every social relation in the modern world. Only the standpoint of the proletariat is able to grasp the social totality. In Lukács, this reduced to moralism: the *real* proletarians, as soon as they are *really* conscious of being proletarian, will act in a *really* proletarian manner to consciously and methodically create the totality of society as a unity – and thereby also to cancel their existence as proletarians by eliminating classes altogether. In Chibber's book, this moralism is reproduced, but without the Hegelian eschatology and mediations. Rather than an expressive totality, we get an expressive monotony.

That the working class is capable of conscious and unified solidarity shorn of all particularism is a matter

to be taken on faith. Any failure to inhabit this interest-based universalism is a failure to comprehend true class consciousness. To ask how this class consciousness is produced from the manifold particularities of workers' local and contradictory situations is to admit that one does not possess this true class consciousness.

Closing the book

Two results follow. First, Chibber's book should put an end to his notion that obsessive attention to culture, ideology and false consciousness only came on the scene when postwar Leftists tried to explain why the revolution didn't happen in the West. The turn to culture is the natural concomitant to positing class interests, rational strategy and class consciousness. 'False consciousness' is the difference between your interests as you currently perceive them and the interests of the class to which you belong, the distance between what you want and what would be rational for the collective action of those in your social position. That is all it has ever been. It wasn't devised by the New Left to explain the failure of Western revolutions. It is inherent in interest-based class politics. That is why Chibber recreates it as quickly as he dismisses it.

Second, attention to culture, ideology and false consciousness need not be a problem. It can be perfectly reasonable to tell people that they should not want what they want because it's bad for them. We can decry 'paternalism' all day long but it doesn't change the fact that we sometimes need to be convinced that we are acting contrary to our own best interests. 'Keep your eye on the prize' is indispensable advice in any political movement. But what is the prize?

Classical Marxists tell their readers forthrightly and repeatedly what the greater good is. They say why it requires struggle, compromise and sacrifice in the present to attain it, and why struggle, compromise and sacrifice is worth it. Because Chibber does not give us a theory of interests, he is also coy about why workers should prefer a strategy of forging a class identity to the strategy of relying on 'networks of kin, caste, ethnicity, race, and so on'. He realises that organising must 'call for some workers *subordinating* their immediate welfare to the larger agenda', but won't say what this larger agenda is or why this subordination of immediate welfare is worthwhile. He only assures us that, 'of course, in the long run, these workers would also benefit in many ways from the security and leverage conferred by membership in the association'. Without a convincing story of interests beyond well-being, welfare and maintaining body and soul, this assurance is empty.

The absence of anything like an emancipatory interest is the void at the heart of *The Class Matrix*. When Chibber introduces the distinction between individualised strategies and solidaristic organisation, he establishes the contrast by saying that workers 'will typically find an individualised course of class reproduction more feasible than one reliant on collective organisation'. Perhaps this is a slip of the pen, but it is also the logical endpoint of his argument. The only alternative Chibber offers to the status quo is 'a course of class reproduction ... reliant on collective organisation'. The political lesson of his book is that workers should organise collectively *for the sake of being workers*.

This is the significance of *The Class Matrix*. For Chibber, the title names a reality from which emancipation is neither possible nor desirable. The only thing left to fight for is an identity politics for workers, a renovation of working class institutions geared toward class reproduction on an expanding scale.

William Clare Roberts teaches political theory at McGill University. He is the author of Marx's Inferno: The Political Theory of Capital *(Princeton University Press, 2017), which won the Isaac and Tamara Deutscher Memorial Prize.*

Producing the intolerable
Anti-prison struggles, abolitionist genealogies
Martina Tazzioli

On September 9, 1971, detainees in the Attica prison in New York organised a collective uprising, seizing control of the building and taking hostage 42 prison staff until September 13 when the collective revolt was repressed by police and 33 prisoners were killed. A few weeks later, in the prison of Clairvaux in France, two detainees took hostage a prison guard, although the revolt was quickly repressed by police. Two months later, in December 1971, a collective uprising took place in the prison of Toul. As Michel Foucault stressed, commenting on the latter, 'the prisoners heard about the Attica revolt; they realised that its problems were their own and that these problems were political in nature'.[1] In the early 1970s, the claims raised by detainees in the US during the wave of collective prison uprisings thus reverberated across the ocean and were relaunched by prisoners in France.

Such uprisings were not unique to France or the US. Two years before, in 1968, detainees revolted in Italy in the prisons of Turin, Milan, Genova and Rome: collective uprisings that were triggered by the social mobilisations which in 1968 spread across the country. Extra-parliamentary parties, like Lotta Continua, and student movements actively supported and amplified those prison revolts: prisoners initially raised very precise claims against the living conditions inside the prison but then expanded these to become a protest about the penal system at large.[2] In the United Kingdom, in October 1969, a prison revolt took place in Parkhurst on the Isle of Wight to protest the brutal violence to which prisoners were subjected on a daily basis.[3] As an article of the time noted: 'the Parkhust revolt was the spark which ignited three years of protests against prison conditions, some of which were organised by the Preservation of the Right of Prisoners, while others were entirely spontaneous'.[4] Prison revolts happened more or less simultaneously in Norway, Sweden and in Portugal also.

The connections, convergences and partial differences between the political genealogies of these struggles within and against the carceral system that took place in many countries between the late 1960s and the mid-1970s have been only marginally discussed in current abolitionist debates. In this piece, I focus specifically on the interconnected political genealogies of the prison revolts in the US and in France, and on the partially different angles of attack and claims they mobilised, bearing in mind that such struggles took place in a larger world context of prison uprisings. While events were unfolding in the early 1970s, the members of *Le groupe d'information sur les prisons* (GIP), or the Prison Information Group, in France referred frequently in their texts to the revolts in the prisons in the US, they supported the Black Panthers, and Michel Foucault himself visited Attica in 1972. Yet, on the US side, the knowledge of what was happening in France was quite limited. This was partly due to linguistic factors – in the US the experience of the GIP was not well known, and their texts were mostly untranslated. Retracing these partially interconnected political genealogies nonetheless enables us to foreground the resonances and mutual influences between struggles that would otherwise remain bounded within national frameworks.

Before proceeding, a methodological clarification is needed: by focusing on the US and the French anti-prison movements in the 1970s, this piece does not engage in a comparative analysis; rather, the goal is to highlight specific similarities, differences and mutual influences between these two political experiences. More precisely, I am interested in showing how those movements articulated their claims in a similar way, even as, at the same time, they foregrounded and challenged different aspects of carcerality. Most obviously, as I will show, while reflections on the racialised nature of punishment and the structural racism that underpins the prison system were at the core of the US movement, such issues remained essentially unaddressed in the French anti-prison movement. Yet, if little has been said about the resonances between these contemporaneous anti-prison movements, affinities and mutual entanglements were, I argue, at stake *irrespective* of the relative lack of actual exchanges at the time. The circulation of knowledge and anti-prison struggles generates what the historian Julius Scott has defined as a 'common wind';[5] that is, a shared political lexicon and ground of tactics, even if, in many cases, these connections and reverberations were not deliberately established nor consciously thematised within the movements themselves.

Such a circulation did not take place only across space, across borders, but also over time: the memory of those anti-prison struggles has sedimented and spread, informing later carceral abolitionist movements as well as anti-racist mobilisations. Forty years on, the mutual resonances as well as the partial affinities and differences between those two anti-carceral movements can be identified more clearly. The anti-prison conjuncture which unfolded simultaneously in many countries in the world between the late 1960s and the first half of the 1970s was intertwined with a broader political turmoil – with the student protests movement, anti-racist claims, strikes in the factories and international workers mobilisations. By connecting these two political genealogies of anti-prison movements what emerges is a common production of the intolerable: that is, anti-prison mobilisations aimed at making the prison system intolerable, unacceptable.

Producing and spreading an *active intolerance* about the prison system, was a deliberate goal of the GIP and of the knowledge production and modes of support they engaged in. The circulation of prisoners' letters and subversive knowledge in the US was driven by a similar purpose: not just informing citizens about the reality of the prison but enhancing collective intolerance towards it. At the same time, multiplying the genealogies of struggles against prisons and showing how these are mutually entangled is crucial, I suggest, for provincialising the current US-centred debate on prison abolitionism.

The piece begins by tracing the influence that anti-asylum movements had on anti-prison mobilisations in the early 1970s. It then moves on to focus on three points that reveal key convergences but also partial divergences between the two movements. First, I discuss the goal of breaking the wall between inside and outside the prison, and the fact that support from outside was conceived by detainees not only as solidarity but also as an active part of the struggle. Second, I show how knowledge co-production served the purpose of producing the intolerable, of rendering the prison system as unacceptable and, therefore, non-reformable. Third, I consider how anti-prison movements from the 1970s have shaped current abolitionist horizons.

The 'common wind'

The radical critique of the carceral institutions that different groups developed in the early 1970s was in part an outcome of the 'common wind' that circulated in the early 1970s, that is, of the knowledge and practice exchanges between anti-prisons and anti-asylum movements. Anti-asylum and anti-prison movements shared a critical analysis of what they defined as total institutions. In Italy and in France particularly, prison revolts and the support from outside that these received should be situated in a specific political conjuncture, when the asylum as an institution was strongly challenged by movements like Psichiatria Democratica in Italy,[6] led by the psychiatrist Franco Basaglia, and by sociologists, such as Robert Castel in France.

The encounter and mutual influence between anti-asylum and anti-prison movements was manifested in several meetings that took place in this period.[7] As reported by Christian De Vito and Silvia Vallani, in 1973 Michel Foucault, Franco Basaglia, Robert Castel and the Norwegian scholar Thomas Mathiesen, as well as members of the British organisation Preservation of the Rights of Prisons (PROP), among others, attended the first Conference for the Study of Deviance & Social Control in Florence.[8] The conference was one of the key occasions on which anti-asylum and anti-prison movements met and exchanged their views.[9] The Manifesto written by the European Group for the Study of Deviance & Social Control clearly showed that both 'crime' and 'deviance' fall under the umbrella of 'abnormality', and denounced the positivist approach then dominant in the social sciences and among policy-makers, for which 'agencies of social control are studied ... from the point of view of how to make them more effective'.[10] Criticising and taking a radical distance from this, the Group was animated by the twofold goal of developing 'a theoretical approach that grants "deviant actors" a conscious past, a present perceived problem and a future praxis', and of elaborating a theory of deviance and crime that 'delineates the nature of the whole society which engenders such problems'.

These connections between anti-asylum and anti-prison movements should not lead us to conclude that there is any simple isomorphism of different struggles against institutions. On the contrary, as Foucault noted, for those in a psychiatric hospital, it is much more difficult to revolt against the asylum and to organise a collective refusal than it is for detainees to revolt against the prison system (although this is what Franco Basaglia tried to do in Italy).[11] Nonetheless, highlighting the mutual exchanges and political affinities between the two movements is key for showing that anti-prison mobilisations did not emerge out nowhere. Nor can they be detached from a broader contestation concerning how the state's violence was exercised in and through total institutions. Indeed, anti-prison mobilisations both boosted and influenced movements against interconnected total institutions and a critical reflection on crime and social deviance from the standpoint of social-economic conditions.

Reconstructing the political conjuncture and the mutual influences through which anti-prison groups emerged in Europe during this period also enables us to foreground the significantly different genealogies of anti-prison movements in France and in the US. Indeed, although, in the US, critical analyses of the asylum were also developed – in particular through the work of the psychologist Thomas Szasz – the main 'common wind' through which anti-prisons mobilisations and prison revolts were connected was set by anti-racist mobilisations, particularly during the period when the Black Panther Party was most active, as the biographies of Angela Y. Davis and George Jackson well illustrate. Equally, despite the different political influences that shaped anti-prison movements in these and other countries, such movements also shared what we might term a genealogy rooted in a 'long 1968', which boosted and informed the anti-prison movement, both because of the widespread radical criticism of repressive institutions and because of the support that detainees received from some radical leftist parties. In fact, many conceived struggles within and against prisons as part of a broader class struggle, as Sante Notarnicola, an Italian detainee who became one of the leader of the prison revolts in Italy in the late 1960s, stressed in his book *The Impossible Escape*: he refused the verdict of the court 'because the police apparatus has been demonstrated to be an instrument for class-based oppression'.[12] Nevertheless, until recently, anti-prison mobilisations have rarely been considered as a political movement as such. For this reason, highlighting their political legacies and retracing their interconnected genealogies is an important task of a history of the present.

Unsettling the inside-outside of the prison

The Prison Information Group (GIP) was founded in December 1970 by former prisoners, and families of detainees, as well as by a group of scholars, including, most notably, Gilles Deleuze, Daniel Defert, Pierre Vidal Naquet and Michel Foucault. Overall, in the first half of the 1970s the anti-carceral movement was characterised by an unprecedented relay between protests inside the prison and mobilisations outside. Importantly, the GIP did not emerge from radical theories about the prison system. Rather, its birth should be situated within a broader political context in which, in the aftermath of the Algerian War of independence (1954-1962), a large number of Algerian citizens were held in French prisons and an important conjuncture of movements was gaining traction: 'the Mouvement de Libération des Femmes, followed by the Front Homosexuel d'Action Révolutionnaire ... and the student and workers' revolt of May '68' were all happening at the same time.[13] The GIP challenged the prison system, above all, by unsettling the boundaries between inside and outside the prison: that is, at the core of their mobilisations was the attempt to break down the barriers to communication, building coalitions and the establishing of connections between people in prisons and those supporting their struggles.

One important observation made by the GIP was that there was a risk that the division enforced by the state between prisoners and free citizens could be replicated also in the anti-prison movement. Political interventions aimed at raising detainees' consciousness could involve inferring that these latter were not themselves aware of their own condition, and that the work of activists and intellectuals were thus needed to achieve this. In opposition to this, the GIP insisted that the point is not 'to raise consciousness among prisoners ... they had this awareness for a long time, but it hasn't had the means to express itself ... individual experiences must be transformed into collective knowledge. That is to say, into political knowledge'.[14] The goal was by no means to explain to prisoners why and how they had to fight, but to give them the floor. The members of the GIP thus aimed at building up transversal alliances between those inside and those outside the jail through practices of knowledge co-production and by amplifying from outside the struggles happening within the prisons' walls. In fact, the mobilisations of the GIP were grounded in the idea that detainees face a double isolation: they were forcibly isolated from the outside and, within the prison, among themselves. Thus, supporting their struggle meant undermining both forms of isolation at once, making it possible for detainees to communicate among themselves and with the outside. Anti-prison mobilisations in France in the early 1970s thereby did more than simply amplify detainees' struggles and spread the news of this outside the prison: the support from outside was in itself constitutive of the struggle against the prison system.

Producing a collective and situated knowledge about the prison system was at the core of the GIP's activities. In a similar way, a central task of the anti-prison movement in the US consisted in breaking the wall between detainees and those outside the prison: by reading the letters written by activist prisoners, including, among others, Angela Davis and George Jackson, what emerges is the urgency of establishing connections with outside the prison as well as with other social movements – such as socialist coalitions and anti-war movements. In fact, detainees were trying both to unsettle the rigid division between inside/outside the prison – pointing to the racialised carceral continuum in the US – and to show mutual entanglements with other social movements that were unfolding at the time. By arguing that 'black revolution and socialist revolution have penetrated the wall',[15] and that the point was not only to struggle against prisons but 'to consolidate and solidify a mass movement with the positive idea of socialism',[16] Davis voiced the way in which struggles within and against the prison system were ultimately fights against class and racial oppression at large.

N. Haroun-Romain. Plan for a penitentiary, 1840.
A prisoner praying in his cell, facing the central surveillance tower.

The particular connections built between abolitionist groups, socialist claims and anti-racist movements were ultimately quite specific to the US context, and were far less developed in the French one. As Gilmore has remarked, 'prisons are geographical solutions to social and economic crises, politically organised by a racial state which is itself in crisis',[17] and the expansion of the prison system in the US is intrinsically connected to broader 'processes of displacement, abandonment and control'.[18] Nonetheless, even if in France claims against structural racism played a marginal role in anti-prison mobilisations, a common thread between the two movements was represented by the effort to demolish the clear-cut division between inside and outside, between detainees and other citizens. This became one of the main goals of the anti-prison movement more generally, insofar as it aimed at undermining and making intolerable the very functioning of the penal system and the basis upon which this was publicly justified as the unavoidable solution for tackling the problem of criminality in society.

Consequently, the multiplication of hierarchies – between inside and outside the prison, as well as among detainees – was directly targeted by the GIP: 'the struggle against the penitentiary system ought to destroy, before anything else, the divisions that the system establishes and that permit it to subsist: the hierarchical divisions inside the prison and the isolation of families outside'.[19] In order to unsettle the twofold isolation inside prisons, solidarity alliances were thus built between detainees and people who supported their struggle, both in the US and in France, by making the uprisings reverberate outside the prison and by articulating punctual demands with broader claims against repression and the social punishing of the poor. Indeed, the struggle carried on by prisoners encapsulated claims and refusals that concerned the punitive society at large and, in the US context at least, the racialised carceral continuum.

Undoing the neat division between detainees and citizens outside entailed showing that the different layers of oppression at play inside the prison were similarly deployed outside its walls and that a fight against these involved targeting all these forms of oppression together. As Daniel Defert put it: 'we must not believe prison is an isolated black hole. In fact, the penal system ... includes three interdependent pieces: the police, the legal system, and the prison'.[20] The revolt in the Toul prison in December 1971 was the first collective struggle led by prisoners in France during which the division between inside and outside crumbled: prisoners went up on the roof and addressed their claims to the public opinion, to the journalists who were there and told them: 'this is what we want'. Indeed, prisoners were aware that, by saying this, 'they would have not found sniggering journalists, nor a hostile public opinion'.[21] The communication with the outside and the very fact of addressing public opinion were central tactics not only for letting people know what was happening inside but, more importantly, for building a platform for collective demands. By breaking down the barriers between inside and outside, detainees' struggles in the US and in France 'disrupt[ed] assumptions such as the idea that politics happens' exclusively or primarily 'in the milieu of the state'.[22]

Intolerance-inquiries and subversive knowledges

The production of collective counter-knowledge about the carceral system played a major role in both the US and French anti-prison mobilisations. In the US, the letters written by prisoners and in particular by prisoner-activists like Angela Davis and George Jackson, had been the main channel through which the reality of the prisons and the struggles against this started to be known. In France, alongside the circulation of prisoners' letters, the GIP initiated a mode of collective inquiry called 'intolerance-inquiry'. The mobilisations organised by the GIP started from the twofold principle that detainees are aware of their situation and of the structural violence at play in the prison, and that, consequently, what was at stake consisted rather in putting in place the conditions for speaking up and for organising collectively. In using the expression 'intolerance-inquiry',[23] they referred to questionnaires, crafted by former prisoners, that were given to detainees and that focused on the living conditions and rights in prisons, including around food, leisure time, visits, work, medical care and access to information and lawyers. In fact, it was by centring on the material living conditions and on what might appear to be small details (such as food quality and quantity, or the cold in the cells) that the questionnaires highlighted the unacceptability of the prison system at large. What they revealed was less the misery and the despair inside the prison than detainees' violated rights. More precisely, through the questionnaires, the GIP discovered 'a whole series of repressions still harder to endure than overcrowding, boredom or hunger',[24] and even harder than the privation of freedom of movement as such. As Foucault asked, if 'detention is in principle the privation of the freedom to leave ... why is it that prison must furthermore lead to the privation of a certain number of other fundamental freedoms?'[25] Thus, the intolerance-inquiry did not function primarily to accumulate knowledge but, rather, to generate an active intolerance towards the prison.

The purpose of intolerance-inquiries was not only to make visible the living conditions of the detainees but, more than that, to start from and point to these in order to illuminate a wide range of substantial violations and privations of freedom, showing their mutual interdependence. In other words, by paying attention to how prisoners articulated both the questions and the answers, the complaints about the living conditions revealed that the prison system was suffocating and, directly or indirectly, killing them. In fact, the wretched material conditions within the prison mirrored the biopolitical tactics for choking and 'crushing the prisoner's sense of self'.[26] As the Organisation of Political Prisoners contended, 'the penitentiary regime marshals all the conditions necessary to break the individual completely, physically as much as morally'.[27] Through the intolerance-inquiry, the GIP radically unsettled the division between detainees and external supporters, since the questionnaires were structured by prisoners and former prisoners in light of what they wanted to make visible and intolerable. Second, the intolerance-inquiry was predicated on non-extractive knowledge co-production, between the detainees and those outside. The intolerance-inquiry did not intend to be an objective description of the prison system. Rather, it was both part of what might be called a militant investigation, to echo workers' inquiries in factories in the 1960s and the 1970s that sought to produce real knowledge about workers' conditions in the factories, and, building on this, to expose the modes of exploitation at stake, and a tool of denunciation, for making the prison system intolerable.

The persistence of the prison system does not only depend on a lack of knowledge and evidence. The question for the GIP was how to transform the evidence into an intolerable reality. Relatedly, the unacceptability of the prison should not be framed in terms of excess (of violence and detention): it is the function of the prison itself which is unacceptable as it serves the purpose of criminalising and controlling a part of the population and of maintaining unequal wealth distribution. Rendering the prison intolerable was not an isolated task: on the contrary, the goal was to produce an active intolerance about 'the legal system, the hospital system, psychiatric practice, military service, etc'.[28] That is, the critique of the prison-system was situated as a part of a critique of the societal confinement continuum: the prison, as abolitionist scholars contend, is in fact the most blatant expression of disciplining and confinement mechanisms that target the lower classes.

Alongside the intolerance-inquiry, the GIP produced leaflets to distribute outside prisons and in cities for amplifying the struggles of the detainees. The letters and the declarations of the prisoners were also circulated widely, in order to let people know about the collective revolts and hunger strikes that were happening in many prisons across France. It is worth remembering that the collective uprisings within French prisons started with political prisoners and then spread across and became a revolt in the name of all detainees.[29] Indeed, while at the beginning their claims concerned the right to be recognised as political prisoners, and not as common criminals, they soon started insisting that their collective struggle was in the service of all prisoners. But what did active intolerance towards prisons mean in terms of transformative politics? It is important to stress that prison reforms were far from the purpose of the activities of the GIP. Indeed, they firmly insisted that reforming the carceral system was not a part of their struggle and that, on the contrary, prison reforms end up in reinforcing the carceral continuum in a disguised way. Rather, as Foucault advanced, the point is to ask, 'can one in effect conceptualise a society in which power has no need for illegalities?'[30]

At the same time that the GIP was producing the intolerance-inquiry, in the US prisoners mobilised with different forms of collective protests as well as by writing letters and manifestos for reaching out and showing the reality of the American prison system. In this respect, George Jackson's activism and the letters he wrote, collected in the volume *Soledad Brother: The Prison Letters of George Jackson*, are well known. Indeed, Jackson, who was killed by the police in 1971 while he was trying to escape the prison, articulated a radical critique of the carceral system, showing that this latter was grounded on racialised punishment and on the criminalisation of the poor: 'most of today's black convicts have come to understand that they are the most abused victims of an unrighteous order. Up until now, the prospect of parole has kept us from confronting our captors with any real determination'.[31] In one of her letters from prison, Angela Davis stressed that 'black revolution and socialist revolution penetrated the walls' of the jail.

For Jackson, Davis and others, the fight against the carceral system was at the same time a struggle against state racism and a class struggle: 'the activity surrounding the protection and liberation of people who fight for us is an important aspect of the struggle, but it is important only if it provides new initiatives that redirect and advance the revolution under new progressive methods'.[32] As Howard Zinn remarked, 'all over the country, prisoners were obviously affected by the turmoil in the country, the black revolt, the youth upsurge, the anti-war movement'.[33] That is to say, not only did the anti-prison movement boost other collective struggles that mobilised for social justice, but detainees and detainees' supporters were in turn influenced by other mobilisations that were taking place outside the prison. Similarly to the French context, this was the basis in the US for an unprecedented solidarity and active engagement with non-detainees; in the words of Zinn, 'on the outside, something new was also happening, the development of prison support groups all over the country'.[34]

Speaking about his time in prison, George Jackson pointed out that 'men are brutalised by their environment, not the reverse';[35] and he explains this statement by illustrating, through a focus on the details of daily life in prison, the extent to which detainees are obstructed and their sense of self-esteem is crushed by the very materiality of the impediments standing in their way and by meticulous disciplinary controls. Such a stress on the biopolitical effects that the carceral system has on detainees' lives, beyond the deprivation of freedom, is an important point of convergence between the anti-prison mobilisations in the US and in France. Nevertheless, the knowledge produced – through detainees' letters, inquiries and reports – and that circulated about and from within prisons, was shaped by different focuses in the US and in France, leading activists in the US to craft a critique of the carceral system which put racism at the forefront.

The antisocial function of the prison in the US was clearly stated by prisoners-activists in the 1970s: while state discourse depicted criminality as a psychological-behaviouralist problem, black prisoners insisted that 'the criminal has nothing to do with breaking the law'.[36] Indeed, first, the acts which are sanctioned by the law are, the argument goes, those commonly perpetuated by the lower classes, as a result of social marginalisation and unemployment. Second, the prison has little to do with law-breaking as long as it is a 'state apparatus employed to maintain exploitative and oppressive social conditions'.[37] For this reason – and this is a key lesson for current abolitionist projects – radical struggles against the prison system cannot be disjoined from an anti-capitalist horizon. The importance of intertwining struggles against capitalism and struggles against the carceral continuum has been constantly reiterated by later carceral abolitionist literature.[38] Such a focus on racialised punishment, and on the need to articulate anti-capitalist struggles and prison abolitionism together, allow us to uncover some key similarities and differences between the anti-prison movement in the US and the one in France.

As part of its intolerance-investigation, the GIP specifically highlighted political oppression as a key goal of the carceral system: the prison's main function is not to punish and correct criminals but, rather, to maintain the oppression and the exploitation of a certain part of the population. The penitentiary system 'forms part of a large, more complex system that we might call the punitive system'.[39] Yet it does not apply to everyone in the same way: it works precisely by strengthening socio-economic differences. The lower classes, the poor, are the target of the prison system. While both in the US and in France anti-prison movements insist that prisons allow the reproduction and multiplication of class differences, in the US this discourse is mainly inflected through the lens of racial capitalism and structural violence, as key components of the carceral continuum. That is, while the race-based functioning of the prison is at the core of the reflection upon the prison system and collective mobilisations in the US, in the French context it is only very marginally elaborated and de facto superseded by considerations on class. The central role played by race and racism in the US anti-prison movement stems in part, of course, from the historical and political legacies of slavery (and the anti-slavery movement) and in part from the pronounced racial composition in US prisons. In 'Racialised Punishment and Prison Abolitionism' (2003), the only text in which she directly engages with Foucault's work, Angela Davis commented that we need a different genealogy from Foucault's genealogy of prisons, which is centred on the history of disciplinary powers: one which 'would accentuate the links between confinement, punishment and race'.[40] In her critique of Foucault's analysis of the prison system, Davis stresses that, first, racism is not a contingent aspect but, rather, a structural component of carceral mechanisms; and, second, she argues that – while for Foucault torture is no longer a part of contemporary modes of punishment – torture actually plays a key role in the functioning of prisons, and is precisely what connects it with the incarceration of slaves.

The nexus between the prison-industrial complex and the slavery system has been stressed by various recent carceral abolitionist scholars in the US, for whom the prison is a form of 'surplus land, capital, labour, and state capacity'.[41] A very similar analysis was present already in the texts written by American prisoners-activists in the early 1970s. For instance, the Folsom Prisoners Manifesto, written in November 1970, define prisons as 'fascist concentration camps of modern America' and as institutions of 'authoritative inhumanity'.[42] The specificity of the US prison system in this respect was also known by the GIP, as Foucault fleshed out after his visit to the prison of Attica in New York: 'American prisons in fact play two roles: a role as a place of punishment ... and a role as concentration camp'; and 'in the United States there must be one out of 30 or 40 black men in prison: it is here that one can see the function of massive elimination in the American prison'.[43] Thus, also thanks to the visits that some members of the GIP – and Foucault in particular – made to US prisons and the exchanges they had with the anti-prison movement there, the specificity of the American carceral system was quite well known.

However, racialised punishment and state racism continued to be largely unaddressed in the GIP's own critique of French prisons.

Abolitionist legacies

Anti-prison mobilisations in the 1970s paved the way for the latest carceral abolitionist projects. Far from constituting a monolithic genealogy, the legacies of past struggles against prisons are inflected by the different ways in which the analysis and the critique of the carceral system was framed. Yet, despite these differences, both in France and in the US, anti-prison struggles shared a refusal to endorse reformist programmes and each firmly challenged the goal of building a better and fairer prison system. Indeed, the purpose of letting people outside know the reality of the carceral system was not to cultivate support for reform programmes but, rather, to render the prisons obsolete.[44] Abolitionism, as Angela Davis has contended, is 'not only a negative process of tearing down, it is also about building up, it is about creating new institutions'.[45]

Prison abolitionism cannot in fact be accomplished without radically changing ways of addressing social phenomena and addressing social marginalisation and poverty, by tackling its causes instead of repressing crime. This would also involve putting in place alternative institutions that could make this possible. In turn, as Davis puts it, prison abolitionism is 'a fundamental requirement for the revitalisation of democracy'.[46] Notwithstanding their differences, the anti-prison movement in France and the one in the US converge in their way of conceiving prison abolitionism. To break down prison walls, writes Jean-Marie Domenach, 'it will be necessary to invent institutions and forms of conduct' that instead of repressing delinquency 'will treat its causes and will thereby compel the transformation of a society that is encouraging crime more and more'.[47] This analysis is in line with the one carried out by activists in the US, according to whom carceral abolitionism entails undoing the modes of labour subordination that underpin racial capitalism. At the same time, it is important not to flatten out the specificities of the struggles against prisons that took place in France (and in Europe more generally) by squeezing these into the terms of the US' carceral abolitionism movement. As discussed above, struggles against prisons in France were not inflected by debates on racialised punishment and the abolitionist agenda was not as explicitly articulated as it was in the US. Highlighting intertwined abolitionist legacies does not mean erasing the specificities of each political context nor does it mean superimposing the North American experience onto all other historical struggles, as a portable template for analysing anti-prison movements happening elsewhere across the world. Rather, it is a matter of amplifying abolitionist legacies beyond the North American context, foregrounding multiple resonances and, at the same time, de-centring the US debate by showing how abolitionist discourses and practices emerged elsewhere and how differently they were articulated.

Carceral abolitionism draws, both politically and historically, on black slave abolitionism. W.E.B. Du Bois' idea of 'abolition-democracy' encapsulates to some extent the very meaning of abolitionist politics in the US. Notably, in *Black Reconstruction in America*, Du Bois retraces the key political steps that led to the official abolition of slavery in the United States. As part of that historical reconstruction, he introduced the notion of 'abolition-democracy' to stress that the abolition of racialised inequality did not end with the end of chattel slavery: rather, it required building up new institutions, and dismantling those that enable the reproduction of racism and slavery.[48] The idea of abolition democracy is importantly connected in Du Bois' work to the active role of the slaves in enacting their own liberation: the general strike that slaves organised in the United States in 1860 constituted a landmark in slaves' struggles for emancipation. Borrowing the notion of 'abolition democracy' from Du Bois, Angela Davis has argued that prison abolitionism does not consist in the mere abolition of the institution of the prison but, rather, it requires the dismantling of the prison-industrial complex as a whole. That is, an abolitionist approach starts from the assumption that the undoing of bordering mechanisms also requires building up and creating new institutions and ways of being-in-common that prevent the formation of social and economic inequalities and racialised punishment. For this reason, carceral abolitionism is not merely about abolishing prisons, and actually it cannot be enforced by shutting down prisons without radically transforming how the production of criminality is addressed: 'abolition is about abolishing the conditions under which prison became the solution to problems, rather than abolishing the buildings we call prisons'.[49] Despite their differences, such a call for transformative political processes echoes, I suggest, the critique of the prison system framed by the GIP. First, as explained above, the members of the GIP refused the idea of prison reforms, as they started from the assumption that 'there can be no reform of the prison without the search for a new society'.[50] This position is not in tension with mobilisations in support of prisoners' punctual demands aimed at improving their life's conditions. Rather, the GIP repeatedly insisted on the importance of keeping the struggle going on both levels – punctual claims and radical critique of the prison system. The 'active intolerance' towards prisons that the GIP aimed at triggering could emerge only by showing that what appear as disparate 'scandalous aspects of penitentiary life' are actually 'impossible to separate'.[51] Struggles for getting better food or hygienic conditions and access to legal aid do not invalidate nor weaken the mobilisation against the prison system as a whole: on the contrary, they enable its grounding in the materiality of prisoners' daily struggles. By no means were detainees' punctual claims a part of a programme for reforming the prison system. Rather, they were raised in response to the unbearable living conditions within prisons. Or, better, the demands raised by the GIP and by detainees could be framed as non-reformist reforms, as they carried on political actions based on what Sandro Mezzadra has defined as a 'split temporality':[52] that is, fighting for the abolition of the carceral system and, at the same time, for detainees' rights inside the prison.

In fact, it can be argued, detainees' collective struggles were actually part of an abolitionist horizon, in which rights claims within the prison – e.g., about medical and psychological support, legal aid and seeing family members – allowed for the exposure of the truly intolerable character of the penitentiary system. An abolitionist approach involves challenging what Gilmore has defined as the 'problem of innocence' which sustains the reformist critique of the prison system. Indeed, the politics of white innocence that Gilmore challenges 'establishes as a hard fact that some people should be in cages ... and it does so by distinguishing degrees of innocence such that there are people, inevitably, who will become permanently not innocent', while, as she argues, it is 'only against this desirability or inevitability [that] some change [might] occur'.⁵³ This echoes Foucault's point about the main political stake of challenging the prison system: speaking about the GIP, he explained that their actions aimed at 'erasing the deep frontier between innocence and guilt'.⁵⁴ By arguing this, Foucault and the members of the GIP took a clear distance from humanist positions that foregrounded human nature as the starting point of their criticism of the prison – stating for instance that even criminals should be respected as human beings.

Past collective struggles within and against prisons have, as I have said, informed current abolitionist projects, through a circulation of a political lexicon and of practical knowledge, as well as through their analysis and critique of the carceral system. The legacy of past anti-prison mobilisations reverberates into the present and, in particular, into the abolitionist projects that in the last few years have animated anti-racist movements, as well as struggles against borders. In fact, I suggest, the legacy of carceral abolitionism movements goes far beyond struggles within and against prisons, as the growing debate on border abolitionism as well as the proliferation of collective uprisings and individual escapes in immigration detention centres imply. The collective memory of racial anti-prisons claims and struggles has enabled the pushing forward of discourses against immigration detention beyond a politics of white innocence – that is, without endorsing the produced opposition between innocent and real criminals or, in this case, between people who committed crimes or otherwise. The interconnected genealogies of anti-prison movements have clearly foregrounded that an abolitionist approach cannot simply be restricted to claims for abolishing prisons. Rather, abolitionism as an analytical-political standpoint involves dismantling the material and political conditions under which the multiplication of borders and the persistence of prisons appear as a condition for people' safety and for the enjoyment of rights.

Martina Tazzioli is a member of the editorial collective of Radical Philosophy *and Reader in Politics and Technology at Goldsmiths, University of London. She is author of* The Making of Migration *(2019) and* Spaces of Governmentality *(2014).*

Notes

1. Michel Foucault, 'Prisons and Revolts in Prisons', in *Intolerable: Writings from Michel Foucault and the Prisons Information Group, 1970-1980*, eds. Kevin Thompson and Perry Zurn, trans. Perry Zurn and Eric Beranek (Minneapolis: Minnesota University Press, 2021), 309.
2. See Christian De Vito and Silvia Vaiani, 'La libertà di lottare. Movimenti di detenuti in Europa Occidentale (1969-1975)', *Zapruder* 16 (2008), 9-23, available at: http://storieinmovimento.org/wp-content/uploads/2017/04/Zap16_02-Zoom1.pdf. The first two big collective protests organised by detainees inside prisons took place in April 1969 in Turin and, a few days later, in Genova.
3. Mike Fitzgerald, *Prisoners in revolts* (New York: Penguin, 1977).
4. Brian Stratton, 'Parkhurst prison revolt 1969', *Fight Racism! Fight Imperialism!* (November 1999), 12.
5. Julius Scott, *The Common Wind: Afro-American Organization in the Revolution against Slavery* (London: Verso, 2018).
6. Psichiatria Democratica was founded by Franco Basaglia in 1973. Unlike the anti-psychiatry movement in the UK, which challenged psychiatry as such, Psichiatria Democratica's goal was to criticise and change psychiatric practices from within, and to challenge the asylum.
7. The exchanges between Franco Basaglia and two of the co-founders of the Prison Information Group, Gilles Deleuze and Michel Foucault (along with Felix Guattari), were frequent over the years. Although this is not the purpose of this piece, and would require a separate analysis, it is important to stress that the mutual influence between anti-prison and anti-asylum movements in France and in Italy was partly due to this also.
8. Michel Foucault, 'Par-delà le bien et le mal' in *Dits et Ecrits I* (Paris: Gallimard, 2000), 1099.
9. In passing, it is worth noting that the positions of Foucault and Basaglia were quite different from the critique of the asylum put forth by the anti-psychiatry movement in the UK. Indeed, Basaglia refused the label of anti-psychiatry, arguing that his goal was to transform psychiatric practices; similarly, Foucault questioned the mere opposition to institutions, contending that this presupposes a repressive and juridical understanding of power that he challenged in his work.
10. European Group for the Study of Deviance & Social Control, 'Manifesto 1974', *Crime and Social Justice* 4 (1975), 47.
11. Ibid.
12. Sante Notarnicola, *L'evasione impossibile* (Milano: Feltrinelli, 1972), 123.
13. Kevin Thompson and Perry Zurn, 'Introduction: Legacies of Militancy and Theory', in *Intolerable*, eds. Thompson and Zurn, 5.
14. Michel Foucault and Pierre Vidal-Naquet, 'Inquiry on prisons. Let us break down the bars of silence', in *Intolerable*, eds. Thomson and Zurn, 109.
15. Angela Y. Davis, *If they come in the morning...: Voices of resistance* (London: Verso Books, 2016), 45.
16. Ibid., 65.
17. Ruth Wilson Gilmore, *Abolition Geography: Essays Towards Liberation* (London: Verso Books, 2022), 135.

18. Ibid., 187.
19. Daniel Defert, 'When information is a struggle', in *Intolerable*, eds. Zurn and Thompson, 72
20. Ibid
21. Michel Foucault, 'La prison partout', in *Dits et Ecrits* (Paris: Gallimard, 2000), 443.
22. Ruth Wilson Gilmore, 'Fatal Couplings of Power and Difference: Notes on Racism and Geography', *The Professional Geographer* 54 (2002).
23. Prison Infromation Group, 'On prisons', in *Intolerable*, eds. Zurn and Thomas, 67,
24. Foucault and Vidal-Naquet, 'Inquiry on prisons', 112.
25. Michel Foucault, 'No, this is not an official inquiry', in *Intolerable*, eds. Zurn and Thompson, 117.
26. Organisation des prisonniers politiques, 'Report on the Prisons', in *Intolerable*, eds. Zurn and Thomas, 58.
27. Ibid., 57.
28. Groupe d'Information sur les risons, 'On Prisons', in *Intolerable*, eds. Zurn and Thomas, 67.
29. The GIP itself was formed at the beginning of 1971 in solidarity with the collective hunger strike of a group of prisoners who claimed political status.
30. Michel Foucault, 'Alternatives to the Prison: Dissemination or Decline of Social Control?', *Theory, Culture & Society* 26 (2009), 24.
31. George Jackson, *Soledad Brother. The prison letters of George Jackson*, available at: https://files.libcom.org/files/soledad-brother-the-prison-letters-of-george-jackson.pdf
32. Ibid.
33. Howard Zinn, 'The US Prisoners' Movement, 1970-1978', available at https://libcom.org/article/us-prisoners-movement-1970-1978-howard-zinn.
34. Ibid.
35. Jackson, *Soledad Brother*.
36. Aptheker, 'The social functions of the prisons in the United States', 53.
37. Ibid., 57.
38. Angela, Y. Davis, *Abolition democracy: Beyond Empire, Prisons and Torture* (New York: Seven Stories Press, 2011); Ruth Wilson Gilmore, 'The case for prison abolition', 2020. https://www.youtube.com/watch?v=1HWqYANmWLY
39. Michel Foucault, 'Pompidou's Two Deaths', in *Intolerable*, eds. Zurn and Thomas, 306.
40. Angela Y. Davis, 'Racialised Punishment and Prison Abolition', in *A Companion to African-American Philosophy* (Malden: Blackwell, 2003), 364.
41. Ruth Wilson Gilmore, *Golden Gulag* (Berkeley: University of California Press, 2007), 28.
42. Folsom Prisoners, 'Prisoners in Rebellion. The Folsom Prisoners Manifesto', in Angela Y. Davis, *If they come in the morning...*, 156.
43. Michel Foucault, 'On Attica', in *Intolerable*, eds. Zurn and Thomas, 295.
44. Angela Y. Davis, *Are Prisons Obsolete?* (New York: Seven Stories Press, 2003).
45. Davis, *Abolition Democracy*, 93.
46. Davis, *Are Prisons Obsolete?*, 39.
47. Jean-Marie Domenach, 'To have done with prisons', in *Intolerable*, eds. Zurn and Thomas, 342.
48. W.E.B. Du Bois, *Black Reconstruction in America* (New York: Routledge, 1998).
49. Gilmore, 'The Case for Prison Abolition'.
50. Foucault, 'Alternatives to the Prisons', 24.
51. Groupe d'information sur les prisons, 'La Santé: Questionnaire and Narratives', in *Intolerable*, eds. Zurn and Thomas, 103.
52. Sandro Mezzadra, 'Double Opening, Split Temporality, and New Spatialities: An Interview with Sandro Mezzadra on Militant Research', *Postcolonial Studies* 16 (2013), 309–319.
53. Ruth Wilson Gilmore, 'Abolition Geography and the Problem of Innocence', in *Futures of Black Radicalism*, eds. Johnson and Lubin (London: Verso, 2017), 234.
54. Foucault, 'Par-delà le bien et le mal', 1099. See also Michel Foucault and J.J. Brochier, 'Prison Talk', *Radical Philosophy* 16 (Spring 1977), 10–15.

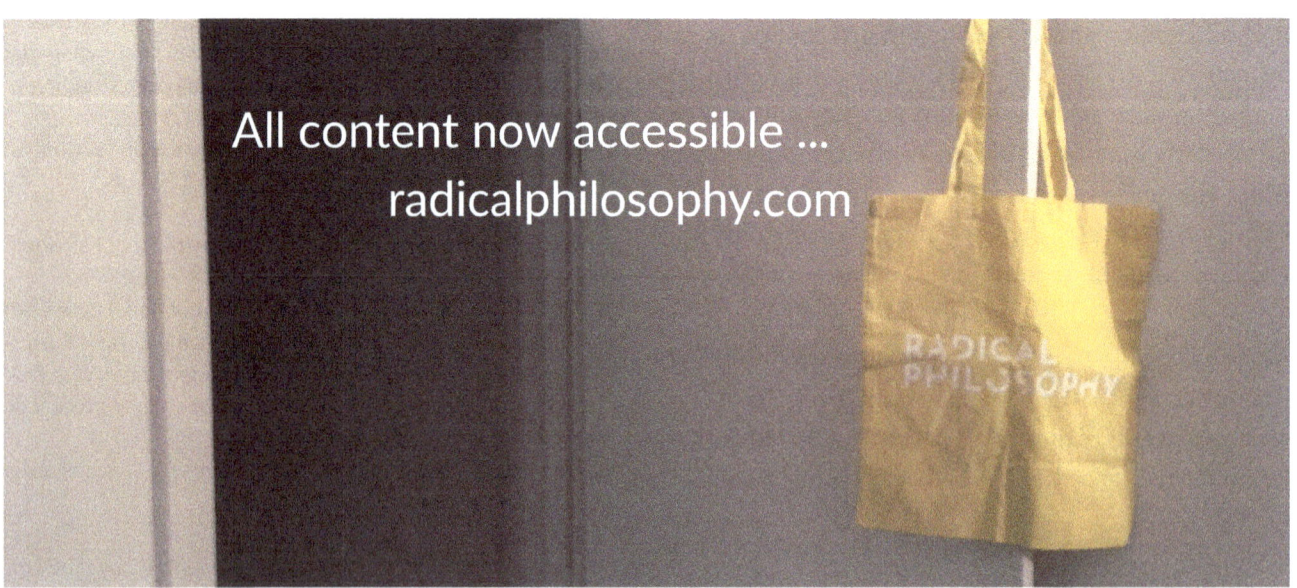

All content now accessible ...
radicalphilosophy.com

Untimely Media
Subversions of obsolescence in decolonial print
Amit S. Rai

'It will keep your secrets. Operate it yourself.'

A. B. Dick Mimeograph Company advertisement in *Life* magazine, circa 1940.

How can we decolonise technics today within, against and beyond Eurocentric teleologies that separate rational humans from savage or inert nature and technological infrastructure assumed to be a 'standing reserve'?[1] The provocative exhibition 'Crafting Subversion: DIY and Decolonial Print', curated by Pragya Dhital at the Brunei Gallery, SOAS University of London from April to September 2022, suggests that there is indeed another history of the tool. The exhibition, as Dhital's accompanying text tells us, 'explores various attempts to forge connections between readers and writers beyond the purview of the state and the logic of the market through the medium of DIY print.'[2] The little magazines from 1960-70s New York and Bombay, samizdat literatures from the former Soviet bloc, anticolonial nationalist and anti-authoritarian antinationalist Indian pamphlets, and Gestetner-mimeograph publications of collective, non-normative, paracapitalist and paralinguistic cultural expression all involved 'direct engagement with lived social antagonism'.[3] In 'Crafting Subversion' these artefacts showcase the untimely history of supposedly obsolete media technologies and what the art collective Alt Går Bra (an inspiration for Dhital's curation) describes as DIY or jugaad media's nonlinear (im)mediations in collective 'experiments with the modes of production of mimeograph publications from the 1960s and 70s'.[4] Jugaad (pronounced ju-gaar) is a colloquial Hindi-Urdu, Marathi, Punjabi and Bengali word for 'playful work-around' or 'everyday hack'. It may also have a Goan genealogy: jugar means play in Portuguese. In this article, I will draw on the political and philosophical resources of this obsolescence, lingering over only a portion of the DIY assemblages that Dhital has through great effort gathered together, and highlighting the materiality of their ecology of sensation and the jugaad strategies of their composition.

The mimeograph revolution

The 'mimeograph revolution' found its living sociality in contemporising gossip, anecdote, assembly, encounter and conversation, in refusing the 'waiting and pleading at the doors of big time publishing', and in refusing the perennial contending with limited resources and obscenity laws that dampened transnational distribution networks.[5] As Lincoln Cushing puts it, 'Before photocopiers took over the short-run end of copy making, messy and relatively inexpensive machines called dittos, mimeographs and Gestetners ruled the earth. Virtually every school, office, and union hall had one in the back room, usually surrounded by reams of paper and the unmistakable odor of fresh solvent.'[6] This lively cultural moment in disparate parts of the world – they were known, for instance, as mimeographs in the USA, Roneos in the UK, and Gestetners in the UK and Europe, stensilmaskin in Norway, nakala in Kenya, toshaban in Japan[7] – saw a proliferation of experiments in artistic and political uses of the mimeograph.[8]

The subversive and at times revolutionary potential of techno-obsolescence is diagrammed today by radical archaeologists of communication and media technology as eruptions of untimely resistances to dominant political ecologies of attention and expression, which, in their very 'figuration of the outmoded', act counter to our times, against our times and for the benefit of times to come.⁹ Joel Burges conceptualises the 'figuration of the outmoded' as a temporality that 'tangibly constellates historical crosscurrents between a bygone modernity and a contemporary horizon as those currents have been stirred up by obsolescence, a complex process of techno-economic transformation that intercalates multiple levels of historical change.'¹⁰

Untimely and outmoded media return to question the relentless presentism of racial capital's current division of labour, its separation of intellectual and manual labour, its treadmill-like commodification of 'new' media, its planned and forced obsolescence, potentialising the relations constituting classes, races, castes, genders and imperial extractivisms.¹¹ The outmoded and the untimely are contemptible, they are 'disattendable' objects (Thomas Hobbes).¹² This disattendability is a critical starting point to decolonise attention itself, given all the obsolete stuff that accumulates through the planned obsolescence of racial capitalist modernity.¹³ As Amy Wendling parses it,

> Industrialization produces monsters with potential. In their constant revolutionizing of the received division of labour, machines have the potential to revolutionize what for Marx is the most important division of labour: the polarizing division between the two classes. Because of this, in Marx's *Communist Manifesto*, machines themselves are key elements of developing revolutionary consciousness as well as the material foundation for the communist mode of production. Habituation to industrial life may produce not only monstrosities, but also liberations from old patriarchal norms.¹⁴

Indeed, the monstrosity of DIY media assemblages may be, and often certainly aspires to be, liberatory, as 'Crafting Subversions' shows to great effect. Such critical vitalisms of technological co-evolution with decolonial, revolutionary and radical movements of resistance and insurgency are not rooted in liberal 'hope'. Rather, taking their inspiration from documenting and subverting the 'random everyday things of the street' – catalogues, posters, advertisements, signboards, street signs, state propaganda, calendar art, film posters and newspaper photographs, as Arvind Krishna Mehrotra of Bombay Poet's little magazine/small press movement notes¹⁵ – DIY media practitioners give free reign to queer and monstrous experimentations with assemblages of (mis)perception and affective cuts into cliched attention, proposing 'models for a future exertion of thought.'¹⁶

Dhital's 'Crafting Subversion' expresses this untimely media history in ways that cause us to question the abject scripts of identity, representation and monumental memory foisted as fate onto workers, women, Dalits, indigenous, queer, neurodiverse and Black folx, people of colour, disabled, disenfranchised and young peoples through public relations firms, libraries, bookshops, publishing houses, cinemas, theatres, galleries, museums, print media (dailies and other periodicals), radio, Internet platforms, television and institutions of higher learning.¹⁷ Installed up the back staircase and across the narrow walkway of the first floor of the Brunei Gallery, as if in silent acknowledgement of the structural marginality of jugaad media assemblages, the art images, political posters, banned pamphlets and Gestetner advertising materials greet curious viewers as living artefacts of the many vibrant DIY media cultures saying (in the title of one little magazine) 'Fuck You!'

In these grim times of creative industries boosterism

and the financialisation of art, platform and surveillance capitalism's naturalised fetishism of the quantified, self-actualising individual, and the mystifying habituations of total market relations as the earth literally burns, 'Crafting Subversion' acts as an iskra, in Lenin's sense: a spark that illuminates and ignites collectively organised assemblages of media, technology and desire. The exhibit highlights entangled media experimentations that wager a subversion of the coloniality of technical Being, repeatedly and perpetually displacing the closures of racial capitalist intellectual property regimes and their individualising subjectivations. This subversion doesn't happen all at once, in some sense it doesn't 'happen' at all, and in another sense is happening everywhere, autonomously and simultaneously. The subversions of jugaad/DIY media assemblages are often indiscernible from their technological infrastructures, in a perpetual and fuzzy reticulation of nonlinear ontological forces and historical tendencies traversing so-called 'formal' and 'informal' economies, the pre-individual and collective. Such DIY media assemblages are entangled in the fugitivity of subaltern ecologies of social reproduction and their subjugated knowledges; as we shall see, the jugaad dimensions of such media assemblages are felt in practices of working around the closures of corporate and private media infrastructures. The values generated through these assemblages in historically specific domains of action and potentialisation are open to neoliberal entrepreneurial capture and capitalist accumulation in the realm of affect.[18] In such ecosystems of media invention and contestation, found materials, low-tech sign reproduction, heat, noise, ink, sweat, dirt, paper, wax, stencil, information and energy form the material conditions of resistance.

The heterogeneous assemblages showcased in 'Crafting Subversions' express the subversive force, sense and value of resistant DIY media cultures under different contexts of state repression, surveillance and control. The DIY publications in various ways refuse the total marketised relations of racial capitalist social reproduction. As I have argued recently in the context of contemporary South Asia, three crucial tendencies of DIY media – political autonomy, temporal untimeliness and technological pragmatism – interact in sensorial interzones that remain only unevenly integrated into digital media industry strategies for profit maximisation, financialisation, monopolisation/oligopolisation, risk management, labour standardisation and increasing value chain efficiencies.[19]

DIY media's ecology of sensation

It is worth focusing on the variable materiality of this eminently analogue media technology: the mimeograph, the world's 'first personal printer'.[20] As Elizabeth Haven Hawley usefully notes, mimeography, as distinct from spirit duplicating, involves creating a stencil from a paper covered in a waxy surface. A ribbon-less typewriter or a stylus can be used to strike or draw upon the stencil, effectively pushing the wax to either side and revealing the tissue paper substrate. Removing the wax allows ink from the machine's printing cylinder to seep through the stencil in selected areas, which forms the image to be transferred. Too much pressure in preparing the stencil can rip the tissue, resulting in ink blobs in bowls of letters where closed areas have been removed completely. Those preparing stencils avoided excessive underlines or cuts of closed circles that weakened the master copy. Complex layouts required careful preparation and handling, at the risk of producing a stencil too fragile to print. Machines printed large areas of colour poorly, as the semi-fluid ink flowed too freely through such cuts. A skilled operator could reuse a quality stencil and produce excellent results consistently, given the proper type of absorbent paper and supplies. In the global North, mimeograph paper could be procured through printers handling relief or lithographic work, and ink – though best when matched to the type of paper and stencil – might even be produced through the dilution of book printing ink with turpentine or gasoline.[21]

The process was not exactly the same everywhere. In early twentieth-century Japan the Horii's mimeograph, also known as the toshaban, developed a stencil duplicating method by film plate process, which does not require large-scale facilities or electrical machines. A sheet of stencil paper is placed on a film plate; the paper, a strong and thin traditional Japanese paper made from the fibre of the Ganpi plant (Diplomorpha sikokiana), is coated with paraffin wax. The wax is then removed with a metal stylus and prints made by exposing the fibres of the paper. A roller covered in ink is used to make a print; numerous gaps among the fibres of the paper allowed ink to pass through, creating a printed copy. What was distinctive about the Horii was that it could reproduce the intricate letters of complex illustrations that came to form the art of the mimeograph in Japan. The ink was oil-based and fade resistant; it was able to print more copies than the printing devices (lithography or typography) used at the time; it was described as 'hard to break and easy enough for anyone to use'; it could also print illustrations alongside characters.[22]

In Dhital's curation, the material specificity of each run from, say, a hand-corrected mimeographed stencil takes on a certain radical contingency, a proliferation of asignifying differences without referent. In the wall text of 'Crafting Subversion', the South Asian publications are contextualised in relation to a wide range of archives produced using different low-tech, sometimes jugaad printing and duplication processes. 'The combination of handwriting and mass-produced ephemera meant that no two versions of the magazine looked the same. (The version of *ezra* held by the British Library ... and the version in the UCL Small Press library, used in the exhibition poster, are clearly non-identical.) Differences in the amount of ink used and pressure applied with each duplication meant that the stencilled text inside was also always different.'[23] This overturns any attempt at the standardisation that formed the sine qua non of the twentieth century's total market media commodity, defetishising it through each labour-intensive blob, glitch and pen mark. What was being decolonised through these analogue processes was habituated attention itself.

A brief media archaeology of DIY/jugaad media

Like all DIY and jugaad media assemblages, Gestetner and mimeograph technologies were developed from previous gadgets and materials for duplicating, evolving through a transnational network of material and intensive flow-and-capture assemblages. A predecessor to the photocopy machine, the mimeograph was invented by Thomas Edison in 1876; as it did not require specialised typesetting or printing equipment, the mimeograph, it is often said, allowed virtually anyone with a typewriter to become a printer.[24] As Dhital clarifies, in the case of Gestetner's paper stencils, these printing innovations were made possible by the import of Japanese paper following the Meiji Restoration of 1868, which had made Japan's economy and society available for Western imperial extraction and expropriation. 'This strong, thin and porous paper could take the impressions of a wheel pen without breaking apart. According to corporate lore, David Gestetner had learned of its properties whilst selling Japanese kites on the streets of New York, where he had fled from Austria as a teenage stockbroker after the 1873 stock market crash. Soon after arriving in London, in 1877, he launched his cyclostyle pen, and in 1885 he patented his first Japanese paper stencils.'

At a particular moment in its rise to ready-to-hand DIY media infrastructure, the Gestetner became associated with global industrial modernity itself. This was explicitly part of its marketing. Gestetner, for instance, hailed the duplicator as 'the pictorial symbol representing the really modern organisation.'[25] As Dhital remarks,

> Its lines are said to represent the modern spirit of industrial design – like a Rolls Royce or the Empire State Building. But the booklet also gives more modest examples of potential uses, such as a self-feeding model described as 'specially for the Gestetner beginner', said to be ideal for the use of schools and small organisations. And this is how the Gestetner is perhaps best remembered today – by the smell of the ink and the feel of the waxed paper used to produce school newsletters and little magazines. Rather than being the product of scientific and technical research, early duplication technology also developed as a result of its practical application by students, clerks and stationers. This is reflected in the examples given in The Book of Ideas, itself produced using a Gestetner: the price list, the invitation card, the information sheet, the direct mail campaign and the sales bulletin.[26]

The *Gestetner Quarterly* and the *Gestetner World in Action* featured examples of Gestetner duplicators being used in various 'exotic' locations: carried in a horse-drawn carriage in the Philippines, sold to monks in Thailand, and demonstrated to members of the Wayana and Trio peoples near the Brazilian border of Surinam.[27] The technology subsequently functioned as a vector of settler colonialism, cultural domination and linguistic systematisation. In one editorial, as Dhital notes, the language of the Wayana and Trio indigenous peoples is said to have 'never previously been put on record. The efforts of the West Indies Mission in Surinam meant that for the first time "the Indians could learn to read their own language." A constant flow of duplicated material ... resulted: "Bible

Tracts, Song Books, Reading Primers, Calendars, instructions in hygiene …".'[28] While the Gestetner became a kind of portable colonial writing technology that was thought to lead to scientific and systematic thinking, or the 'domestication of the savage mind', it was also simultaneous with the emergence of the Brazilian mimeograph poets movement which used this same technology to evade state censorship and devise a new poetic language.[29] As Alt Går Bra points out, the mimeograph turned out to be the ideal clandestine printing device, lightweight and compact enough to be easily moved from place to place, avoiding confiscation and censorship, also suitable for producing a reasonable amount of copies with reasonable print quality.[30] Indeed, in many parts of the world Gestetner-produced, self-published work enabled aesthetically and politically radical collectives to escape or work around the scrutiny applied to works printed at formal production facilities.[31] From Ukrainian prisoners of war during World War II making mimeograph newsletters, to its use among politically engaged artists in Mexico from 1968 until the 1980s, to mimeographed children's books by the Black Panthers in northern California, DIY media assemblages have consistently blurred the boundaries between intellectual and manual labour in the social production of print, developing printing techniques that were only available outside print shops.[32] As Hawley argues, 'Accessible and localized, this form of self-publication connoted rejection of external control over a community's message and production of self-determined cultural content … From the Black Arts Movement to feminist presses, mimeography linked marginalized groups to a recurring motif of independence and aided in the construction of community.'[33]

The question concerning gender and the division of labour involved in DIY media is also subtly highlighted in 'Crafting Subversion'. In one photograph reproduced as a large poster-sized image that meets one at the top of the back stairs at the Brunei gallery, Joan Grand, who worked in the publicity department at the Gestetner works in Tottenham between 1934 and 1964, demonstrates a Stencil Lightbox, also known as a Gestetner Scope. 'This was used to trace clip art, drawings, or lettering on a stencil, a more complex form of duplication than the flatbed process David Gestetner had popularised in Britain. Gestetner had first patented his cyclostyle, a wheel pen for writing on stencils, in 1881, one of several versions of this tool and technique invented in the last decades of the nineteenth century. The most well-known of these is probably Thomas Edison's mimeograph (1880), and many works produced using Gestetners are described as mimeographed.'[34] What of Joan's labour? The image is telling: as she works away at the tracing, her face illuminated by the lightbox, a group of white men stand around her in judgment of her work, as if coaxing her on to better hand discipline, withholding and withdrawing approval and attention while appropriating the products of her labour. This gendering of the actual work of the mimeograph, or the Gestetner, is noted only in passing by Steven Wright in his otherwise brilliant history of militant publishing projects in Italian far-left workerist movements:

> Potere Operaio was not immune from the phenomenon of the 'Gestetner angels' [*angeli del ciclostile*], an expression coined during this period to designate the comrades (typically women) 'doing behind-the-scenes support work for those (mostly men) who had a public presence as leaders, speakers, and writers'. The words of Stefania Sarsini suggest that the gender relations within Potere Operaio were then par for the course within the Italian far left as a whole: 'Lucia, despite her militancy, always remained Scalzone's woman, as I was Verità's woman, and Grazia Zermann was Daghini's woman: we were all "the woman of". Our identity as persons didn't exist and this made militancy all the harder. No documents were elaborated by women. And the "gratification" of cyclostyling leaflets until late at night, or of cleaning a branch office soiled by the [remnants of] sandwiches and cigarette stubs smoked by dear [male] comrades intent on staying awake so that they could elaborate revolutionary theories, was certainly rather minimal for a revolutionary militant'.[35]

In India, this gendering would be articulated specifically with caste and class in the little magazine movements. I return to this below.

Fuck you to damn you to Unfuck you

Another historically significant example of DIY print featured in the exhibition is *Fuck You/A Journal of the Arts*, edited, published and printed from 1962–65 by Ed Sanders, from what he described as 'a secret location' in New York's Lower East Side. Gwen Allen, in 'The Poetics and Politics of the Mimeograph', helps us to contextualise these DIY and jugaad media assemblages in 1960s

America. These assemblages created 8.5-by-11 inch mimeographed, stapled publications, a low-fidelity format that was nearly identical to that of dozens, if not hundreds, of similar poetry magazines that sprung up in New York and elsewhere at the time. 'The dizzying proliferation of small-circulation presses and mimeographed magazines – including *C: A Literary Review*, *Poems from the Floating World*, *Umbra*, and *Fuck You: A Magazine of the Arts*, to name just a few – were central to both the aesthetic innovations and the social world of second-generation New York School poetry.'[36] These magazines were deeply embedded in unofficial networks of friends, interlocutors and acquaintances constituting both their contributors and readers, thus placing their ecology of practice within a social context of chance meetings, conversations and other publications.[37] As Allen argues persuasively, through the rapid, low-cost dissemination of poetry, these publications also shaped the social milieu in which this poetry was written and read; indeed, the relative speed and spontaneity of the mimeograph encouraged experiments in styles of spontaneity, collaboration, appropriation and cut-up methods of composition.[38] Daniel Kane notes how rapidly and inexpensively produced mimeographed publications brought the experience of the printed page – DIY media's immanent ecology of sensation – 'closer to the impromptu nature of the live poetry reading itself, capturing something of the informal, social atmosphere of these gatherings ... Rexograph sheets were passed out at readings, to be drawn or written on, or taken home and typed on, and then submitted, and the resulting magazine would be brought back and distributed the following week.'[39]

Allen and other media archaeologists help us to appreciate what I have been calling the jugaad aspects of DIY media assemblages. Anderson notes how mimeograph magazine production was frequently completed at night and on the sly with available office and church mimeographs, linking its ecology of practice to protest press and underground newspaper production.[40] Vito Acconci and Bernadette Mayer printed a poetry magazine called *0 to 9*, which, in the words of Caroline Reagan, was 'jarring in its resistance to readability. Pictures, with a few exceptions, are notably absent. Text assumes eccentric forms, resembling encoded maps. Oftentimes, words coalesce into intimidating, rambling chunks.'[41] In a fine example of a jugaad, Acconci and Mayer would 'drive to a friend's father's office in New Jersey, arriving after closing at 5 pm, and work until dawn, typing the stencils and running off and collating the magazine, sometimes with the help of friends or relatives.'[42] As Allen notes, the rough analogue quality of the mimeograph process, its resonant ecology of sensation, lent the publication a 'distinct materiality, rife with smudges and blobs, incompletely formed letters, uneven ink distribution, and other flaws due to imprecision in the stencil-cutting and printing process.'[43] These de-habituating sensations of reading experimental printed matter stirred up associations with political broadsides and other radical publishing practices, and the 'unrefined appearance' gave language a kind of 'weight and corporeality' in keeping with the poetic investigations published in the magazine.[44] 'Nothing was perfect about the *0 to 9* in its mimeograph form', Mayer observed. 'We were trying to get far away from the idea, so promulgated, of the perfection of the poem with white space around it, set off from other things.'[45] Bringing poetic sense to its unrefined infrastructure of sensation, *0 to 9* creates events of poetic language not as pristine or idealised, but as messy, unruly, untimely vectors that disregard 'conventional spacing and margins, to say nothing of proper grammar and syntax. Words do not remain well-behaved and silent couriers of meaning, but seem to make noise, to act things out.'[46] The magazine's messy materiality references its printing process. More, *0 to 9* also made the subscribers of the magazine into potential contributors, 'since the stencil could, in theory, be removed, typed on, and sent back to the editors for publication in the next issue.' While this possibility remained largely symbolic, it expressed a certain reciprocity between the production of the magazine and its reception and the participatory community *0 to 9* strove to create among its readers.[47]

Sanders stencilled the *Fuck You* journal in the offices of the *Catholic Worker*, where many contributors also worked. Sanders printed around 500 copies of each issue on flecked, coloured Granitex paper 'borrowed' from the *Catholic Worker* and gave them away for free. He also mailed out copies to Pablo Picasso, Samuel Beckett, Jean Paul Sartre and Fidel Castro.[48] The second issue (April 1962) was dedicated in all caps to:

PACIFISM, UNILATERAL DISARMAMENT, NATIONAL DEFENSE THRU NONVIOLENT RESISTANCE, MULTILATERAL INDISCRIMINATE APERTURAL CONJUGATION,

ANARCHISM, WORLD FEDERALISM CIVIL DISOBEDI-
ENCE, PROJECT MERCURY, PEACE EYE, THE MARGARET
SANGER INSTITUTE, OBSTRUCTERS & SUBMARINE
BOARDERS, AND ALL THOSE GROPED BY J. EDGAR
HOOVER IN THE SILENT HALLS OF CONGRESS.

Fuck You became one of the most famous magazines of the North American 'Mimeograph Revolution', infused with the spirit of iskra, the spark talked about by early Russian revolutionaries, which for Sanders could burst 'out of a poetry café on Second Avenue' to 'inspire a network of minds and sweep America to Great Change'.[49]

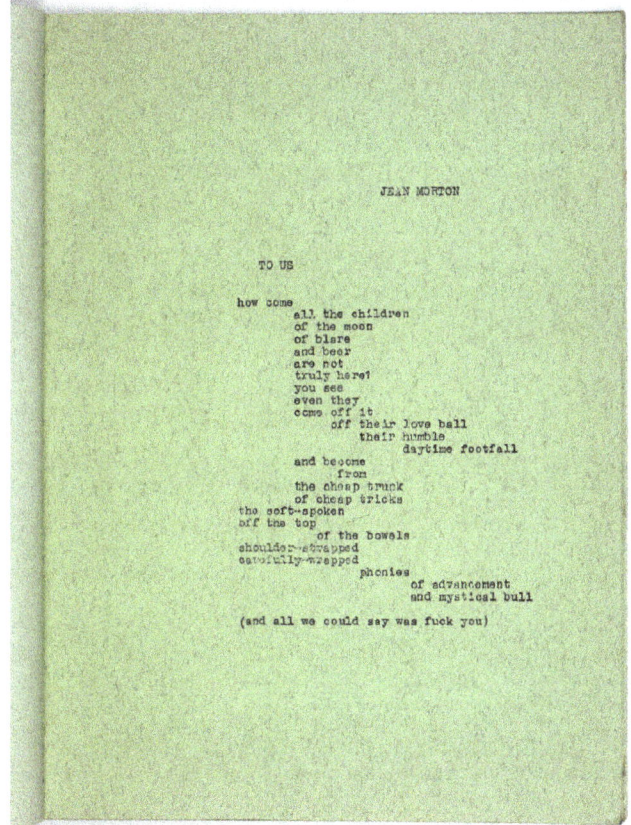

Sanders's *Fuck You* also resonated with DIY/jugaad media cultures across the world, such as that of the Indian poet Arvind Krishna Mehrotra in Allahabad, north India. As Dhital observes, news of *Fuck You* reached Mehrotra in the early 1960s through a write up in the *Village Voice* sent by an uncle of two of his friends studying in New York. With these two friends, the brothers Alok and Amit Rai (no relation to the author), Mehrotra was inspired to set up his own journal, *damn you/ a magazine of the arts*. Their first issue was published in September 1965 using a dusty Gestetner in the office of the Rais' father, a publisher. 'One hundred copies were printed to be sold at a price "commensurate with your dignity and ours." Subsequent editorials discussed the difficulties the editors faced producing and distributing their work, and celebrated achievements such as the inclusion of illustrations in the second edition of damn you, following the discovery of stencilling pencils in a local stationery shop.'[50] Sanders and his collective had incorporated Egyptian hieroglyphics into the design of *Fuck You*. In a resonant line of flight, Mehrotra drew upon an 'eclectic range of sources, spanning regions and epochs.'[51] In an editorial statement in the sixth and final issue of *damn you* published in 1968, Mehrotra situated his media assemblage in the ancient town of Allahabad, 'far from the "skyscraping" places of the world. Specifically, from 18 Hastings Road, home of the Rai family and office of the damn you press.'[52] Sonal Khullar has argued that instead of the rupture of pictorial space pursued by artists in Brazil and Japan, the Bombay poets and painters of this time sought its 'enrichment and intensification through careful attention to process, material, bodily presence, and detailed description, and they chose aesthetic contemplation as the means to a social and political critique.'[53] They developed media assemblages of 'lifting – documenting and defamiliarizing – their environment by citing and subverting street signs, advertisements, state propaganda, calendar art, film posters, and newspaper photographs, and took to loafing – a mode of critical observation and analysis and the pursuit of committed deprofessionalization and translation across spaces – by mobilizing the ordinary, yet extraordinary, spaces of the paan shop and the Irani restaurant in order to reinvent artistic sociability and subjectivity.'[54] We can certainly question the gendered, sexual and caste dimensions of these 'ordinary' spaces, their accessibility to only a narrow segment of upper-caste, homosocial male Indian society.[55] Clearly, the figure of the loafer, as a social type distinct from the flaneur of nineteenth- and twentieth-century Paris (the hero of Baudelaire and Benjamin), served as a model and norm for (classed) creativity and (caste-based) citizenship in the work of the Bombay painters and poets. In this work, even as it rein-scribed normative gender, heterosexual, class and caste power, the city became a 'resource to rethink the relationship of art and politics, experience and imagination, power and marginality in modern India, and to link visual and literary worlds through a translation between spaces, media, languages, and forms.'[56]

In my interview with him, Mehrotra stressed the transnational, trans-temporal dimensions of what the three, and later himself with the Bombay-based magazine *ezra*, were doing. This was immediately tied to the material quality of DIY/jugaad publishing. Looking over a page from *damn you* (6) reproduced on the writing archaeology website 'Artefacts of Writing', one gets a feeling for what Mehrotra and the Rais had to learn to publish *damn you*:[57]

> Each issue was improvised depending on what was available … or depending on what one felt like or one's finances. You know sometimes it was determined by … We might have found a stack of green paper somewhere in some stationery shop, in Bombay I'd pick up paper from the raddiwala (waste paper seller), sometimes they would have a whole stack of green paper or blue paper lying around, and you know you just picked up fifty sheets very cheaply for a few annas, and that was why the cover of *ezra* 1 was pink, they must have been cut offs from something else … they were sold by weight … I would just walk into those lanes behind what used to be Wayside Inn, Rhythm House [the Kala Ghoda area of Fort, Mumbai], and buy a rupee worth of foolscap paper and that would give me fifty sheets, which didn't weigh very much, and you could make two covers from one sheet … And I would buy stencils … from one of the shops and then take them to where I was staying, to Mulund, in Deep Mandap, far from central Bombay … I would work on an ancient Royal Typewriter bought by my mother's father in the late 1940s in Simla, I always had it and carried it around so that's how I started writing using the typewriter … I would type up these poems, and then take them back to the cyclostyling shop, ask them to run the stencils. [When we worked on *damn you*] Amit Rai had his typewriter, and I had my own typewriter in my room in Hastings Road. So we would divide what we had to type, I would bring home a stencil, and take it back and print it out on the machine in the Rais' home. The cost was only the cost of paper and the purchase of stencils, you could get ten stencils for a rupee. So it didn't cost very much. If you were to go to a professional typist then they charge you per page. They were cutting stencils all the time, either typing or cutting stencils. If I had gone to a professional I'm sure the images would have come out more clearly, but since I was doing it at home … and because the round of the letters would clog with the ribbon, so they had to be cleaned. So you were always there with a safety pin, you went on removing [the ink] … [laughing] I remember doing that … when you type the letter 'g' the top half of the 'g' would just be a black blob … this is crazy. People don't believe this, you went with a pin removing the flint from the d, c, g … A lot of time went into cleaning the keys. Which partly accounted for the less than perfect … Whatever was completely illegible those pages we had to throw away. When we were doing it ourselves we didn't know how to ink the thing so the page would just come out black, completely black. Or we got bits of ink somewhere or the other … We tried to be as neat and as clean as we could. But they were slightly illegible … You mean even *Fuck You* had that problem? Oh, I'm pleased [laughing] … I thought they'd be doing it better in New York than we were in Allahabad![58]

Vrishchik (Year 1, No. 11–12), reproduced with permission of Gulammohammed Sheikh and

One can conjecture about the caste and class background of these cyclostyle shopwalas – were they India's version of Italy's Gestetner Angels? The breakdown of the division of intellectual and manual labour, and by extension the assumption of a certain able-bodiedness, also returns here to question the usefulness of a phrase that appears often in DIY media discourse: anyone could operate one. For Mehrotra and his friends, connecting up with and then featuring an unknown poet from Fort Lauderdale, or with the not-so-distant Ezra Pound, was a thrill and a spark of inspiration for a kind of undercommons movement of avant-garde aesthetics and DIY/jugaad media assemblages.[59]

The DIY movement continues

We can say without hyperbole that what was at stake in several of the DIY/jugaad media assemblages gathered together by Dhital in 'Crafting Subversion' was the potentiality of a people-to-come to express a revolutionary becoming in and for itself. For example, in a moment of 'Great Change' in India, from, say, 1967 to 1977 (from the onset of the Maoist Naxalite insurgency to the 'end' of the Emergency) – which was certainly marked by betrayals and great failures of solidarity – when this potentiality hinged on the collective construction of a revolutionary conjuncture precariously relating rural militants, the industrial working classes, Dalits, a refashioned Hindu right, and minorities of all stripes, Indira Gandhi's authoritarian state literally turned out the lights. About a decade after Mehrotra was publishing *damn you*, as Dhital reminds us, Indian political activists, such as the Lok Nayak (People's Leader) Jayaprakash Narayan and, earlier, socialist leader Rammanohar Lohia were deeply involved in anti-Congress agitation and a perhaps too facile practice of lokniti (people's politics).[60] Narayan's movement for 'Total Revolution', which some on the far left in India today consider symptomatic bourgeois upper-caste eyewash, covering over the dangerous compromises with the Hindu right at the time in forging an anti-Congress movement, generated their own DIY media assemblages, which some continue to believe sought to produce resistant knowledge and a transformed sense of social practice.[61] A fascinating part of the exhibition in this respect is from the collection of Ram Dutt Tripathi (born 1950), a former-BBC journalist imprisoned for his role in the resistance to the Indian Emergency of 1975-77 (and digitised by the University of Göttingen).

As Dhital's wall-text reminds us, one of Prime Minister Indira Gandhi's first acts on seizing state power on 25 June 1975 was to completely shut off electricity for the newspaper district in New Delhi and take control of the national radio station, 'leaving Indians to look for alternative sources of news'.[62] One of Tripathi's first acts of resistance after the Emergency was imposed was to buy a flatbed cyclostyle duplicator and produce newssheets containing information about what was happening in Delhi and the locality. He and his friends in the Yuva Sangharsh Samiti (Youth Struggle Association) would then sell these for a small profit to support themselves whilst underground. In the exhibition, Dhital carefully juxtaposes Tripathi's archive and a selection of nationalist literature from the British Library's collection of publications proscribed in colonial India. As she notes, the Narayan-led anti-Congress movement for 'Total Revolution' styled itself as the second independence struggle, and Indira Gandhi's autocratic actions seemed to prove that a change of leadership was insufficient to bring about decolonisation.

> A more thoroughgoing transformation of society and decentralisation of power was required. Much of the visual and verbal rhetoric of this movement also drew upon earlier periods of protest. The image of Mahatma Gandhi, prominent in Congress literature produced during the colonial period, recurs in anti-Congress publications distributed during the Emergency. During the Independence struggle various groups had also issued 'calls' for Indians to refuse to cooperate with the government.

The exhibition displays two such pleas. In one (in English) the Hindustan Seva Dal (Indian Service Party, Meerut), a grassroots wing of the Congress Party, urges Hindu and Muslim government workers to remember the anti-British uprising of 1857 and unite in opposing the Government machinery. In another (in Hindi), Indumati Goyanka of the Rashtriya Mahila Samiti (National Women's Association) calls on Indian 'brothers' working in the police force to quit, or at least vow not to inflict violence on their 'mothers and sisters'. Dhital highlights that a similar plea for the 'police and army to revolt by hero of the Independence struggle and leader of the movement for Total Revolution, J.P. Narayan, was the immediate context for proclamation of Emergency in 1975.'[63]

The movement continues. Recently, an artist collective calling itself the Bombay Underground started publishing a zine with the title *a5*, its first issue cover reading UNFUCKYOU, in seemingly explicit dialogue with both Sanders and Mehrotra. I was able to buy a copy for a few rupees at the extraordinary People's Freedom 75 event on 7 August 2022, 'somewhere in Mumbai'. The brilliant gathering/event/exhibition showcased art self-curated by a collective of artists who had come together in resistance to and refusal of Hindu totalitarianism.[64] While not much can be said about the event (to protect those whose data-identity is being tracked, quantified, and cross-referenced quite meticulously by the Hindutva surveillance state),[65] the zine and its DIY publication process bears witness to an iskra that has not dimmed in its revolutionary becoming.

Untimely subversions of obsolete media

Today, it is difficult to imagine a smart phone company advertising its neuro-fetish cum portable data mine with the tagline: 'It will keep your secrets. Operate it yourself.' But this was precisely what made the mimeograph and the Gestetner valuable, indeed forceful in DIY media assemblages across the globe. The mimeograph revolution reverberates today in jugaad and DIY assemblages in radical undercommons, in revolutionary energies and becomings that break down the binary between intellectual and manual labour – the mimeograph, and by extension the DIY revolution, is a continuation of class war by other means, intimately tied to class/caste/gender/racial struggles for emancipation.[66] As Hawley puts it more modestly,

> Mimeography captured the imagination of potential self-publishers. Advertised as simple in design and operation, the equipment proved accessible to nonprofessional printers. Writers, activists, and other amateurs learned printing skills or gained access to friendly machine owners through the widespread presence of these machines in offices around the country. The skills to run a machine were readily gained through programs run by the A. B. Dick Company or training on the job. These low-cost, reliable machines for duplicating one's own original material have been associated closely in fact and public perception with publishing undertaken outside commercial printing channels, as well as through mainstream printers and business offices.[67]

Today, this assumed accessibility must be put under erasure through subaltern histories and subjugated knowledges of norms of able-bodiedness in DIY media cultures globally.

This able-bodied norm in the relationship of humans to technology is legible all the way back to at least Hegel. For instance, in Alt Går Bra's tribute to the subaltern mimeograph cultures that proliferated throughout the world in the twentieth century, the art collective confesses to a Hegelian inspiration, citing the philosopher reflecting on the tool: 'In the tool the subject makes a middle term between himself and the object, and this middle term is the real rationality of labour ... On account of this rationality of the tool it stands as the middle term, higher than labour, higher than the object (fashioned for enjoyment, which is what is in question here), and higher than enjoyment or the end aimed at. This is why all peoples living on the natural level have honoured the tool.'[68] Hegel articulates a classical Eurocentric teleology of the relation of human practice to technology, and in the romanticism of the peoples without history 'living on the natural level', in the insistence on the role of technical mediation between the unhappy subject-supposed-to-know and 'his' bad object choices, in the supposed discovery/recovery of the real rationality of labour in the 'honoured' tool – an entire, if ambivalent program of instrumental reason lies in wait. 'In this humanism', writes Wendling, 'objectification is the foundational moment of human subjectivity, and human beings are set over against nature rather than viewed in continuity with it.'[69] This is the still unfolding history of what Stefano Harney and Fred Moten call the white science of logistics in racial capitalism: technology as congealed dead labour, fixed capital, a crucial part of the technical, organic and value compositions of capital for Marx, and yielding for Heidegger the ready-to-hand standing reserve, the essence of which is nothing technological.

This intersects with projects that would decolonise racial formations in and through DIY media. In Adorno's (anti-)Hegelian yet thoroughly Eurocentric aphorisms in *Minima Moralia*, he writes that

> Progress and barbarism are today so matted together in mass culture that only barbaric asceticism towards the latter, and towards progress in technical means, could restore an unbarbaric condition. No work of art, no thought, has a chance of survival, unless it bear within it repudiation of false riches and high-class production, of colour films and television, millionaire's magazines and Toscanini. The older media, not designed for mass-production, take on a new timeliness: that of exemption and improvisation. They alone could outflank the united front of trusts and technology. In a world where books have long lost all likeness to books, the real book can no longer be one. If the invention of the printing press inaugurated the bourgeois era, the time is at hand for its repeal by the mimeograph, the only fitting ... unobtrusive means of dissemination.[70]

As in most of Adorno's writings, there is something

profoundly repugnant and no less compelling here (a few pages later, he will go on to argue why 'Savages are not more noble').[71] Ambivalently refusing both (racialised) barbarism (which one?) and progress (Euro-capitalism's own), he celebrates the soon-to-be obsolete, humble mimeograph. In Joel Burges's gloss on this jarring passage, he notes that mimeographs were hardly obsolete in the late 1940s, enjoying extensive currency in businesses and schools as a copying technology, yet it must have seemed outdated almost since its inception in the late nineteenth century, 'as if it were a stopgap solution on the road to a better copying technology for the masses.' Adorno attempts to turn the mimeograph untimely in a utopian fashion, to become strategically nonsynchronous with the techno-economic interests of (racial) capitalist modernity, refusing its total market culture, and offering up a 'critical temporality of outmoded media … a figuration of the outmoded is a temporal constellation in which past and present are agonistically juxtaposed by crisscrossing … "transient elements within an accelerating sequence of displacements and obsolescences".'[72] The agons proliferate as Dhital's 'Crafting Subversion' documents so well. Untimely questions of gender, ability, race and caste will have returned to push DIY media assemblages toward other ecologies of attention in revolutionary becomings yet to come.

Amit Rai is Reader in Creative Industries and Arts Organisation at Queen Mary University of London, and the author of Jugaad Time: Ecologies of Everyday Hacking in India *(2019).*

Notes

1. Martin Heidegger, *The Question Concerning Technology, and Other Essays* (New York: Harper Collins, 2013).
2. Pragya Dhital, 'Crafting Subversion' Exhibition Wall Text, 1.
3. Stephanie Anderson, '"Crowded Air": Previous Modernisms in some 1964 New York Little Magazines', in *The Mimeograph: A Tool for Radical Art and Political Contestation*, ed. Alt Går Bra (Bergen: Alt Går Bra, 2016), 111.
4. Alt Går Bra ed., *Mimeograph*, 9.
5. Anderson, '"Crowded Air"', 111.
6. Lincoln Cushing, 'Cranking it out, Old-School Style: Art of the Gestetner', in *Mimeograph*, ed. Alt Går Bra, 120. Cf. Henri Lefebvre, *Rhythmanalysis: Space, Time and Everyday Life* (London: Continuum, 2004), 14; Ari Jerrems, '"An Opening Toward the Possible": Assembly Politics and Henri Lefebvre's Theory of the Event', *Global Society* 34:2 (2020), 233.
7. Elizabeth Haven Hawley, 'Revaluing Mimeographs and Other Obsolete Things: An Introduction to Media Archaeology', in *Mimeograph*, ed. Alt Går Bra, 23, 63.
8. Alt Går Bra ed., *Mimeograph*, 11. For instance, the pioneering LGBT publication *The Ladder*, whose audience was mostly lesbian identified, was published using mimeography. Cf. Hawley, 'Revaluing Mimeographs', 23.
9. For a spatial interpretation of technological obsolesce in Hindi cinema see Ranjani Mazumdar, 'Technological Obsolescence and Space in Bombay Cinema', in *A Companion to Indian Cinema*, eds. Neepa Majumdar and Ranjani Mazumdar (Chichester: Wiley, 2022), 540–568.
10. Joel Burges, 'Adorno's Mimeograph: The Uses of Obsolescence in *Minima Moralia*', in *Mimeograph*, ed. Alt Går Bra, 33–39.
11. Amy Wendling, *Karl Marx on Technology and Alienation* (Basingstoke: Palgrave Macmillan, 2009), 196. See Wendling's gloss on Postone's notion of capitalism's treadmill effect: 'Because the means of production are constantly being transformed and machinery improved, articles are produced with constantly increasing rapidity. This leads to a dialectic between the labour accomplished in, say, one hour and the socially necessary labour time that determines this same hour. The effect of this dialectic is to constantly increase the intensive magnitudes of the abstract units. This year's hour is socially determined to be more labour-intensive than last year's, and this year's hour becomes the new baseline for determining what an hour means. Postone calls this "the treadmill effect". In capitalism, this effect constantly ratchets up the intensity of labour that is socially expected to be performed in a given unit of abstract time. One must run for twenty minutes, just as before, but at a faster pace, because "twenty minutes" has come to be more intensively determined by social necessity.'
12. Sianne Ngai, *Ugly Feelings* (Cambridge, MA: Harvard University Press, 2005), 336–337; quoted in Burges, 'Adorno's Mimeograph', 36.
13. Burges, 'Adorno's Mimeograph', 36.
14. Wendling, *Karl Marx*, 172.
15. Laetitia Zecchini, '"We were like cartographers, mapping the city": An interview with Arvind Krishna Mehrotra', *Journal of Postcolonial Writing* 53:1–2 (2017), 199. Cf. Sonal Khullar, '"We Were Looking for Our Violins": The Bombay Painters and Poets, ca. 1965–76', *Archives of Asian Art* 68:2 (2018), 113–15.
16. Theodor Adorno, *Minima Moralia*; quoted in Alt Går Bra ed., *Mimeograph*, 34.
17. See Stephen Wright, *The Weight of the Printed Word: Text, Context and Militancy in Operaismo* (Leiden: Brill, 2021), 109.
18. Patricia Ticineto Clough, Karen Gregory, Benjamin Haber and R. Joshua Scannell, 'The Datalogical Turn', in *Non-Representational Methodologies: Re-envisioning Research*, ed. Phillip Vannini (London: Routledge, 2015), 156–174; Stefano Harney and Fred Moten, *All Incomplete* (London: Minor Compositions, 2021).
19. Amit S. Rai, 'DIY Media in South Asia', *BioScope: South Asian Screen Studies* 12:1–2 (2021), 64–67; cf. Amit S. Rai, *Jugaad Time: Ecologies of Everyday Hacking in India* (Durham, NC: Duke University Press, 2019).
20. Excerpt from Alessandro Ludovico, *Post-Digital Print: The Mutation of Publishing since 1894*, in Alt Går Bra ed., *Mimeograph*, 18.

21. Elizabeth Haven Hawley, 'Revaluing Mimeographs as Historical Sources', in *Mimeograph*, ed. Alt Går Bra, 24.
22. Ueno Hisami, 'Toshaban: On the Development of the Mimeograph between Printing and Art in Modern Japan', in *Mimeograph*, ed. Alt Går Bra, 71
23. Dhital, 'Crafting Subversion', 2.
24. Excerpt from Gwen Allen, *Artists' Magazines: An Alternative Space for Art* (Cambridge, MA: MIT Press, 2011), in Alt Går Bra ed., *Mimeograph*, 104.
25. Dhital, 'Crafting Subversion', 4.
26. Dhital, 'Crafting Subversion', 4.
27. Dhital, 'Crafting Subversion', 5.
28. Dhital, 'Crafting Subversion', 5.
29. Dhital, 'Crafting Subversion', 5.
30. Alt Går Bra ed., *Mimeograph*, 18.
31. Hawley, 'Revaluing Mimeographs', 23.
32. Nicolas Pradilla, 'A Ubiquitous and Feared Tool: Collective Editorial Practice by a Generation of the Crisis', in *Mimeograph*, ed. Alt Går Bra, 12.
33. Hawley, 'Revaluing Mimeographs', 23.
34. Dhital, 'Crafting Subversion', 2.
35. Wright, *The Weight*, 33.
36. Allen, *Artists' Magazines* excerpt, 104–105.
37. Allen, *Artists' Magazines* excerpt, 106.
38. Allen, *Artists' Magazines* excerpt, 106; Anderson, '"Crowded Air"', 111.
39. Daniel Kane quoted in Gwen Allen, 'The Poetics and Politics of the Mimeograph', in *Mimeograph*, ed. Alt Går Bra, 105.
40. Anderson, '"Crowded Air"', 111.
41. Caroline Reagan, 'The lost '60s magazine that gave artists Sol Lewitt and Adrian Piper true conceptual freedom', accessed 3 September 2022, https://www.documentjournal.com/2020/03/look-inside-0-9-the-radically-experimental-magazine-that-broke-all-the-rules-of-language/.
42. Allen, *Artists' Magazines* excerpt, 105.
43. Allen, *Artists' Magazines* excerpt, 105.
44. Allen, *Artists' Magazines* excerpt, 105.
45. Bernadette Mayer quoted in Allen, *Artists' Magazines* excerpt, 105.
46. Allen, *Artists' Magazines* excerpt, 105
47. Allen, *Artists' Magazines* excerpt, 105
48. Dhital, 'Crafting Subversion', 5–6.
49. Dhital, 'Crafting Subversion', 6.
50. Dhital, 'Crafting Subversion', 6. Cf. Arvind Krishna Mehrotra, *Partial Recall: Essays on Literature and Literary History* (New Delhi: Permanent Black, 2012), 59–62.
51. Dhital, 'Crafting Subversion', 7.
52. Dhital, 'Crafting Subversion', 7.
53. Khullar, '"We Were Looking for Our Violins"', 112.
54. Khullar, '"We Were Looking for Our Violins"', 113.
55. Cf. Shilpa Phadke, Sameera Khan and Shilpa Ranade, *Why Loiter?: Women and Risk on Mumbai Streets* (New Delhi: Penguin Books, 2011).
56. Khullar, '"We Were Looking for Our Violins"', 113.
57. See Artefacts of Writing, 'Webnotes', accessed 5 September 2022, https://artefactsofwriting.com/webnotes/.
58. Interview with Arvind Krishna Mehrotra, 5 September 2022. Cf. Mehrotra, *Partial Recall*, 65.
59. Interview with Arvind Krishna Mehrotra, 5 September 2022.
60. After the early 1950s, Narayan opposed lokniti (people's politics) to rajniti (party politics). Cf. Daniel Kent-Carrasco, 'A Battle Over Meanings: Jayaprakash Narayan, Rammanohar Lohia and the Trajectories of Socialism in Early Independent India', *Janata Weekly*, 20 October 2019, https://janataweekly.org/a-battle-over-meanings-jayaprakash-narayan-rammanohar-lohia-and-the-trajectories-of-socialism-in-early-independent-india/.
61. Anderson '"Crowded Air"', 112.
62. Dhital, 'Crafting Subversion', 9.
63. Dhital, 'Crafting Subversion', 10.
64. I use this word advisedly: in conversations with Indians from different backgrounds in three different cities recently 'totalitarian' (in English) was the word they used to describe Narendra Modi's authoritarian state. Many if not most of the poems published in the little magazines of the era would not be circulated today for fear of censorship and legal prosecution, harassment and, increasingly, arrest.
65. A postcolonial genealogy of this uniquely South Asian relation to surveillance and identification technology is staged in the Raqs Media Collective's installation 'Untold Intimacy of Digits' (2011) at the 'Crafting Subversion' exhibition. In it they animate an artefact from the Francis Galton Collection (University College London), a handprint taken in 1858 in lieu of a signature, to affix the identity of a Bengal peasant, Raj Konai, to a document. In their animated facsimile, Konai's blue handprint is made to gesture at how counting numbers is taught to children throughout much of India. Their concept brings together the invention of fingerprinting in Bengal (which only later went to England) with a critique of Modi's Aadhaar identification program, itself based on fingerprinting. The authoritarian aspiration to quantify biometric identity has remained constant from Konai's handprint to Aadhaar's biometrics. Interview with Shuddha Sengupta of the Raqs Media Collective, 29 August 2022.
66. Wendling, *Karl Marx*, 68; cf. the discussion of Walter Benjamin's encounters with avant-garde aesthetics and technological reproducibility in the 1920s and 1930s and his notion of 'the revolutionary energies that appear in the "outmoded"' in Burges, 'Adorno's Mimeograph', 33.
67. Hawley, 'Revaluing Mimeographs', 23
68. G. W. F. Hegel, *System of Ethical Life and First Philosophy of Spirit* [1802–04], quoted in Alt Går Bra ed., *Mimeograph*, 9.
69. Wendling, *Karl Marx*, 65.
70. Theodor Adorno, *Minima Moralia: Reflections from Damaged Life*, trans. E. F. N. Jephcott (New York: Verso, 1978), 50–51; Cf. Burges, 'Adorno's Mimeograph', 34. Adorno's method was 'schooled' by Hegel's dialecticism, but he remains quite critical of the master.
71. Adorno, *Minima Moralia*, 52–53.
72. Jonathan Crary, *Suspensions of Perception: Attention, Spectacle, and Modern Culture*, quoted in Burges, 'Adorno's Mimeograph', 34–35.

Reviews

Knowing looks

Tom Holert, *Knowledge Beside Itself: Contemporary Art's Epistemic Politics* (Berlin: Sternberg Press, 2020). 278 pp., €22.00 pb., 978 3 94336 597 9

Tom Holert remarks near the beginning of *Knowledge Beside Itself* that art has traditionally been defined in contradistinction to knowledge, at least scientific or systematic knowledge. How then to understand the proliferation of discourses of 'knowledge' and 'research' in contemporary art?

This is visible, Holert indicates, in 'curatorial statements, advertisements for art institutions, art criticism, and writing by artists', where artistic practices are described with increasing frequency as research practices; and in the way that contemporary art spaces provide platforms for 'various kinds of study, investigation and experimentation'. Museums and galleries act more and more 'as providers of critical discourse and sites of knowledge production. With their educational and discursive programming, as well as a curatorial approach interwoven with academic theorizing, museums of contemporary art [...] deliberately transform themselves into institutions of knowledge production and management'. As Holert points out, this tendency is connected to the rapid expansion since the 1990s of 'fine art PhD programs, "artistic research" as the new normal of higher education in the arts, and the presumptuous trope of art as "knowledge production".' The growing use of such terminology is in part an effect of the 'university-isation' of the art school and increasing incorporation of contemporary art into the academic protocols of research and teaching in the neoliberal university, at least in much of Europe.

The book also frames these issues in relation to transformations in art and economy since the 1960s – specifically, postconceptual art's tendency towards a 'drastic boundlessness', conditioning its expansion into spheres where knowledge is at stake either directly (its increasing transactions with 'theory' or pedagogy) or indirectly (archival or activist turns); and a post-Fordist shift towards the 'knowledge economy' and creative industries, which Holert talks about in terms of 'immaterial labour' and 'cognitive capitalism' taken from post-autonomist Marxist theory. The parallels and transactions between these two tendencies have been explored at length elsewhere by other art historians and theorists, such as Dave Beech, Helen Molesworth and Marina Vishmidt. For Holert, the rising importance of 'information' within capitalism means that knowledge becomes a site of political struggle, for instance in relation to intellectual property and the 'knowledge commons'. In this context, what Holert calls the 'epistemisation' of art takes on critical stakes, enabling contemporary art to engage in 'knowledge politics'. It is the task of getting to grips with this complicated cluster of developments that the book sets itself. In the process it mentions an extremely wide range of ideas and practices, from decolonial epistemology to the ethics policy of the British Academy.

The titular idea of 'knowledge beside itself' suggests a productive non-identity between art-as-knowledge and knowledge-as-knowledge. On this model, art scrambles, dislocates, reconfigures, interferes with and opposes the forms and contents of knowledges; it 'purposefully fails, neglects, queers and ultimately overwrites [their] protocols'. As Marina Vishmidt puts it, in a phrase Holert quotes, art 'defers, inverts, implodes knowledge'. This is an essentially negative relation to knowledge that is actually one of two perspectives on the art-knowledge relation threading through the book. The other, a positive one, is also implicit in the idea of 'beside itself', and concerns art's ability to generate or act as a platform for alternative ('subjugated' or 'minor') knowledges. Both models have valid potentials: critique or deconstruction in the first instance, subcultural or para-academic counter-production in the second. Both have possible drawbacks. The first might lead to a nihilistic or cynical game in the debris of research, or acting as a playful but harmless poetic companion to 'real' knowledge (as sometimes seems the case in collaborations between artists and academics), or even – more problematically – functioning as a sort of blue sky thinking for knowledge production, a 'disrupter' (to use the business jargon). The second might lead to a logic where art is only justified when it produces some determinate knowledge, and in the context of academia, feeds smoothly into the notion of the artwork as 'research output'. (Elsewhere, Vishmidt writes that 'research-as-art works best when it's breaking down', and the implication here for art to apply the negative function above to any positive knowledge it produces seems like an important rule of thumb.)

Despite acting as a primer covering important ground, the book is constrained by the fact that although it recognises the existence of an antinomy – the tension between 'art-as-research' as a potentially radical critique and expansion of art, and 'art-as-research' as the subsumption of art under neoliberal forms of measurement and control – it only seems able to repeatedly point it out, rather than providing an analysis that yields further understanding of its determinants and effects, or gives a sense of how the two apparently contradictory tendencies might interact. This antinomy, which appears several times throughout the book in slightly varying guises, is clearest in chapters one and three. In the first of these, 'Artistic Research: Anatomy of an Ascent', Holert begins from neo-avant-garde claims – forwarded by US artists such as Allan Kaprow, associated with Fluxus, and pre-Situationist International groups in Europe such as SPUR and the International Movement for an Imaginist Bauhaus – for art as a type of unruly, deviant research. Such a polemical identification of art with research, continued in conceptual art, was an anti-aesthetic, anti-autonomy gesture. While such ideas may be in the background of current discussions, Holert argues that there is no direct line between them, given that 'the signifier "research" ... has, in the hands of many educators and administrators, become a key discursive instrument in the administration and management of artistic production in the realm of higher education and beyond'. In this chapter, as well, Holert makes an important point about the colonial history of 'research', the way that anthropology and sociology have provided conceptual underpinnings for colonial biopolitics; a history that, as Linda Tuhiwai Smith says (quoted by Holert), makes research 'one of the dirtiest words in the indigenous world's vocabulary'.

Holert persuasively states that at their best research-centred artistic and curatorial projects 'produce a specific knowledge that exhibits rather than conceals the tortured materiality of the objects on display and the practices of the institutions involved ... Following Roland Barthes, it can be said that these projects successfully unsettle the fiction "that research is reported but not written".' However, as Holert acknowledges, 'the institutionalization of artistic research' often has an opposed effect, one of 'domestication and pacification' of the un- and anti-disciplinary features of the artistic research suggested by groups like SPUR. Indeed, reversing Barthes's terms, it could be said that in many cases art-as-research results not in the exposing of 'research' to the 'writing' or 'text' that it is underpinned by but represses, but instead a move in the opposite direction, with artworks seen as primarily representations of a reified content, as in the tendency to overly describe artworks and exhibitions in terms of the subject matter they are 'about'.

A similar structure is visible in chapter three, 'The Problem with Knowledge Production'. Here, Holert cites relevant debates within Soviet Productivism in the 1920s. As Holert characterises these, Boris Arvatov argued that in order to enter industrial production, artists first required technical retraining to obtain practical skills and knowledge. In contrast, Varvara Stepanova argued that artists' 'objective knowledge of external forms' already enabled them to actively enter production, as a more experimental complement to the engineer. Meanwhile, Boris Kushner's position was a compromise between these two, claiming like Stepanova that artists could already make this shift, but to do so it was necessary for them to learn some 'auxiliary knowledges'. Holert then shifts to tracing the term 'knowledge production' to, interestingly, the work of Fritz Machlup, a 'champion of neoclassical microeconomic theory' who argued that knowledge was a valuable commodity. The reappearance of the term 'knowledge production' in 2002 in Documenta 11, curated by Okwui Enwezor, Holert argues, might seem curious, since knowledge was clearly not meant here as a commodity. Instead, it was the critical potential of making art a space for generating knowledges that was foregrounded. For Holert, this 'semantic recoding' of the term was done by shifting the emphasis to knowledges from the global periphery, although it is a shame that Holert does not spend more time analysing the discourse around Documenta 11, given its prominence in his argument and in the recent history of contemporary art.

Across the chapter, the same antinomy again emerges. On the one hand, a Productivist or neo-Productivist emancipatory desire to link art to social revolution by connecting it to knowledge and material production; on the other, the 'institutional convergence of art and research' leading to a managerialist quasi-Productivism. As Holert is aware, the attempt to realise the Productivist programme under late capitalism tends to simply instrumentalise art in the service of the value-form. Holert states that 'the case is far from settled', but instead of interrogating it further, the problem is left hanging. Symptomatically registering the tension between emancipatory and instrumentalist aspects of art-as-research/art-as-knowledge is a limit point that the book seems unable to pass beyond.

The other chapters are primarily structured around case studies of artworks. The most interesting of these is on 'Knowledge Politics in the "Middle East"'. Although Holert does not explicitly frame this in terms of Edward Said's account of Orientalism, his discussion of works by Adelita Husni-Bey and Tony Chakar as resisting a Western, imperialist 'will-to-knowledge' could be understood in these terms.

Overall, the book is a frustrating read, in large part because it suffers from an apparent anxiety to mention everything related to the topic at hand. While countless writers, artists and topics are cited, key problems are not interrogated thoroughly. Distinct positions tend to be conflated because they are not explored in enough depth for significant differences to emerge. The strategy is collation rather than theorisation proper. The lengthy 'Bibliographic Addendum' to chapter one is a miniature image of this: attempting to provide a definitive biblio-

graphy of artistic research since 2000, it both acts as a useful resource and flattens the works listed.

Another case in point is the discussion of Pierre Macherey's *A Theory of Literary Production* (1966) that appears unexpectedly at the end of chapter three. Holert argues that Macherey is 'neo-Productivist', but it is hard to see how, unless two very different definitions of Productivist are in play. Macherey's understanding of literary 'production' is basically a formalist, Althusserian one, where 'production' means any transformation of a 'material' into a 'product' through determinate 'means' (an activity that can take place entirely in thought), whereas in Soviet Productivism it refers to the relations of material production. (A third, more strictly Marxist definition of 'production' as the production of value hovers in the background of the book, but is never quite invited to announce its presence outright.) Meanwhile, Holert seems to understand Macherey's notion of the 'object of knowledge' as evidence that Macherey sees art as an epistemic activity, but Macherey's (Althusserian) object of knowledge belongs to the critic, not the artwork. Macherey's arguments are constructed on a categorical distinction between art and science, in fact, which sets them at a distance from the claims of Soviet Productivism, and inflects any appropriation of them in relation to questions of art-as-knowledge.

In general, despite its caveats, the book is overly generous to the art institution. Holert's solutions to the problems he raises are often voluntarist and idealist. What is needed is an analysis that is more structural. (Stewart Martin's essay for Documenta 12 (in *RP* 141), and Peter Osborne's recent text on the subsumption of research (in the collection *The Postresearch Condition*) contribute to this.) This is a necessarily bleaker analysis, but this does not mean there is no space for new artistic practices. Indeed, such analysis should also orientate itself by current or recent practices that take up critical and reflexive inquiries into knowledge – Harun Farocki or Ultra-red, for instance. Holert raises the possibility of artworks carrying out a new form of institutional critique – in relation to academia rather than art – but implies, rightly, that this shouldn't be limited to a narrow form of critique that disenchantedly enumerates the ways in which art production is enmeshed in the neoliberal university. Instead, he points to Vishmidt's notion of 'infrastructural critique', an expansion of institutional critique that locates art in an expanded social and material field and can take 'immanent' or 'transversal' forms. This does indeed offer a productive way of conceptualising the intervention that critical art practices may make in the present. But after Holert's book, there is still plenty of space open for theorising art's interfaces with research and knowledge production.

Nicolas Helm-Grovas

Climate struggle

Matthew T. Huber, *Climate Change as Class War: Building Socialism on a Warming Planet* (London: Verso, 2022). 320pp., £16.99 hb., 978 1 78873 388 5

The US Congress passed its largest ever investment in clean energy in August – the Inflation Reduction Act (IRA) – and yet it remains impossible to shake the feeling that, as Matthew T. Huber puts it, 'the climate movement is losing' in both the US and globally. Fossil fuels still provide the vast majority of the world's energy. Pipeline protests and youth climate strikes, irrepressible in 2019, have seen their momentum scotched by the pandemic. The Russian war in Ukraine now provides a national security pretext to 'drill, baby drill' in the US, UK and elsewhere, as supply shortages drive record profits. Even the IRA represents a victory not so much for the 'climate movement' as for investors in 'green capital', who stand to benefit most from new clean energy tax credits. Meanwhile, climate disasters multiply, and the people who dragged the world into planetary catastrophe still call the shots.

Given the venality of the global ruling class, content to place scattered 'green' bets while sucking every last dollar out of fossil fuels, the way for the climate movement to start winning is to treat climate change as a class struggle, Huber argues in his new book, *Climate Change as Class War: Building Socialism on a Warming Planet*. 'Capitalists who own and control the means of production *produce* climate change', Huber writes. Only the working class has the numbers and leverage to challenge these capitalists at 'the point of production', he argues, and only a climate politics anchored in traditional labour demands for *more* – money, safety, and control over production – has a chance of winning workers to the cause. For Huber, slashing personal emissions, pricing carbon, or, really, doing anything that does not build up the power of capital's primary antagonist – labour – is fiddling while the planet burns.

Reviews of *Climate Change as Class War* have mostly focused on Huber's ideas about how to build a working-class climate movement in the US. I address some of these ideas, but focus on Huber's theoretical points – both because Huber offers a persuasive rebuke to liberal environmental as well as eco-Marxist thinkers and because a coherent theory of class clarifies why a working-class climate program is necessary not just for workers but for everyone.

Huber is hardly the first to blame climate change on capitalism. He is, however, refreshingly specific about why capitalism is to blame. The problem is not rich people's SUVs, 'growth' in the abstract or market inefficiencies, which might be 'corrected' by factoring ecological costs into the price of carbon. The problem is the class structure of the global economy, which concentrates power with 'a small minority of owners who control … the production of the energy, food, materials and infrastructure society needs to function', and who use that control to extract more value from workers than they pay in wages. Labour exploitation is bad for workers on its face. It is bad for the climate because capitalists have come to rely on coal, oil and gas to deepen exploitation – to squeeze more and more value out of the workforce.

Marx observed that capitalists can squeeze workers in two ways. They can extend the working day or use machines to increase how much workers produce per unit of time. Because increasing worker productivity (or, 'relative surplus value') has historically meant using fossil-fuelled machines, 'Capital's drive for *relative surplus value* – that is to say, their drive to increase *exploitation* – ultimately entails more fossil fuel combustion and intensification of the climate crisis'. Here Huber follows Marx's *Grundrisse*, as well as Andreas Malm's argument in *Fossil Capital*: the capitalists who built up the English factory system in the early nineteenth century traded water mills for steam engines not because coal was cheaper than water, but because the portability and energy density of coal allowed them to submit workers to the rigid discipline of urban factories running day and night. Mechanisation also cheapens commodities churned out by the industrial system, including food, driving down the socially necessary wage any given capitalist must pay workers. This too increases relative surplus value while baking carbon burn into the reproduction of everyday life.

This is not the standard eco-Marxist account. Represented by figures like James O'Connor and Jason W. Moore, the usual eco-Marxist critique holds that capitalism produces ecological crises because capital plunders its 'outsides': 'cheap' labour, land and resource frontiers, including the carbon capacity of the atmosphere, which capital both needs and tends to destroy. It is hard to dispute this account; from petrochemical 'sacrifice zones' in Louisiana to clearcutting in the Amazon, examples of capital's ecological parasitism are everywhere. For Huber, though, traditional eco-Marxists stray too far from 'the hidden abode of production' – a tendency he, like Ellen Meiskins Wood, blames on neoliberalism's scrubbing of class struggle from the political imagination. In foregrounding the destructive *effects* of capitalism away from the shop floor, eco-Marxists presumptively deprioritise the class best positioned to address destruction's *causes* at the point of production: the working class.

Crucially, class is neither an identity nor an income bracket but a social position, defined by one's relationship to the 'means of production', as Huber stresses. If you own land, factories, mines, apartment blocks, software patents or money for investment, you belong to the capitalist class. If you do not – and so get what you need to live by trading your labour for money which you then trade for food, shelter, energy and the like – you belong to the working class. If you work to live but your work mostly involves ideas, symbols and images, you might belong to a segment of the working class Huber, following Barbara Ehrenreich, calls the 'professional class'. Each class has firmly objective interests. Capitalists want to extract surplus value from workers. Workers want more resources, power and control over their lives. Capital and labour are thus at war. The socialist view is that trying to win this war – by organising to claw back power from the capitalists, ultimately to make the economy serve the common good rather than private gain – is the best way to satisfy workers' immediate interest in material security and *everyone's* long-term interest in a livable planet.

Pulled mostly from the ranks of the professional class, mainstream climate activists have largely avoided class warfare in favour of various forms of sacrifice – from limiting personal consumption to campaigning for carbon pricing. Even the climate movement's more radical currents – fossil infrastructure saboteurs, for instance – tend to position themselves against abstractions like growth, slipping into a 'politics of less' that denies the necessity of securing more material wealth for the majority of people. In worst case scenarios, such a politics fuels populist anger more readily captured by the Right than the Left, as France's 2018 Yellow Vest protests, sparked by a fuel tax hike, suggest. In best case scenarios, it aims to redistribute resources from the rich to people who directly experience worsening weather – the so-called frontline communities routinely spotlighted by the professional-class climate movement.

These frontline communities are owed a tremendous climate debt, but, for Huber, the climate movement's alliance with frontline groups (more often rhetorical than real) is a strategic mistake. People who depend on 'resource-based livelihoods', especially, may be most deserving of resources for adaptation and repair, but this does not make them the best equipped to wrest those resources from a powerful global ruling class. 'While socialist politics must always assert the right to self-determination of land-based peoples, a majoritarian popular climate politics will not emerge from those directly experiencing its worst effects', Huber writes. A majoritarian climate politics can only emerge from the majority – a broadly conceived working class, whose relationship to capitalism is defined not by a direct connection to the environment, but by 'profound *alienation* from the ecological conditions of life itself.'

Workers' separation from the conditions of life is the basis of what Huber calls 'proletarian ecology'. Echoing Italian communist Laura Conti's 'ecology of class', 'proletarian ecology' defines the working class broadly: the mass of people who lack direct control over land, housing, energy, mobility, and so on, and so must work for money to buy commodities to live. Because workers' access to resources is mediated by the commodity system, the working class has an interest in 'decommodification' – not just free or affordable housing, electricity and food, but social ownership of the means of producing what one needs to live well. Social ownership is also a solution to climate change; the tendency to deepen exploitation for profit is, after all, what drives accelerating combustion. For this reason, Huber argues, appealing to working people's interest in decommodification – even if, at first, this simply looks like public power or free mass transit – is key to building a climate movement sufficiently large, committed and powerful to demand a just transition to a non-fossil economy.

Huber's defence of the working class as an agent of decarbonisation and climate justice is a necessary rebuke to the view that labour is too committed to jobs – and thus industrial growth – to lead a movement for ecological repair. At the same time, Huber understates the compatibility of a working-class climate politics and one emerging from the frontlines. Labour exploitation and plundering the land are two moments of the same process – one that involves violently transferring ownership of the means of life from the mass of people to a handful of capital owners, making reproduction contingent on selling one's labour on the market. Any movement that opposes capital's exclusive control of the means of life – whether made up of waged workers, unwaged workers, land-based populations, anti-colonial fighters, or something else – is struggling against the same enemy. In focusing principally on how climate activists claim an alliance with frontline communities to promote a politics of less, Huber downplays the many examples of land-based struggles, from Standing Rock to southwestern Bangladesh, fighting for precisely the thing Huber suggests the labour movement also wants: popular control over production.

Though Huber undersells it, the compatibility of working-class and land-based struggles lends weight to one of the book's most important and controversial claims: the particular interests of the working class – social ownership of the means of life – are the interests of the human species as a whole.

Species is a loaded word. Dipesh Chakrabarty put the concept back on the critical map in his 2009 essay 'Climates of History', which argued that climate change reveals the species to be an agent of 'geological' change. The essay, which also popularised the Anthropocene concept, invited a rush of critiques and awkward neologisms: capitolocene, plantationocene, and others, all of which observe that the species is internally stratified, with some bearing outsized responsibility for climate change and others bearing outsized burden. Huber inherits a version of this critique, stressing that most planet-warming emissions trace back to a handful of capital owners who 'have names and addresses'.

But Huber also wants to claim a universalist politics. Unlike the bourgeois universalism of the Anthropocene, however, whose insistence that 'we are all in this together' papers over actually existing hierarchies, Huber's socialist universalism holds that social equality is possible only on the condition of material equality – when no single class, by virtue of its monopoly over land and other assets, can exert control over any other class. In this fairly orthodox Marxist view, the working class is the 'class to end classes', first, because it has a material interest in doing so and, second, because its position in modern economies, i.e., the source of all capitalist profits, gives workers the leverage needed to actually pull it off.

Beyond this, the labour struggle is a struggle for universal liberation because capital is a universalising force. Capital subsumes difference into itself by turning human effort into a commodity (labour power) that becomes the measure of value in general – a means of 'universal convertibility' allowing qualitatively unlike things to be exchanged. This unleashes capital's expansionary potential, driving capitalists to scour the Earth for anything they can seize and sell. The universalising thrust of capitalism begins, in other words, with the labour contract. For this reason, workers' fight against exploitation is also a fight against capitalism's imperialising tendencies, including its tendency to exhaust the capacities of 'women, nature, and the colonies', as Maria Mies put it. This is what makes working class interests the species' interests: the source of workers' oppression – the commodification of labour, which entails the commodification of life – is the source of capitalism's full gallery of horrors, including those, like planetary heating, that appear to unfold far from the shop floor.

At the same time, labour power is the source of modernity's triumphs: 'Capitalism has ushered in real historical possibilities for human emancipation'. Yet such possibilities remain only that, possibilities, so long as wealth produced by workers' collective efforts remains in private hands. Replacing capitalism with more democratic forms of political economy is key not only to curbing ecological destruction, but also to making the possibilities for abundance contained in modern machinery and infrastructure serve common rather than private ends. This is not to say that today's global network of factories, mines, fields, ports, wires, algorithms, and so on should be preserved *tout court*, with workers replacing capital's representatives at the helm. The architecture of modern capitalism has a tendency to degrade workers and the environment regardless of who holds the deeds. A socialist economy has to change not just *why* we produce but also what and how if it is to serve human needs into the future. The socialist wager is that a consciously and democratically planned economy, accountable to ordinary people, is infinitely better suited to achieving long-term human well-being than an economy ruled by and for the few.

Bringing this vision into being requires an organised and militant working class. As Raymond Williams put it in a 1984 lecture to the Socialist Environment and

Resources Association, building a sustainable and democratic system of production can only be achieved by 'the force which is rooted in the majority interest and in the indispensable livelihood of all the people in the society, and that, ideally ... is the labour movement.'

Looking to the US, Huber suggests first organising electricity workers – a strategy he calls 'socialism in one sector'. Ditching fossil fuels will require widespread electrification under any scenario; organisers should work with electric utilities workers, already heavily unionised in the US, to use strikes, slowdowns and work-to-rule campaigns to fight to nationalise electricity production, with an eye towards improving working conditions, providing electricity as a human right and transitioning the grid to non-fossil sources. Building this sort of programme will require sustained workplace organising focused on connecting workers' interest in workplace safety (consistently a top priority) with their positional interest in control over the environments in which they live. If such organising succeeds, a nationalised electricity sector might form 'the core of a public sector-led decarbonization program'. Longer term, the 'disruptive capacity' of electricity workers might supply the muscle for working-class voting majorities persuaded to support Green New Deal-type programs. FDR struck the New Deal under pressure from a broad working class backed by industrial workers on strike. Who says it can't happen again?

There are many reasons to doubt the odds. Despite excitement around the 2021 'strike wave' and successful union drives at Starbucks and Amazon, union density and strike activity remain at historic lows in the US. Even if workers have a material interest in 'decommodification and decarbonization', the two core planks of capitalist ideology – the free market is good; there is no alternative – remain sturdy enough to block any quick conversion of the US workforce into a class *for itself*. More insidiously, the materials, machines and infrastructures that make capitalists powerful (and heat the planet) are also the materials, machines and infrastructures ordinary people rely on to survive. To live in a fossil capitalist society is to live under a threat: no fossil fuels, no work.

The hope is that labour militancy can answer this threat with its own: no workers, no profits. More than anything else, then, building a working-class movement for post-carbon democracy means supporting militant labour actions, however small, that demonstrate working people's power to disrupt the economic and political order and remake it in some other image. As Huber suggests, there is no better way to get a feel for labour's power than unionising your workplace.

Casey Williams

Frames of modernity

Susan Buck-Morss, *Year One: A Philosophical Recounting* (Cambridge, MA: MIT Press, 2021). 416pp., £28.00 hb., 978 0 26204 487 5

Philosophers of the enlightenment such as Rousseau, Kant and Hegel imagined their projects as universal in reach and scale. Whether these philosophers were writing about the social contract, the foundations of moral law or the progression of spirit, the idea that the whole world could be understood from a universal perspective was taken for granted. In the twentieth century, postcolonial theorists have argued that this 'universal perspective' was inspired by specific, local or provincial European imaginaries. Reading postcolonial theory, one has learned to be cautious of the way universal modes of thought risk imposing one culture's values and norms onto all other cultures. Yet in an increasingly divided yet 'globalised' world we might ask: Are there ways of recuperating universal forms of inquiry from this dubious history? If so, how would we navigate the risk of imposition and reduction? What kind of philosophical project could be both global in its reach and sensitive to particularity, contingency and difference? What kinds of projects could create *new* visions of universal thought and history? For the last two decades, the philosopher and historian Susan Buck-Morss has been tackling precisely these questions.

In Buck-Morss's hands, universal history does not name a desire for sameness, homogeneity or subsumption, but an attentiveness to moments of *commonality* that cut across national, cultural and racial divides. In *Hegel, Haiti, and Universal History* (2005), Buck-Morss argued that the 1791 Haitian revolution – the first successful campaign for freedom by enslaved peoples – was an event of *universal significance*. Hegel, for example, learns about the revolution in the journal *Minerva* and the vision of freedom developed in the *Phenomenology of Spirit* is created in the shadow of the struggles of enslaved Haitians. The Haitian revolution, for Buck-Morss, challenges the idea of an isolated and uncontaminated Western modernity and is one of the key sources of a *global* modernity.

Universal history, on this account, is not only found in philosophical reflections, but embodied in the lives of ordinary people. Buck-Morss draws our attention to quotidian moments of cross-cultural recognition such as when French soldiers sent by Napoleon to quell the unrest of the Haitian revolution come across slaves singing 'La Marseillaise' and sense that they might be fighting on the wrong side. Or a Polish regiment who refused to drown 'six hundred' enslaved Haitians because they felt a sense of alliance with this struggle for human freedom. Such 'moments of clarity' do not belong to a national culture, but a universal one. In this way, Buck-Morss imagines universal history outside of its traditional parochialism.

'Common humanity', writes Buck-Morss, 'exists in spite of culture and its differences. A person's nonidentity with the collective allows for subterranean solidarities that have a chance of appealing to universal, moral sentiment, the source today of enthusiasm and hope. It is not through culture, but through the threat of culture's betrayal that consciousness of a common humanity comes to be.'

This sensitivity to subterranean solidarities, which cut across cultural difference, resonates throughout Buck-Morss's writing. *Dreamworld and Catastrophe: The Passing of Mass Utopia in East and West* (2000), for example, underscored the commonality between communist and capitalist dreamworlds and *Thinking Past Terror: Islamism and Critical Theory on the Left* (2003) illustrated the shared hopes and aspirations of Islamic and European critical theory. Buck-Morss's latest book *Year One: A Philosophical Recounting* (2021) expands upon this compelling vision of universal history.

Year One opens by asking: How do modern readers engage with the first century? What kinds of origin stories do we tell about this century? Are these stories based in historical fact or fiction? In *Year One*, Buck-Morss takes readers to an epoch that is used to generate mythical origin stories of cultural, religious and national division. Our modern conceptions of time, Christianity and Judaism, law, war and apocalypse can trace their origins to the first century. Ambitiously, Buck-Morss returns to this century to tell another story – one that emphasises commonality over division, contingency over solidity, and multiplicity over linearity.

The first chapter focuses on ideas of time in the first century. Buck-Morss demonstrates how the standardisation of time – the use of *anno domini* signifying the years after Christ's birth – would not have been recognisable to people living in this period. People living in the first century navigated multiple temporal orientations. Some forms of marking the passing of time focused upon the seasons, while other forms focused upon the renewal of imperial titles. In times of civil unrest – such as in the first Jewish-Roman War – coins were minted which reset time and proclaimed a new year one. Thus, Buck-Morss casts this period as one in which multiple visions of temporality were circulating. By emphasising how the form of time we inherit from the first century was unfamiliar to those living during this period, Buck-Morss introduces the central argument of her book: the first century is not the place we imagine it to be and modern readers have, systematically, imposed their cultural biases onto this early period. 'It is possible to colonize time', writes Buck-Morss, 'as well as territory. It happens when particular collectives claim a specific, vertical slice of history, set upon it a flag of national or religious belonging, and control the production and distribution of the meanings that are mined within it.'

The second chapter, focusing on Flavius Josephus' *Judean War*, provides an example of how national and religious origin stories distort interpretations of first-century texts. Josephus' *Judean War* has been important to Christian readers as it provides non-biblical evidence of Jesus' existence. And, it has been important to Jewish nationalist scholars who trace the loss of a Jewish 'national existence' to this war. Against such identity-based readings, Buck-Morss argues that modern understandings of religious identity, state structures, law and politics, do not easily align with Josephus' world. Reinterpreting the meaning of the Greek word *stasis*, Buck-Morss shows that Josephus' writing does not tell the story of a clash of identities or cultures, but rather focuses upon the dangers of 'factionalism' in political and social life.

In a similar manner, the third chapter focuses on the question of disciplinary knowledge through the writing of Philo of Alexandria. Buck-Morss emphasises the way Philo incorporated mathematics, musicology, theology, biology and humanistic exegesis into his thought, and uses this as an example of a philosophical method that does not abide by the strict demarcation of realms of knowledge. Unlike Kant, who sought to differentiate between 'scientific truth', 'ethical practice' and 'aesthetic judgment', Philo's method creates creative "analogies" among different forms of knowledge. Buck-Morss concludes the chapter by asking if such a transdisciplinary method might be useful to contemporary debates around climate disaster.

The fourth chapter turns to John of Patmos, author of the book of Revelation. Buck-Morss reconstructs the 'historical reality' that informed John's writing and thought. Rather than reading the book of Revelation as an eternal meditation on the return of a messiah, Buck-Morss argues that John was concerned to critique forms of human power (such as the Roman imperial cults), which acted as if they were divinely empowered. Once again demonstrating how modern categories do not align with the historical experiences of first-century writers, Buck-Morss demonstrates how the book of Revelation does not create hard distinctions between 'Jew versus Christian, heretic versus true believer … sinner versus saved.'

The concluding chapter, 'Constellations', turns to the question of translation as a method of reading history. In this chapter, Buck-Morss brings together first-century writers – particularly John and Philo – alongside theories of reading from Zora Neale Hurston to Reinhart Koselleck. History, for Buck-Morss, can be used to escape the myths, stereotypes, and binary divisions that haunt our contemporary moment. Throughout the chapter, Buck-Morss emphasises the importance of paying attention to how words in historical texts are translated. On the importance of translation as a method of writing history, Buck-Morss writes,

> In the double vision of history suggested here – not only as critique of history-become-myth, but also as philosophical rescue of material traces it provides – the first task is to translate words in a way that lets the past escape the impositions that have been placed upon it, allowing historical details to slip out of the conceptual frames that have carried them forward. The evidence … recedes from the horizon of modern understanding because the past and the present do not align. The part that vanishes from modern optics is its most valuable aspect because it challenges the inherited traditions of power. Rather than attempting a full recuperation, we enter into the text in order to decipher the transitory history encoded in the words. The experience de-reifies, de-ossifies, de-bakes the hardening of the past into concepts, making legible something that cannot otherwise be read. How to 'tilt the hermeneutic mirror' so that it does not reflect an immediate image of ourselves? How to extend the conditions of possibility that condense in our own moment in time, rather than using the past to naturalize the present along with the concepts and categories used to describe it?

In this sense, for Buck-Morss, reading historical texts can be compared to learning a foreign language. The task is to learn the new syntax, the new grammar, and new idioms of historical writers and philosophers. Translating past worlds into the present, in this account, is not about finding direct correlations, but meditating on the *gap* between the language of the past and the language of the present. Within this gap, a new kind of opportunity emerges: to let go of or escape the modern myths that divide humanity and to free up space for us to ask new questions and tell different stories.

'Any search for origins', writes Buck-Morss, 'will discover at the source, not the purity of identity categories but the moment of these categories' disappearance.' Like her previous books, *Year One* is animated by the desire to think anew about universal history. This project is not guided by the desire to find one common origin story or myth. Rather, *Year One* invites us to think about the universal as a loss of origins, an inaugural ambiguity, and a multiplicity of differences at our supposed genesis: 'Here is the wager: if the first century can be reclaimed as *common ground* rather than the origin of deeply entrenched differences, then its very remoteness in time has the potential to lift modernity's self-understanding off existing foundational constraints … A tiger's leap. The task is to liberate the past from the concepts that purport to contain it; to suspend the structuring schema of history as modernity's content. To fall out of modernity itself' (emphasis mine).

Year One, then, leaves its reader asking where such a fall out of modernity might take us? What kinds of community emerge from the disappearance of origin stories? What forms of historical writing can both accept the dispersion of entrenched differences and refuse reductive homogeneity?

One potential weakness of *Year One* is its emphasis on transcendence. Buck-Morss casts modernity in an almost entirely negative light and, therefore, argues that we must move beyond its terms absolutely. Yet we might ask: Has identity (a key term of modernity for Buck-Morss) not also produced forms of emancipatory politics? Are all adoptions of modernity's terms equivalent? How do we think about feminist, postcolonial or diasporic writers who have immanently reclaimed modernity's terms? Buck-Morss avoids these difficult questions by refusing to engage in key contemporary debates and, instead, turning to an 'outside' of modernity through the first century.

On the other hand, the strength of *Year One* is its commitment to a new vision of philosophy, history and politics. *Year One* seeks to remind us that we need not think of the past or the present as ossified. We can discover unexpected worlds in historical archives. And, inspired by these discoveries, we can think in a radically different manner about disciplinary structures, the future of the humanities, and the binds that connect us across space and time.

Nasrin Olla

Earth systems

Dipesh Chakrabarty, *The Climate of History in a Planetary Age* (Chicago: University of Chicago Press, 2021). 296pp., £76.00 hb., £20.00 pb., 978 0 22610 050 0 hb., 978 0 22673 286 2 pb.

The bright red time ball atop Flamsteed House at the Royal Observatory in Greenwich rises halfway up its mast each day at 12:55 p.m., to the top of the mast at 12:58 p.m., and drops suddenly to the bottom at exactly 1:00 p.m. Like the BBC's famous pips, the ball is what is called a time signal – a visual or aural sign used to synchronise time across sometimes vast geographical distances. When first used in 1833, the time ball signalled the time to merchant vessels, fishing boats and warships on the Thames. Before the near-instantaneous communication offered by the telegraph, watchmakers would travel to Greenwich to synchronise their goods, and one enterprising London family offered this service for a fee. Such temporal synchronisation is measured in relation to a single line that still serves as the reference point for global spatial and temporal coordinates: the Greenwich Meridian.

The global spatial and temporal ordering of the earth marked by the Meridian, whose location was decided on by delegates from twenty-six states at the 1884 Meridian Conference in Washington, D.C., is the culmination of centuries of European imperial voyages that aimed to map and conquer the so-called 'free space' of the globe outside Europe. Today, scientists are hard at work trying to establish a new measure of earthly time in the form of a geological time signal: a Global Boundary Stratotype Section and Point (GSSP) for the Anthropocene. Otherwise known as a 'golden spike' after the bronze discs geologists use to mark GSSPs, the term refers to a section of rock that designates 'the lower boundaries of stages on the geologic time scale'. GSSPs are rock strata that contain common or distinctive fossils or other material that signal a global change that marks the start of a new geological time period. Proposals for an Anthropocene GSSP range widely, from particulate matter linked to the burning of fossil fuels to the global dissemination (and disposal) of the iPhone. Whatever geological phenomenon is chosen as the Anthropocene time signal, it must exhibit a 'globally synchronous' marker of humans' geological impact on the earth.

These time signals – Meridian and GSSP – might, in Dipesh Chakrabarty's terms, mark the difference between the global and the planetary, human time and earth time. Though universal or 'Cosmic' time, as it was called by UK Meridian Conference delegate Sanford Fleming, is today synchronised by satellite signals, the vision of the spherical globe agreed to in 1884, as Chakrabarty reminds us, is not an artefact of a bygone age but remains the basis of Google Maps software and Geographical Information Systems today. Chakrabarty's globe represents the modern humanism that he argues is giving way to 'the planetary' as a result of a growing consciousness of anthropogenic climate change. This 'new historical-philosophical entity called the planet', according to Chakrabarty, is a view of the earth as a single interconnected system – the 'Earth system'. Given that 'the age of the global as such is ending' and 'we are on the cusp of the global and the planetary', the task for historians, Chakrabarty argues, is to relate these two models of humans' relationship to the earth and life on its surface. Yet their shared commitment to global synchronicity suggests that the planetary age may end before it begins.

It is around the time of the 1884 Washington Conference, when European colonisation had reached its apex, that the international political system is said to have become a fully global political order. Hedley Bull, a key figure in the 'English School' of international relations, wrote in 1977 that 'throughout human history before the nineteenth century there was no single political system that spanned the surface of the world as a whole', but that 'since the late nineteenth and early twentieth century there has arisen for the first time a single political system that is genuinely global.' Prior to this political globalisation, in Bull's view, 'world order was simply the sum of the various political systems that brought order to particular parts of the world', whereas the expansion of international society across the globe means that 'order on a global scale ... is the product of what may be called a world political system.'

Not coincidental, then, is the coincidence of talk of global warming and globalisation in the 1980s and 1990s. It is only once climate begins to be conceptualised as a systemically interconnected unity rather than in local or regional terms that it becomes an object of concern for the UN and other international institutions. This happened alongside the conceptual separation – still refused by climate deniers – of climate from weather, a distinction that rests on understanding climate as systemically connected rather than a simple aggregate of local weather patterns. The Intergovernmental Panel on Climate Change, for example, drew on computer models of earth's atmosphere to understand climate as a dynamically interconnected global system not reducible to regional weather and thus as a force that has significant effects on the earth as a whole.

This kind of global unity is the object of earth systems scientists and the emerging planetary boundaries framework. Originated by Johan Rockström and colleagues at the Stockholm Resilience Centre (SRC), the framework (the subject of a recent Netflix documentary called *Breaking Boundaries* featuring Rockström) posits nine planetary boundaries that establish a 'safe operating space' for the human species. These geophysical systems range from ozone depletion, climate change, biodiversity loss to global phosphorous and nitrogen cycles threatened by industrial use of agricultural fertilisers. Five of the nine boundaries – climate, biodiversity, land use, nitrogen and phosphorous cycles and chemical pollution – have already been broken with the rest rapidly approaching. The SRC reported in January that the chemical pollution boundary is the latest threshold crossed as plastics and other toxic human-created compounds accumulate in the biosphere at an unprecedented rate.

Earth Systems Science (ESS) is organised around the view that anthropogenic climate change caused by political and economic globalisation has transformed the human species into a geological force. For Chakrabarty, this disturbs the distinction between humans and the natural world central to many modern claims to political authority. Scientists' claim that humans have 'become a force capable of changing ... the climate system of the planet as a whole' challenges the distinction between natural and human history that informs most historical scholarship. There is a dizzying variety of terms used to signal this shift, like Capitalocene, Cthulucene and Eurocene, each of which emphasise a different cause or characteristic of the contemporary predicament. Chakrabarty prefers Anthropocene, a condition marked by the shift from a global to a planetary conception of the earth.

This preference is linked to Chakrabarty's insistence that the problems brought into view by the planetary are irreducibly collective. The key feature of the planetary is that it decentres the human by placing the species against a backdrop of geological processes that take place on vast timescales that are not normally the subject of historians' attention. While histories of capitalism, for example, provide partial explanations of planetary warming on earth, the history of climate change, Chakrabarty maintains, is not synonymous with the history of capital. ESS, he points out, is not specific to earth but is a 'planetary science' that studies earth as one among innumerable other planetary bodies in the universe. From this perspective, 'our current warming is simply an instance of what is called planetary warming.'

Chakrabarty locates the origins of earth systems science in the planetary focus of NASA scientist James Lovelock and his 'Gaia Hypothesis', which conceived of the earth as a single geophysical system. But while scientists at NASA were looking skyward, the government that funded it was looking East to a raging cold war in which NASA was a significant weapon. US and Soviet military funding spurred research on earth systems in the 1950s and 60s as Cold War militaries sought meteorological, oceanographic and geophysical knowledge to control the weather, develop submarine routes, study new theatres of war like the arctic and predict the fallout effects of a possible nuclear conflagration. This research led to computer modelling of geophysical systems of the kind eventually used by the Intergovernmental Panel on Climate Change. While Chakrabarty may be right that there would be no climate discourse without ESS, it is hard to imagine ESS without states and their imperial ambitions. The science of climate, like the science of space that resulted in the Greenwich Meridian, is entangled with war and empire.

The Climate of History in a Planetary Age, however, is not a history of climate change, climate science or climate historiography but an analysis of the consequences of the growing consciousness of humans' status as a geological force for the practice of history as an academic discipline and a form of popular knowledge. The planetary enjoins historians to 'connect deep and recorded history' by placing human history within the geological history of the earth and the history of life on its surface. It is in this sense that 'one can ... read Earth System Scientists as historians working within an emergent regime of historicity.' The category 'planet' emerges when history is practiced simultaneously on the 'two registers' of earth history and the human history of modern empires and their globalisation.

Relating these two registers reveals how recent and precarious is the life of the human species on earth. The lesson of the planetary is that 'we cannot afford to destabilize conditions that ... work like boundary parameters of human existence.' At the same time, Chakrabarty admits that human endangerment is an eminently political question that cannot be decided by scientific expertise alone. In this sense, 'the entity to which climate change pose[s] a real threat [is] human civilization as we have come to understand and celebrate it.' The 'parametric conditions' that global warming threatens are conditions 'for the existence of institutions central to our idea of modernity.' The human of the planetary boundaries framework is a specific kind of modern subject secured by the political, economic, social and technological institutions that have developed on earth over the last five centuries. Is it the human as such that the Anthropocene threatens, or the human that brought about the Anthropocene and its terrible effects?

The problem of climate change, Chakrabarty found, could not be addressed with the 'theories of globalisation, Marxist analyses of capital, subaltern studies, and postcolonial criticism' with which Chakrabarty has built an impressive body of historical and philosophical writings. The question is 'how do we relate to a universal history of life … while retaining what is of obvious value in our postcolonial suspicion of the universal?' As political battles are fought between the 'lumpers' and the 'splitters', as Chakrabarty calls advocates of universality and particularity, the task remains to negotiate the relationship between the twin facts of unity and diversity on earth.

This question is especially acute in the context of 'climate justice', the idea that states should be held responsible for mitigating climate change to a degree proportional to their responsibility for causing it. Inequality in this respect is extreme. Climate justice is closely tied to the idea that the modernising projects of postcolonial states should continue. How can India's growing middle class be denied the air-conditioners that contribute to climate change but also keep them alive in increasingly unbearable temperatures? Rather than dismiss the aspirations of 'anti-colonial nationalism' which 'remains programmatically committed to modernization', even in the context of a warming world, Chakrabarty argues that the 'ethical aspects' of these still-powerful desires for global modernisation must be addressed 'if one is to plumb the depths of the human predicament today.'

The planetary also enjoins historians to consider humans' entanglements with the non-human – living and otherwise. Alongside the environment, in Chakrabarty's view subaltern studies pays insufficient attention to specific inequalities like caste rather than general categories like class. Chakrabarty reflects on caste by drawing on his experiences as a youth in Kolkata in an essay on the 'Dalit body' as an example of human intertwinement with the non-human. While 'marginalized because of its forced contact with death and waste matter', Chakrabarty prefers to see in the Dalit a 'planetary body' that spurs thinking on the entanglement of humans with their others. The problem is the way modern political aspirations to freedom, equality and self-determination depend in some respects on a vision of the human autonomous from nature and thus 'how difficult it still is to "politicize" this connected figure of the human.'

Yet human embeddedness in 'deep time', as Chakrabarty points out, is a feature of European political philosophy from the eighteenth century, when there was a broad shift from classificatory systems of nature, like those of Linnaeus, to a view of nature as dynamic and evolutionary, in which organisms are subject to development over time. This view of natural history can be found as early as Aristotle's writings on politics. For Immanuel Kant, a figure emblematic of this transformation alongside others like Buffon and Humboldt, enlightenment and progress are only possible collectively, at the level of the human species. This framing of human possibilities on earth involves teleological conceptions of progress that produce hierarchies built on categories like race and civilisation. These are present both in Kant's work and in nineteenth-century geopolitical thought in which geological processes are considered central to human political life.

Geographer Friedrich Ratzel, for example, father of German *Geopolitik*, argued that 'Man' must be studied 'as a life phenomenon of the earth'. Writing in 1902, Ratzel explained that 'Cosmic influences may broaden or narrow the districts within which Man is able to exist, as was experienced by the human race during the glacial period, when the ice sheet first drove men toward the equator, and, later, receding, enabled them once more to spread out to the north.' Questions about the formation of the earth's crust cannot be 'left to geology' because they concern the geographical formations that influence the character and limits of human political communities. Though no prophet of climate change, Ratzel connects geological, biological and human history to draw conclusions about the limits of human political life on earth. Ratzel's work, and his now-infamous concept of lebensraum, would be used in the twentieth century to justify German genocide in South West Africa and Nazi imperialism in Europe.

This history makes Chakrabarty's lament that 'we don't yet know how' to understand ourselves 'as a species deeply embedded in the history of life' ring hollow. The relationship between human beings, the earth and political authority has been the subject of philosophical reflection for centuries. The likelihood is rather that it is specific answers to this question that have led to the current predicament, rather than their absence. More compelling are the images included in the book of a child playing with earth-moving vehicles in a sandbox that Chakrabarty argues demonstrate the naturalisation of humans' 'geomorphological agency'. This aligns with the way species thinking infuses contemporary politics, from biologically reductionist visions of race and nation to categories in international law like crimes against humanity. Moreover, humans' vulnerability to wider astrophysical forces drives scientific efforts to defend the planet from asteroid strikes and telecommunications networks from disruption by solar flares. This view is of course also present in the widespread alarm about the catastrophic environmental effects of political and economic globalisation.

This alarm tends to be channeled in two ways. The first is a narrow, technocratic response that asks how best to source the energy needed to continue the project of global modernity. The second sees the Anthropocene as an 'ecological overshoot on the part of humanity', indicative of a 'shared predicament' among life on the planet. Here Chakrabarty departs from the earth systems scientists who inspire his reflection. While *Breaking Boundaries* concludes with Rockström calling for the planetary boundaries problem to be taken up by the United Nations (UN) Security Council, Chakrabarty suggests that the UN may be closer to the problem than any solution. While UN negotiations take place on an 'indefinite calendar', climate presents an urgent problem that calls for action on finite timelines. 'It is entirely possible', he writes, 'that planetary climate change is a problem that the UN was not set up to deal with.' The problem of temporal scale might also be posed in terms of the relatively short time horizon in relation to which UN decisions are made, which rarely points beyond the current century. Compared to the geological timescales that characterise the planetary, decision-making at the UN is all too human.

Despite Rockström's call for Security Council action on planetary boundaries, states so far remain uninterested in the location of the Anthropocene GSSP. Climate accords like the Paris Agreement, however, suggest that the limits earth systems impose on global political and economic order are now recognised by most states on earth. Perhaps soon they will convene to weigh in on the question of an Anthropocene time signal. Whether this should be feared or celebrated depends on one's answer to a question likely to animate the world politics of this century: who has authority over the earth?

Regan Burles

God's away

Willem Styfhals, *No Spiritual Investment in the World: Gnosticism and Postwar German Philosophy* (Cornell University Press, 2019). 306pp., £112.00 hb., £32.00 pb., 978 1 50173 099 3 hb., 978 1 50173 100 6 pb.

Willem Styfhals' new book offers a conceptual history of Gnosticism within a deceptively narrow discursive field. Though Gnosticism re-emerged and become a relatively widespread term in German thought from the end of the nineteenth century onwards, gaining particular prominence in the interwar period, Styfhals takes as his principal focus the philosophical debates around Gnosticism that took place after 1945.

At the core of this decision, and central to the concerns of the book, is the radical caesura in the theoretical usage of Gnosticism engendered by the events of the Second World War, and the atrocities of the Holocaust. What emerges through this combination of conceptual historiography and comparative analysis of the 'Gnostic moments' in German thought is an account of the ways the term Gnosticism became bound up with the philosophy of modernity and its on-going self-definition and self-periodisation.

The most prevalent feature of the post-war shift was a turn away from any perceived radical political potential of Gnostic thought towards the notion of Gnosticism as a diagnostic catch-all for the problems of the present epoch. The radically divergent (and often deeply contradictory) positions that germinated from this re-excavated term lead Styfhals to suggest from the outset that rather than a concept in the more narrowly philosophical sense, Gnosticism might better be understood as a 'metaphorical motif of modernity'. The subsequent analysis is divided into six chapters, each highlighting one particular facet of this nebulous and shifting deployment of Gnosticism: Crisis, Eschaton, Subversion, Nothingness, Epoch and Theodicy. The recurrent thinkers throughout the book are ones whose work ranges over interdisciplinary ground, with admixtures of the theological, philosophical and historical to varying degrees: Hans Jonas, Jacob Taubes, Karl Löwith, Eric Voegelin, Hans Blumenberg, Gershom Scholem and Odo Marquard, as well as (more peripherally) Walter Benjamin, Martin Heidegger and Ernst Bloch.

Styfhals draws attention to the terminological diffusiveness of Gnosticism even in its everyday theological sense. Gnosticism 'is not and has never been a category that signifies a well-defined historical phenomenon'. Rather, it is an early modern or even nineteenth-century application to those early Jewish and early Christian heresies predicated on a radical separation [*Krisis*] between transcendence and immanence: a retrojected unity of distinct and disparate heresies. More specifically, it is a term used to denote sects that attested to God's absolute withdrawal from the world, a withdrawal which gives creation over to the devil and leaves the world fallen and evil. Re-coded in the domain of the political, this point of *Krisis*, enacted by the awareness of divine absence from the world, demands the birth of a new epoch, one whose historical urgency may be located in the *Kulturkrise* that swept German cultural life in the twentieth century. This relationship to crisis, that sprung from 'heretical undercurrents of Western monotheism' was vital for making Gnosticism an intellectual resource and object of fascination for Jewish and Christian thinkers in the interwar period. It was also what would lead to its use as a diagnostic term for the crisis of late modernity.

Styfhals excels in his genealogical presentation of his object of study, despite the often murky conceptual terrain he has to navigate where definitions and usage not only of Gnosticism but of terms like: 'eschatology', 'secularisation' and, of course, 'modernity' are both stratified and precarious (even within the work of a single author). This is evidenced most clearly in the section on Eschaton, which primarily stages a confrontation between Taubes and Löwith and demonstrates the inextricability of Gnosticism from the discourse of secularisation.

Styfhals presents their shared conviction in the theology of salvation as initiating a break with 'classical' cyclical time, inaugurating the idea of time as a progressive evolution – and, further, that this structure of linearity still determines the contemporary experience of time. The key difference for Styfhals lies in the *legitimacy* of the secularisation of this eschatological line, with Löwith viewing it as an illegitimate de-formation, negating Christianity's transcendent God, and descending into groundlessness, and Taubes conversely identifying in Gnostic eschatology a radical anti-totalitarian potential. Löwith's thought is therefore in line with Christian eschatology, whereas Taubes moves towards apocalypticism. For Taubes the eschatological resurgence in modernity is a legitimate transformation. In fact, his thought is characterised as one where 'the end of time structures the entire history of the West'. This idea of chthonic subversion puts Taubes at radical odds with Löwith, for whom it was the 'modern eschatological structure of hope itself' that had rendered these atrocities possible, but draws him into the orbit of Scholem whose influence on the philosophy of the Frankfurt School (and in particular Walter Benjamin) is well documented.

As Styfhals shows, Taubes and Scholem are alike in seeking to expound the radical potential of Gnostic heresy through a 'deconstruction' of orthodoxy, each developing a negative political theology (grounded respectively in an apocalyptic reading of Paul's theology and a messianic anarchism) oriented toward an absolute destruction of the political as such.

Scholem's notion of heresy, as a form of self-assertion whose radical messianism destabilises orthodoxy and any claims it has to authenticity, places its redemption outside of history. It has nothing to do with immanent development but rather is 'transcendence breaking in upon history'. This focus on the necessity of catastrophe for redemption sets paradox at the heart of Scholem's political project: it is the inner logic of the messianic. In Scholem's work this Gnostic force remained circumscribed by Jewish messianism, with Christian inwardness radically distinguished from the political, public messianism of the Jewish faith. It is here that Taubes aimed his radical critique: arguing for the messianic as a real historical force, one that was informed and transformed by historical contexts and events. Going beyond the merely historiographical, Styfhals here elucidates how Taubes utilises the deconstructive operations of Scholem's orthodoxy/heresy binary to problematise both the distinction the latter author makes between the Christian and Jewish salvation *and* between the religious and secular as such. The interiorisation of salvation in Christianity was, for Taubes, merely another historical transformation of the messianic.

The destruction of law and the political brings Styfhals to the question of nihilism. Through the motif of 'Nothingness', Styfhals elaborates a conception of *religious nihilism*, a constellation of Gnostic positions producing theologies after the 'death of God'. The classic reception of Nietzsche's phrase is as a wholesale rejection of any legitimating transcendent beyond that structures the immanent world. In Heidegger's words, we are left with a world where 'the supersensory world has no effective force'. Understood this way, nihilism and Gnosticism, in their denial of an ontological relation between the transcendent and immanent, share a rejection of the intrinsic value of the natural world and any form of moral law. The divine withdrawal of God (conceived as *das Nichts der Welt*) and the non-existence of God as anything but a figment of the imagination end on the same destitute plane.

Benjamin enters Styfhals' analysis explicitly here, through a discussion of the 'Theological-Political Fragment' and the paradoxical dynamics of the messianic and profane. Rightly noting Benjamin as anti-gnostic, Styfhals explicates Benjamin's dialectical recovery of the messianic-profane by grounding the former in the transience of the latter. Benjamin's readers have often tended either to over- or underemphasise Benjamin's nihilism (usually in line with their position on the materialism-theology spectrum which haunts all approaches to his work) but Styfhals' reading, whilst (given the book's context) remaining theologically inflected, makes a strong case for the dynamic, dialectical relation at work in the messianic. History's 'weak messianic power' finds its index of redemption in its unending passing away. Rather than Gnostic separation producing an all-encompassing nihilism, in what Styfhals terms *religious nihilism*, nihilism itself becomes the method of the messianic, the striving for the destruction of modes of being that gives rise to a history not of victory or progress but 'discontinuity, catastrophe and decay'.

With the final two chapters centred on Voegelin and Blumenberg, the metaphorical horizon of Gnosticism as a term reaches its widest arc and its most determinate application to the present epoch (*Neuzeit*). Both are critical of Gnosticism as such but whereas for Voegelin modernity is a Gnostic age, for Blumenberg, it is Gnosticism's very overcoming. Styfhals here draws out a dichotomy of uncertainty and absolutism that exemplifies the problem of modernity, even if this problem remains under-developed. Voegelin sets uncertainty at the very heart of Christianity as the absolute correlate of faith, rendering the origin of the movement of secularisation interior to Christianity itself. Through Gnosticism then, Christ's de-divinisation of the world (in contrast to the preceding polytheistic and pagan religions) becomes spuriously re-divinised through its rendering immanent of the possibility for mystical knowledge. For Voegelin, the existential certainty of divine withdrawal which Gnosticism posits constitutes a failure of will. Further, this secularised pseudo-religious truth becomes the ground for totalitarianism over and against the relative temporal legitimation of Christian politics. Modernity illegitimately attempts to secularise Christian mystery into the realm of human action.

Blumenberg conversely sees the project of the 'atheological theodicy' of modernity as the legitimation of the world as it is. The modern age 'begins with an act of theodicy' in that it attempts to overcome the resurgent Gnosticism whose forces seek to divest the world of meaning and coherence. What Blumenberg finds in this atheological theodicy of modernity is an attempt to render life liveable and nature reliable, to legitimate 'the possibility of human existence and self-assertion'. Being faced with divine absolutism, human life becomes impossible. This, for Blumenberg, unites both myth and reason, in that they serve to discharge the absolute, a reduction of reality necessary for life.

Styfhals suggests in the book's introduction that his investigative method parallels Blumenberg's 'metaphorology' in its exploration of the German *reception* of Gnosticism. However, this isn't quite carried through theoretically and feels like a missed opportunity to draw together the earlier thinker's metaphorics of post-Kantian concept formation and the intellectual history of modernity.

The conclusion, certainly the book's weakest section, makes some reference to Blumenberg's 'background metaphorics' in relation to secularisation, but not a reflection on the question of metaphor, the de-formation of the concept of Gnosticism into a 'pseudo-concept', as a constituting feature of the internal structure of the modern itself. For all his exceptional insights, metaphor is the term which Styfhals receives and leaves underdeveloped.

If there is a weakness in the book then it lies in a certain withdrawal of philosophy from Styfhals' own method. Metaphor remains either too vague or risks becoming synonymous with vagueness. The closing remarks, which turn to Arendt, the question of the Holocaust and the failure of conceptual thought to comprehend, evidence this most clearly. What Styfhals addresses is an undeniable *reticence* on the part of those discussing Gnosticism, even critically, to deal directly with the Holocaust (as opposed to thinkers like Arendt who did), despite the Nazis' destructive totalitarian regime largely confirming some of the Gnostic paradigms the various authors explore. The question from the book's opening gambit – why Gnosticism operated metaphorically and 'why this space was not able to be thought conceptually' – is examined on *historical* but not *philosophical* grounds. The question of metaphorical truth runs across Nietzsche's fundamental metaphorics, whereby metaphor is a constituent component of perception, the hermeneutics of metaphor and, in the wider context of the critique of epistemology, the link between epistemic and historical violence. The question that Styfhals provides a great deal of evidence for, and suggestive argumentation towards, but finally leaves unanswered is: what can the caesura in the theoretical discourse of Gnosticism engendered by the Second World War reveal about the status of metaphorical truth in modernity?

Despite this 'failure of will' (or perhaps of time), *No Spiritual Investment in the World* remains an invaluable contribution to understanding the complex conceptual history of Gnosticism, sitting alongside Benjamin Lazier's *God Interrupted* (whose primary focus is the preceding interwar period) and within the wider context of work examining the theological undercurrents of modernity. By writing a book which covers so much philosophical ground, Styfhals illuminates the complex position of Gnosticism within the German tradition, and provides ample evidence for why the problems it sought to address – modernity's on-going problem of self-definition, the destruction of theology as a possible communicative mode of historical experience, and the struggle to find a legitimate ground for meaning – remain our problems today. *No Spiritual Investment in the World* makes Gnosticism a living metaphor, even if it stops short of investigating how this might transform our understanding of why 'metaphor is living'.

Daniel Fraser

Sunstruck

Oxana Timofeeva, *Solar Politics* (Cambridge: Polity Press, 2022). 140pp., £9.99 pb., 978 1 50954 965 8

Since Antiquity, the sun has been tied up with earthly and divine authority. The solar god Sūrya, a Hindu deity, was worshipped in sun temples across India. In the fourth century, under Roman Emperor Julian's rule, the ancient Helios, like Sūrya depicted with a radiant crown and a horse-drawn chariot, became the central divinity. Fatally stabbed from behind, a few days after the summer solstice in 363, Julian flung his hands towards the sun, speaking his last words to Sol Invictus: 'Oh Galilean, you have conquered!' The ultimate source of life on earth, nourishing and disastrous, the sun continues to play a key role in radical politics today, from ecological utopianism to Solarpunk.

Written in times of global environmental crisis and pandemic, Oxana Timofeeva's *Solar Politics* is a bold, provocative attempt to fundamentally shift perspectives on ecology and radical politics. Taking the reader from the unbuilt City of the Sun in the Kazakh steppe to Hegel's *Phenomenology*, the book aims to unveil the relevance of Georges Bataille for contemporary environmentalism. His general economy, driven by generosity and exuberance, is presented as an alternative to capitalism's restrictive economy, based on expansive colonisation.

For Timofeeva, all utopian visions unite in a 'spirit of solarity'. Defeating exploitation, solarity creates a sense of 'cosmic solidarity' between human and nonhuman beings. Accordingly, solar politics 'breaks the promethean vicious circle of worship and extractivism, begins from the recognition that the sun is neither a master, nor a slave.'

What Timofeeva envisions is not the return to an idealised, pastoral state where people live in harmony with nature. Neither does she claim to colonise the sun as the final stage of the Anthropocene. Solar politics is a kind of in-between path that radicalises existing visions of solarity and transforms them into praxis. Unlike other environmentalist philosophies such as the Gaia paradigm, solar politics does not abandon the promethean tradition but aims to overturn it from within: Solar Politics moves from rethinking climate change as a rebellion of the colonized Earth or revolutionary movement of oppressed nature to the development of the general strike as the solar strike, and decolonizing struggles and revolutionary movements as unavoidable climate change.

However, what Timofeeva shares with other ecological projects is her distinct focus on nonhuman agents. Rather than objectifying the sun, or extracting energy from it, solar politics treats the sun as a radiant comrade. In short, solar politics aim to decolonise the sun. But what might this radical politics look like? And what does it mean to treat the sun as a comrade? To gain more clarity, we need to look at Timofeeva's conceptual framework that takes Bataille's general economy as a blueprint. In the introduction, 'Two Suns and the City', Timofeeva retraces a 'solar utopian tradition' from Book VI in Plato's *Republic* through the Renaissance thinkers Marsilio Ficino and Tommaso Campanella to Bataille's experimental writings from the 1930s.

The central symbol in this tradition is a strange doubling of the sun. In the *Republic*, preceding the famous cave allegory, Socrates distinguishes between the visible and the invisible, the physical and the spiritual sun. Timofeeva reads Plato's solar metaphysics dialectically, stating that 'the sun and the eye communicate as if they are looking into each other through the layers of things encompassed by light, and the one reflects the other.' We keep staring at the sun and, through our eye, the divine eye of the sun looks at itself – although, as Timofeeva quotes Bataille, it is blind. In Timofeeva's view, Bataille, in his theory of general economy, was the first to develop a truly cosmic perspective on the sun. In the decentred universe presented in *The Solar Anus* (1931), the sun's 'luminous violence', like an eruptive volcano, penetrates the earth with its solar rays.

Timofeeva distinguishes the violent, dark sun appearing in *Rotten Sun* (1930) from later appropriations in neo-reactionary movements, such as Nick Land's *The Dark Enlightenment*. Radical theories, she states in another section, are always at risk of being misused. Therefore, it is our responsibility to fight for the legacy of ambiguous ideas. Bataille's black sun, in her view, points to the inescapable bond between humanity and solar violence. The entanglement between the human and the nonhuman, which already surfaced in her previous book *The History of Animals: A Philosophy* (2018), again takes centre stage in *Solar Politics*. Timofeeva's fascinating twist is that she situates nonhuman alterity within ourselves. Thinking solarity means to find 'an inhuman element within the human, which will connect me to the serpent, the volcano, or to the sun.'

In the first chapter, 'Two Kinds of Violence', Timofeeva undertakes a daring yet at times drawn-out reading of Georges Sorel, Walter Benjamin, Hegel, Frantz Fanon and Bataille, illustrated by various examples – for instance, the Sisters Khachaturyan who made headlines in Russia for killing their abusive father. Her analysis of emancipatory violence in her home country, such as the protests in Moscow against fake elections in 2019, has become even more relevant after the Russian invasion of Ukraine. Shortly after 24 February, Timofeeva, a Professor at the European University at St. Petersburg and member of the artistic collective 'Chto Delat?', was among the first intellectuals based in Russia who openly spoke out against the war. In *Solar Politics*, she appeals to protest against increasing oppression, terror and police violence. And after all, she jokes, there is always the possibility to leave Russia or Belarus to settle on Mars in the near future.

Emptying the concept of violence from moralistic dogma, she develops a definition encompassing both anthropogenic and nonhuman activity. She distinguishes between two types of violence, oppression as 'negation' and revolutionary violence as the 'negation of negation'. The left, she claims, should embrace 'a new common sense of revolutionary violence, the justifiability of which is debated with regards to historical precedents.' This rather open definition seems a slippery slope, potentially justifying all kinds of violent acts. While her analysis is provocative, it is, moreover, not immediately clear what place it occupies in a project of solar politics. Above all, where is the sun?

Some hints towards solarity are made in her interpretation of Bataille's non-anthropocentric concept of 'sacred violence.' This imaginary type of violence belongs in the realm of animality. While a spider or serpent may not do any harm, they still scare us. Their violence is uncontrollable because it is 'without a subject: no one really commits it, no one is to blame.' Here, her argument gains momentum again:

> The divine violence of the nonhuman that affects us can really be anything. A serpent, a spider, a new bacterium or virus, a hurricane, permafrost melting in Siberia, radioactivity, forest fires, methane blow-outs: all these present us with an image that differs from our conventional understanding of violence as a negative agency of certain individuals or groups of human beings, including anthropomorphic gods.

In a cosmic framework, not just anthropogenic climate change is considered violence but also nonhuman excesses of energy that bring changes on a planetary level.

This line of thought continues into the second chapter on 'General Economy', where we finally return to the sun. Timofeeva argues here for the relevance of Bataille's unfinished project of a universal science for contemporary 'energy humanities', a new field that looks at ecological issues, such as global warming, waste or water pollution, from an interdisciplinary perspective. While Timofeeva refers to Imre Szeman's project, we might also think of Michael Marder's *Energy Dreams: Of Actuality* (2017). While energy is often regarded as a limited resource, Bataille emphasised 'the excess of energy, the ultimate source of which is the sun.' General economy, for Timofeeva, is driven by cosmic expenditure, generosity and surplus.

This 'superabundance of energy' is the main drive of a solar economy that models itself after the sun that 'gives without ever receiving'. At first sight, this project seems paradoxical as it aims to think beyond growth while promoting 'nonproductive expenditure'. However, with examples from wombats to the COVID19-virus, it becomes clearer what Timofeeva has in mind. The pandemic 'demonstrated how everything is connected on multiple levels – people and other animals, weather conditions, surfaces of objects, interfaces and infrastructures, currency rates, science, emotions, air pollution, cultural developments, and industry machines'. Where governments shut down their borders to protect their restrictive local economies and the bodies of their citizens, the virus travelled freely, indicating that the destructive excess of nonhuman violence is already at work.

The inherently solar nature of the universe is a kind of nonhuman, 'primordial togetherness', a collective life based on generosity, gratuitousness and solidarity. While contemporary capitalism is considered a 'restrictive economy', a revolutionary, solar economy in the spirit of Bataille suggests, for example, an immediate 'transfer of American wealth to India without reciprocation'. This claim might sound naive if we think of world economy as being shaped by nation states. It is not however from the perspective of the sun. If we take Bataille's claim seriously, it unveils the limitations and hypocrisy of ecological thought under global capitalism. For instance, environmentalists campaign globally to protect Brazil's Amazon, which is abundant with unused resources crucial for our ecosystem. On the other hand, the country is a developing economy that works towards catching up with the West. In the framework of restrictive capitalism, Brazil's economic development goes hand in hand with the destruction of the rainforest. Is not solar generosity as radical redistribution a reasonable solution here? Solarity both liberates the rainforest from being an exploitable resource and rebuts a capitalist myth of progress.

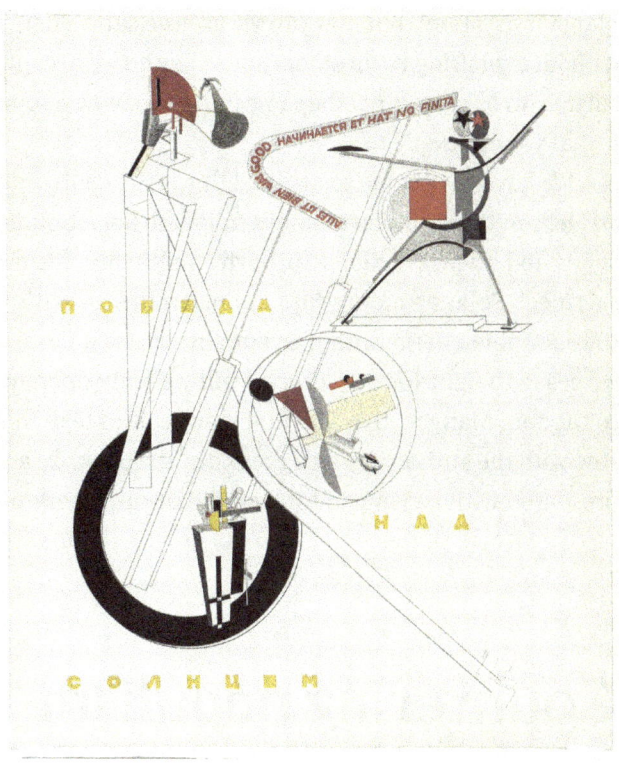

In the third chapter, 'Restrictive Violence of Capital', Timofeeva claims that phenomena like the pandemic or climate change, catastrophic for human life, are direct reactions of the nonhuman against 'the banal, normative, restrictive violence of capital.' As explored in the example of the Gaia paradigm, we should not read solar violence through an anthropomorphic lens. Solarity is not some wilful act of cosmic punishment but nature's indifference which poses a serious political threat to global capitalism. Another crucial point here is that solar generosity – or what she later calls 'sacrifice' – is unthinkable in a restrictive economy. We do not learn how to share by donating or working in co-working offices. These practices are 'a parody of gifts just as team-building in the office is a parody of collectivity.' Under capitalism, if we were as generous as the sun or the phoenix, 'alight like a living sun', we would ultimately die.

Instead of celebrating the sun, humanity traditionally aimed to colonise it, a tendency particularly central for early Soviet ideology of the new man, as exemplified by Russian Cosmism, astronautics and the futurist opera *Victory over the Sun* (1913). Timofeeva argues that a 'hypermasculine image of humanity as an all-powerful conqueror of the universe' persisted in both communist and capitalist modernity. This will to power makes sense in an economy with growing demand of energy. After all, the sun is 'the most powerful fusion reactor in our planetary system'. But how can we use the sun's energy without exploiting it? In other words, how do we become solar, if 'to be solar is not the same thing as having a solar cell in your pocket'?

We have to become solar – and this is the controversial lesson that Timofeeva draws from late Soviet philosophy and science-fiction – through an ultimate 'cosmic sacrifice'. Solar economy does not mean the transition to renewable energy within a capitalist system. Only if we cease to fight for our survival will we truly open up to the sun. Many readers will find it difficult to take this step with the author. Towards the end of the book, we are presented with a vision of total annihilation, emerging from Evald Ilyenkov's 'Cosmology of the Spirit'. In her reading, this heretical text of late Soviet Marxism marks 'a dialectical passage from the restrictive economy to the general on the cosmic scale.' In other words, we become solar through our own self-destruction, the entropic 'fire' which consumes our universe.

Is this all we are left with? Our political actions are nothing but 'offerings to the planetary debauchery irradiated by the sun'? This would be an underwhelming if not alarming diagnosis. The conclusion, 'The Sun is a Comrade', does not offer a more satisfying resolution either. Highlighting the significance of nonhuman violence for emancipatory struggle, *Solar Politics* instigates an important, refreshing shift of perspective on the disastrous ecological crisis we are facing. Yet how solar politics might concretely tackle this crisis remains a mystery until the end. Maybe efficient political action itself, and this might be one reading of the book, already vanished when viewed at a cosmic scale. Now, humanity has to facilitate its final transition into the nonhuman sphere, gloriously illuminated by the sun.

Isabel Jacobs

Countering populism

Paul K. Jones, *Critical Theory and Demagogic Populism* (Manchester: Manchester University Press, 2020). 288pp., £85.00 hb., £25.00 pb., 978 1 52612 343 5 hb., 978 1 52616 373 8 pb.

Jeremiah Morelock, ed, *How to Critique Authoritarian Populism: Methodologies of the Frankfurt School* (Chicago: Haymarket Books, 2022). 502pp., £25.99 pb., 978 1 64259 767 7

Although there is now a massive literature on the right-wing populisms that have reshaped politics over recent decades, debates continue as to whether we have really understood these movements, and the nature of their parties and leaders. Two new books consider how the Frankfurt School tradition, in particular, can help us assess – and oppose – today's authoritarian or demagogic populisms.

In *Critical Theory and Demagogic Populism*, Paul K. Jones focuses on the Studies in Prejudice programme which members of the Institute for Social Research worked on between 1943 and 1950, during their exile in the USA. He argues that whilst resulting work, especially *The Authoritarian Personality*, 'continues to exert influence in social psychological and political psychological studies of authoritarianism, it has rarely featured in the contemporary literature on populism'. Jones sees this as a field in which political science and political theory are unfortunately privileged over work by sociologists or social psychologists.

Jones draws on the Institute's analyses to illustrate certain shortcomings which he identifies in 'orthodox populism studies'. These include an underestimation of the role of modern media in shaping what Theodor Adorno called the 'physiognomics' of demagogy and the ways this is enabled by 'the culture industry'; populism's social psychological dimensions; and the importance of understanding any particular form of populism in relation to its specific political and social context, rather than presenting it as a phenomenon which disturbs that context as if from outside.

In substantial early chapters, Jones considers connections and differences between the most influential assessments of populism and critical theory. This allows him to correct some misrepresentations. Against those who say that critical theorists in the 1940s overemphasised individual psychological susceptibility to racism, Jones notes the 'division of labour' within Studies in Prejudice between research on 'followers', which is the focus of *The Authoritarian Personality* by Adorno and his co-authors (1950), and work on 'leaders', the best-known example of which is *Prophets of Deceit* by Leo Löwenthal and Norbert Guterman (1949) (both of these books were reissued by Verso in recent years).

He usefully highlights Adorno's argument that 'liberal exposure' or 'truth propaganda' is insufficient as a response to right-wing demagogy. Too much of the opposition to reactionary populism assumes that it can be discredited by calling out the cynical character of leaders' rhetorical devices or the 'incoherence' of their positions. Notions that Trump's appeals to his supporters or the 'attractions' of Brexit promoted by Farage and Johnson could be countered by 'fact checking' involve an over-reliance on liberal norms of journalism and imply the existence of an ideal 'informed citizen'. Overcoming this naivety, opposition to right-wing demagogy needs to recognise the powerful socio-psychological mechanisms which it activates and mobilises, for 'reasoned argument' is not effective, in itself, to resist the appeals of paranoia and 'false projection'. Jones notes the positive example provided by Adorno's tone and positioning: his critique is always 'directed against the contempt that the demagogue holds for the audience, rather than against that audience itself'.

This approach of continuing to respect people who fall under the influence of right-wing populists is exemplified in a previously unpublished version of the foreword to *Prophets of Deceit* by Adorno (1949), which Jones provides as an appendix. Adorno explains how racist demagogues' 'performance offers the audience vicarious gratifications', as they direct their appeal towards peoples' 'inner and largely unconscious mechanisms'. These are manipulated in ways which mean that they 'are to stay unconscious' so that audience members are 'prevented from gaining insight' into their 'real social interests'.

Across two chapters, Jones assesses the work of Ernesto Laclau and Stuart Hall, asking whether it is possible to bridge the 'considerable gulf' between their 'Gramscian' approaches and the Frankfurt School's work. He tracks the different positions taken by Laclau, Hall and Nicos Poulantzas at various times. One of his conclusions is that both Frankfurt School theorists and followers of the 'diverse Gramscian legacy' recognise the strong intersections between fascism and populism – a dynamic which 'completely vexes' today's 'orthodox' theorists of populism.

Part two of *Critical Theory and Demagogic Populism* explores how 'the culture industry' often serves 'as an alternative "crucible" of demagogues to the orthodox political sphere'. Jones takes account of the ways that cultural forms and communication technologies have developed over recent decades, including the shift away from serious journalism as 'the central means of political communication'. He begins with nuanced observations about how Adorno and Max Horkheimer actually conceived of 'the culture industry', as opposed to a 'cultural populist' caricature of their position as 'elitist' (Jones also makes careful distinctions between theorists and historians who have varied relationships to 'cultural populism'). Once onto his main theme, Jones argues that if the culture industry can indeed generate demagogues, then contestation of 'bad populism' needs to take 'a different shape from that usually advocated by critical analysis'. This 'usual' shape, which is in Jones' view largely ineffective, is that of 'learning and emulating "populist logics" as a counter-hegemonic practice' – a strategy that he identifies with the work of Hall and Laclau.

What should be done instead? Jones considers attempts to oppose demagogic populism through popular art. His examples include Edward R Murrow's television journalism which discredited the anti-communist Senator McCarthy in the mid-1950s, Elia Kazan's film *A Face in the Crowd* (1957) and The Who's 'rock opera' *Tommy*. He then provides a short but well-focussed account of 'Trumpian psychotechnics', underlining the extent to which Trump built on his reality TV profile and depended on Twitter and the Fox news channel. Jones concludes that, for all its new features, the dynamic of Trump's successes 'uncannily resembles' that identified by the

Institute for Social Research in the 1940s.

Given the 'integral relationship between modern means of communication and demagogic populism', recent and ongoing changes in the character of cultural production and the media raise new threats and questions. These are explored in Jones's final chapter (in which he also justifies his book's focus on the USA as a 'pivotal case' for the issues he has covered). Engaging critically with some of Jürgen Habermas's concepts, Jones notes that developments including the proliferation of private television channels and the growth and character of social media tend to disintegrate and splinter whatever was left of any shared 'public sphere'. Mainstream political communication 'faces the harsh reality that the "agenda-setting" role of journalism has declined dramatically and the institutional resources sustaining political journalism have shrunk'. This changing structural context adds to the risks of populist movements being captured by demagogic reactionaries: any potential counterforce provided by what remains of liberal and well-informed 'public sphere' resources is severely weakened, and we are without 'a global -counter-demagogic tradition'.

Jeremiah Morelock builds on his well-received collection *Critical Theory and Authoritarian Populism* (2018) with the pieces assembled in *How to Critique Authoritarian Populism*. Like Jones, Morelock aims to show how techniques and methodologies drawn from the Frankfurt School can be used to address reactionary politics today. The book's opening assertion that 'no other school of thought has focused so thoroughly on understanding and critiquing how authoritarian movements come to be embraced within liberal democracies' is tied to a three-fold explanation of why, nevertheless, this tradition remains on the margins rather than being in the mainstream of social sciences: its indigestible radical 'boldness'; its troublesome interdisciplinarity; and the ways it rejects the alternative 'poles' of positivist, empirical methodology and of interpretivist approaches which reproduce the relativism of postmodernism, at the same time as refusing the 'lazy pragmatism' which Morelock

(with Daniel Sullivan) defines as the currently dominant research paradigm, one which he castigates as a 'threat to the reflexive dialogue that actively promotes quality in academic work' and to critical thinking more generally.

It's in the nature of an edited collection that none of the twenty-three contributors have space for the complexity and detail which is found in Jones's arguments. If this makes most chapters in Morelock's book relatively accessible, this sometimes comes at the cost of oversimplification. (At the same time, there are some passages where tighter editing could have made unnecessarily difficult expositions considerably clearer.) The book's most regrettable stylistic-political misstep is that a couple of chapters conclude with attempts to cultivate the consolations which come from weakly-grounded optimism, a stratagem which was always foreign to Adorno and Horkheimer.

Most of the pieces, however, are clear and focused, accurately describing the arguments of a range of Frankfurt School figures and discussing these in relation to current challenges. In the book's first part, on 'philosophical methodologies and foundations', David Norman Smith provides interesting historical information. Detailing how understandings of commodity fetishism and characterological authoritarianism were properly elaborated for the first time in the 1920s, Smith highlights the contribution of lesser-known activists and scholars to the Frankfurt School's early work, including Hilde Weiss and the School's benefactor, Felix Weil. Smith also underlines the significance of two Marxists who are very well known, but whose direct contribution has routinely been downplayed. The standard histories by Martin Jay and Rolf Wiggershaus record that Karl Korsch and Georg Lukács spoke at the 1923 Marxist Study Week which effectively inaugurated the Institute for Social Research, but I had not registered, until reading Smith's chapter, that 'between them, [Korsch and Lukács] contributed nearly twenty per cent of the total pages' to the Institute's journal between 1924 and 1931. These essays on 'reification, alienation and commodity fetishism ... sprang from and shaped Institute preoccupations'. (Another unfortunate editorial lapse means that such important points are not easily re-referenced: there is no mention in the index of Korsch, Lukács, Weil or Weiss).

Lauren Langman and Avery Schatz provide one of the key chapters in the second part of the book, drawing out the importance of psychoanalytic thought in Frankfurt School work. They focus on the interplay between 'irrational claims', conspiracy theories and authoritarian politics, building on a clear statement of the widely-held understanding that 'times of crisis evoke ... fear, "extinction anxiety", anger, *ressentiment*, and shame' which are then projected onto enemies – so-called elites 'above' and, 'below', minority groups who already face multiple forms of discrimination, marginalisation and oppression. Langman and Schatz trace how 'psychodynamic processes transform both the emotion (from shame to anger ...) and intentional object (from self to other) with the purpose of protecting the vulnerable self'. Authoritarian populists consciously craft their rhetoric to connect to these processes: 'repressed shame therefore constitutes a social mechanism that may mediate between the emotional patterns of contemporary society ... and support for right-wing populist parties'.

Gregory Joseph Menillo develops this theme with a consideration of 'the psychoanalytic framework' which key members of the Institute for Social Research used to 'link the culture industry with fascism'. In the decades after the Second World War, Adorno applied the concepts of standardisation and 'pseudo-individualisation' in his insistence that 'modern, mass consumer culture' is 'animated by ... authoritarian dynamics'. Menillo quotes Fredric Jameson's observation that Adorno saw the Allies' 1945 victory as involving 'the triumph of the culture industry over Nazism', so that the shift from the 1930s-40s to the 1950s-60s was 'perhaps better understood as a "variation within a single paradigm, rather than the victory of one paradigm over another"'.

Rudolf J Seibert, Michael R Ott and Dustin J Byrd seek to combine Frankfurt School approaches with critical political theology, drawing from the work of Johann Baptist Metz and others. They propose that religion continues to carry the 'potential for the revolutionary creation of a more reconciled, humane and peace-filled society'. Realising this would mean translating the 'liberating, prophetic, Messianic and eschatological substance of religion into rational, revolutionary secular theory and praxis of societal change'. By contrast, A K Thompson's arguments on religion are more concretely grounded. Considering the importance of a version of Christianity to 'the historical bloc now galvanised around the Republican Party', he notes that the religious beliefs which are organised in this way are 'internally riven and politically ambivalent'. This creates the possibility of progressive activists 'exacerbating the factional schisms' within the 'current Christian bloc', a task which Thompson argues would involve 'provisionally accepting the desires that animated the initial wishful attachment' to Christianity before demonstrating that these 'desires ... cannot be resolved within the terms set out by Christianity itself', thus pushing 'toward left conclusions'.

The book's main theme is resumed in part three, which surveys empirical work carried out by Frankfurt School figures, including Erich Fromm's 1930s study of working-class attitudes in Weimar Germany, the United States programmes and the 1950s 'group experiments' back in Germany, which revealed the ongoing persistence of authoritarian attitudes in spite of 'de-Nazification'. These extensive studies, which have been relatively little considered, provide evidence that the 'pessimism' and critical insights of Horkheimer and Adorno were grounded in concrete research to a greater degree than allowed by 'conventional narratives', which suggest that they 'abandoned empiricism ... in favour of pure theory'. Sullivan argues that there is still much to draw from this work, not only through recovering the riches of raw data held in archives, but more importantly by learning from 'the methods' which Frankfurt School researchers 'constructed for probing the interplay between unconscious individual and mass-sociological factors in the emergence and sustenation of authoritarianism'. Christopher Craig Brittain's chapter is a stimulating illustration of how such methods can be deployed, showing how Trump's unclear and inconsistent rhetoric helped him engage his audiences, not in spite of but *because of* the 'uncontrollability' of his messages.

The fourth and final section of *How to Critique Authoritarian Populism* examines 'strategies for interpreting different types of media artefacts and discourses'. It takes in discussion of Siegfried Kracauer's work on film, and insights into how the categories used in *Prophets of Deceit* can be 'extrapolated' to identify 'agitator-like qualities' in politics today. Stefanie Baumann critiques contemporary documentary films: she observes that a significant number of 'big commercial productions' have uncovered 'shocking scandals', arguing that their format can nevertheless work against the cultivation of critical thinking, by inciting 'the viewer to subordinate herself to the authority of the provided information and its explanation rather than leaving space for her own interpretation'. Panayota Gounari offers a reading of Herbert Marcuse in order to pinpoint features of 'one-dimensional discourse' which can sharpen our analysis of the styles and languages of social media 'in the context of authoritarian capitalist societies'. These include dehistoricisation, operationalist and aggressive language, the cultivation of the self as a brand, and the 'discourse of amusement'.

Douglas Kellner's short afterword emphasises the current relevance of *How to Critique Authoritarian Populism*. As Morelock and Sullivan argue, the volume demonstrates that the legacy of the early Frankfurt School is an important resource, 'a massive, powerful, multi-dimensional, transdisciplinary collection of methodologies to aid in the ongoing struggle against authoritarianism and authoritarian populism in late capitalist society'.

Recent events underline how important that struggle is. The electoral success of Giorgia Meloni's Brothers of Italy proves that activists with neo-fascist roots can come in from the margins to displace 'mainstream' politicians. The current moment in the (dis) United Kingdom's ongoing 'great moving right show' illustrates that long-established parties can be reshaped around ever-more regressive policies. Both books reviewed here direct us to what are therefore urgent problems: what explains the attractions of authoritarian reaction? How do we act through our politics, social movements and cultural interventions to effectively counter the right and advance a progressive agenda? Jones and Morelock provide rich evidence that the concerns and arguments which Horkheimer, Adorno, Löwenthal and their colleagues developed seventy years ago and more can offer starting points to meet key challenges of our time.

Mike Makin-Waite

Cracks and crevices

Sebastian Truskolaski, *Adorno and the Ban on Images* (London: Bloomsbury, 2021). 232pp., £85.00 hb., £28.99 pb., 978 1 35012 920 7 hb., 978 1 35012 9 221 pb.

These notes are from Beethoven's Fifth Symphony in C Minor, written between 1804 and 1808. Even listeners who do not read music can easily recognise the melody. It is so easy to understand and memorable, that, as a joke, in a season 16 episode of *The Simpsons* called 'The Seven Beer Snitch', the audience leaves after the first four notes are played, having heard 'the good part'. Theodor Adorno was opposed to those types of works. In his view, they represent an objective, rational and organised form that create an illusion of utopia, of natural harmony between the individual and the whole, which leads to the assimilation of the individual and thus also to their suffering, both physically and mentally.

While many studies have been conducted on the importance that Adorno attributed to breaking this kind of representation in music (after all, he dreamt of becoming a composer himself and wrote more essays about music than any other field), *Adorno and the Ban on Images* focuses on a matter whose significance has been largely overlooked: Adorno's criticism of images, or as Sebastian Truskolaski puts it, the image ban 'as a leitmotif in Adorno's thought'.

The book glides smoothly and clearly between Adorno's infamously difficult writings, his more and lesser-known works, his discussions of philosophy, art and politics, the critiques of his predecessors and dialogues with his acquaintances, and reconstructs Adorno's philosophy so that it answers what Truskolaski sees as the central challenge of modern philosophy: 'how to imagine a world beyond suffering and injustice, without simultaneously, betraying its vital impulse'. In order to answer this question, the book offers a rearrangement of Adorno's 'uneasily systematic anti-system around the notion of imagelessness', that is, around 'a thinking which resists representation'. This resistance is precisely what allows the kind of philosophy that Adorno wishes to practice: 'the attempt to contemplate all things as they would present themselves from the standpoint of redemption', as Adorno puts it in *Minima Moralia*.

The book sets out from the biblical story of Moses descending from Mount Sinai after receiving from God the tablets containing the Ten Commandments, only to find the Israelites worshiping a golden calf. Moses then smashes the tablets in anger, and commands in the name of God: 'Thou shalt not make unto thee any graven image'. Adorno's invocation of a biblical motif is rather surprising. Religion didn't play a major part in his upbringing, and, as Truskolaski points out, Adorno's understanding of Judaism and Christianity 'owes more to the acquaintance with Benjamin and Kierkegaard respectively, than it does to the Talmud or any catechism'.

Truskolaski nevertheless transforms Adorno's image ban into a 'potent philosophical device', which signals Adorno's commitment to a mode of philosophical critique 'which aims to hold open the possibility that things might yet be otherwise'. He suggests using the commandment against making images to short-circuit the historical dynamic outlined in *Dialectic of Enlightenment*. It is possible, in other words, 'to invoke the image ban – in its capacity as a philosophical-historical marker, rather than a theological edict – to formulate a critical theory of the present'.

For Adorno, this present included two world wars, the Holocaust and totalitarian regimes, as well as repressive features of everyday life under capitalism, in which the individual was more isolated than ever, alienated from nature, society and himself. It is the grave cost of the long-lasting struggle of man against nature depicted in *Dialectic of Enlightenment*. Human beings assert their place in the world through the mastery of nature, and by doing so denying their own ties to nature. This struggle 'must also be seen as the struggle against oneself'. The internalised sense of domination, in other words, returns as the calamitous revenge of repressed nature: the domination of human beings over each other.

As analysed in the book, this dialectics of human control over nature, which returns to it like a boomerang, was made possible by the asymmetry between subject and the object, as subjects find different and more efficient ways to exploit objects. Truskolaski interprets and illustrates this issue, showing how, for Adorno, different theories of representation approached the relation between subjects and objects (be they political, grammatical or epistemological) in a way that only widens the asymmetry between them. In Lenin and Engels' views, for example, the 'external world' appears as a mere fact, a rigid system wherein humankind is 'limited to a mere mirroring of the factual'. This elevation of matter to an ontological invariant is used, in Adorno's view, to justify a political configuration where 'governmental terror machines entrench themselves as permanent institutions' thus 'mocking the theory they carry on their lips'. Kant's view is given as another example of the deterioration of the relation of subjects to objects. Kant's theory that the world appears before us as formed by our sensory and intellectual perceptions, so that the objects within it as they are in themselves are unknowable except through an extra-human perspective, which we have no access to, leads to a reification of the subject: 'Subject reduces the object to itself; subject swallows object, forgetting how much it is object itself'.

The book also restructures Adorno's critique of religious representations. Adorno addresses not only the attack of faith by reason in eighteenth-century Europe, but also the turn to religion out of a dissatisfaction with reason in 1950s West Germany, which he interprets as a 'false sense of consolation' and, ultimately, a 'capitalist cult religion', as Truskolaski puts it with a nod to Walter Benjamin. Religion designates what Freud has called a 'system of thought', and, in any case, for Adorno and Horkheimer, there can be no positive representation of 'the absolutely good'. For Truskolaski's Adorno, the yearning for transcendence is potentially emancipatory, but it too runs the danger of reverting into its opposite. The image ban might thus be read as an expression of the sense that something more may be possible.

And so, there is supposed to be another possibility to rethink the subject's coercive gaze, its exploitation of objects, and its positive representations, which only reinforce the damaged life. 'Such a relation between subject and object is not set in stone', but in order to change it, we must reject certain modes of representation, as well as the systems they prop up, and at the same time change our perspective, our standpoint. Instead of trying to represent an external object, be it nature or God, we think the possibility of social transformation from within, through the 'rifts and crevices' of damaged life, or – as Adorno puts it in 'Notes on Kafka' – through the 'cracks and deformations of the modern age'. This will be the standpoint of redemption.

Adorno's goal, as Truskolaski interprets it, is thus to find a different way of thinking, and the image ban is a 'strategic, provisional figure for the kind of thinking that Adorno has in mind'. This point, too, is convincingly demonstrated throughout the book. It is a type of thinking that rejects 'representational thinking', a thinking that thinks thought 'against itself'. This rejection is precisely where Adorno's utopian dimension is realised, as this un-representation, or negative representation, manages best to express the aforementioned 'rifts and crevices' of damaged life. It manages to intimate 'what *ought* to be: a world free from domination, coercion and suffering'.

One of the quotes most identified with Adorno appears at the end of his essay 'Cultural Criticism and Society', where he claims: 'To write poetry after Auschwitz is barbaric'. This is a statement he would later retract. 'Perennial suffering', he says in *Negative Dialectics*, 'has as much right to expression as a tortured man has to scream.' Adorno goes on to formulate a 'new categorical imperative': 'to arrange their thoughts and actions so that Auschwitz will not repeat itself, so that nothing similar will happen'. In order to represent suffering, or 'the voice of the victim', as Adorno puts it in one of his lectures in 1958, one must ban positive representations of what is to take its place. As Truskolaski puts it: 'Presenting what *is* in such a way that it yields what *ought* to be is the basic movement of Adorno's thinking'.

Works of art, as shown in the book, must follow this guideline. Art is perceived by Adorno as a kind of immanent overturning of ideology, which is viewed as 'untruth' or 'false consciousness' forced from the top down, expressing the attempt of the powers-that-be to justify the capitalist mode of production in order to maintain the existing social order. Art 'manifests' and 'criticises' this ideology of untruth from within, if it manages to present what *is* in such a way that it yields what *ought* to be. That is, art, in its status as an independent cognitive action, is ascribed a principled oppositional task in relation to the contemporary social being. Being autonomous, it embodies opposition to reality and negation of the existing social situation. 'The profound force of resistance' that Adorno ascribes to certain artistic renditions lies in their particular ability to 'negatively intimate an "imageless image of Utopia" as something beautiful'.

Much criticism of Adorno, much of it justified, is that his theory remains a mere theory without providing ways for action, and, moreover, that his theory thwarts the possibility of action. When asked in an interview with the German magazine *Der Spiegel*, three months before his death, 'But how would one go about changing societal totality without individual action?', he replied: 'I do not know. I can only analyze relentlessly what is. In the process, I am reproached in the following manner: "If you criticize, you have to say how to do better", but I consider this a bourgeois prejudice.' Truskolaski is of course aware of this criticism, and cites Adorno's words from 'Marginalia on Theory and Praxis' where he identifies the division between thought and action with the separation of subject and object. 'Just as the division of subject and object cannot be revoked immediately by a decree of thought, so too an immediate unity of theory and praxis is hardly possible: it would imitate the false identity of subject and object and would perpetuate the principle of domination that posits identity and that a true praxis must oppose.'

Truskolaski's book offers, on behalf of Adorno, another answer to this critique, an answer that is a kind of compromise between passive theory and active action: active thinking. As opposed to Beethoven's Fifth Symphony in C Minor, Arnold Schoenberg's music is given by Adorno as an example of a music that manages to dismantle the sense of cohesion and organicity in Western classical music, thus representing the continuing suffering. Adorno's admiration for the composer stems from Schoenberg being able to shatter the familiar experience, the pleasant melody, and demand the listener's active participation. It 'requires the listener to spontaneously compose his inner movement and demands of him not contemplation but praxis.' Adorno's image ban, as the book shows, does exactly this: it requires from us an active way of approaching and thinking about nature, images, representations, and thus serves as a philosophical critique 'which aims to hold open the possibility that things might yet be otherwise'.

Hedy Cohen

Witchcraft as praxis

Jack Z. Bratich, *On Microfascism: Gender, War, and Death* (Philadelphia: Common Notions, 2022). 240pp., $20 pb., 978 1 94217 349 6

Unacquainted readers may think that 'microfascism' is perhaps analogous to contemporary terms such as 'microaggression': the prefix 'micro' implying a simple reduction in scale and scope for actions representing larger systems. But *microfascism is not just small fascism*. If fascism is a certain arrangement and organisation of material, political and social institutions, microfascism is relegated to the realm of subjectivity. Inspired by Deleuze and Guattari's exploration of the idea, Bratich gives three main characteristics of microfascism: '1) it takes place "before" but really *in* excess of the state; 2) it exists in minds but moreover in desires, bodies and practices; and 3) it is composed in culture to create individual and collective actions with their own specific fascist results'. Microfascism does nevertheless have common traits with its ideological namesake. The driving philosophical motor behind both fascism and microfascism is the same: palingenetic restoration/renewal – or, in other words, 'the continuous revival and return of the "original"' – and eliminationism.

In a fascist framework, these terms can be grasped with basic examples. One could equate palingenetic restoration/renewal to the obsession with enabling the 'Aryan race' to thrive through military power and geographical living space. Palingenetic eliminationism can be understood as the attitude Nazi Germany would have towards various groups that were deemed antagonistic toward Aryan flourishing: Jews, Roma, the disabled, communists, homosexuals, etc. What becomes more difficult is understanding these terms in a microfascist framework, which is what most of the book aims to achieve. The object of restoration/renewal is much more elusive within microfascism because it is the individual subjectivity of each microfascist. The palingenetic restoration/renewal of individual subjectivity results in what Bratich calls the 'autogenetic sovereign', more commonly known as the 'self-made man'; or the 'subject [that] can create itself *ex nihilo*'.

Palingenetic eliminationism also receives an extra layer of complexity when moving into microfascism. Under fascism, enemies are eliminated through various means of total annihilation: extermination, euthanisation and castration. Under microfascism, however, simple annihilation is no longer possible. Bratich argues throughout the book that within microfascism, the primordial antagonism, the dialectical *sine qua non*, is gender. Autogenetic sovereign men are carrying out eliminationism against women. The problem, then, is simply logistical: men cannot annihilate all women because they are required for the perpetuation of humanity. But for Bratich, gendered eliminationism doesn't have to be an unequivocal death sentence. It can be a long term neutralisation, a 'slow death' or 'a reduction of capacities *towards* the null'. The microfascist is thus in a constant struggle to the death with women without having the option of adopting the large-scale, industrial eliminationism seen under twentieth-century fascism. From this tension comes a new form of eliminationism: microfascist *flight*. Following Julius Evola's teachings, the microfascist views the material realm as the 'domination of Mother Earth and the Mothers of life and fertility'. The trajectory of microfascism is that of a 'flight from materiality into abstractions, even spiritual forms'.

In addition to a philosophical analysis of microfascism, Bratich looks at various real-world expressions of it. These examples are not purely pedagogical. Indeed, there is a sense of urgency and responsibility to Bratich's project which is found within the first pages of the introduction. He argues that fascism is elusive and constantly undergoing transformations in order to survive, an idea which is at odds with how fascism is commonly seen historically: that is, as an event of the first half of the twentieth century, in the past, to be studied. For Bratich, fascism is much more resilient than conventional historical narratives would imply, and so, as with fascism, it is important to understand microfascism as it exists in the present. To do so, he explores the three main areas of microfascist expression: gender, war and death. He is careful to use contemporary examples in each section to reinforce the idea of an alive and present threat.

For gender, one of the most insightful examples Bratich looks at is that of the problem of female reproductivity. Indeed, the need for women to (ironically) produce self-made men is a barrier toward eliminationism. Due to this, microfascism seeks to take control of women's power of reproduction, to the point where 'females [are made] redundant in the very sphere where they are made indispensable – that of reproduction'. This is perhaps the primary goal of patriarchy as a whole: disempowering women to the point where they can no longer contest men over matters of reproduction. Because if women have any degree of autonomy over reproduction, then men are bound to the material world. In claiming the power of reproduction for themselves by eliminating women (either literally or effectively), men will vanquish materiality and enable a deeper dive into abstraction. One tactic is to culturally control women's sexuality, to promote a kind of sexuality that is suitable to the microfascist, and to severely punish dissidents. Such a reaction was seen in the 2021 Atlanta spa shootings which were carried out due to the killer's 'need to eliminate temptation by sex workers'. The shootings were also a retaliation against the women's autonomy over their bodies, which are inseparable from reproductive power for the microfascist. Bratich shows that when the slow (cultural) death is not sufficient, current-day microfascism can turn to the physical annihilation typical to twentieth-century fascism.

Despite never entering an all-out military war with its foes (unlike fascism), microfascists constantly define themselves through the language of warfare. This is because microfascism relies on a state of perpetual struggle; without struggle there is no space for the material man to renew himself through abstraction and become the autogenetic sovereign. Bratich will look at the different formations microfascists take in preparation for war: the decentralised, but not isolated, lone wolf; the mass shooter as influencer or 'inspo-shooter' for future shooters; the 'loosely auto-organized … and quasi-independent' groupuscules; and the cultural unit of the squad. Each formation will come with its own empirical examples, from shooter manifestos to the 'Army for Trump'. But of all these formations, the most interesting is undoubtedly that of the Männerbund. Translated typically as '"warrior societies", "warrior bands", "military confraternities", or "men's societies"', the Männerbund combines at once the gender and war aspects of microfascism. While the other formations do not require a certain relationship with gender, the Männerbund is defined by it. Looking once again at Julius Evola, Bratich finds that 'entry into the Männerbund is thoroughly masculinized against the feminine, resulting in a "higher man" who functions via war as autogenetic sovereignty'. Bratich looks at contemporary forms of initiation into the Männerbund, most notably redpilling. What he finds is that these warlike initiation rituals revolve once again around a specific 'gender conversion', where men undergo a 'manospheric metamorphosis' upon seeing the 'truth' about 'feminism's pernicious effects, grounded in misandry'. The gendered aspect of microfascism is both fundamental and ubiquitous.

The last element of microfascism that Braitch studies is necrotics or, more simply, death. Death is central to the microfascist dialectic. Bratich relates various elements of socio-political life to death through contemporary terms and some neologisms: 'necropolitics' and 'necropolitical sovereignty'; microfascism as a 'deathstyle' rather than a lifestyle; 'necrocapitalism' and 'necro-economics'; the 'Necrocene' instead of the Anthropocene; and, finally, the heavily gendered 'necrophilia'. The picture that Bratich paints is clear – under microfascism, everything is made to die and death is what gives the microfascist his *élan vital*. The creation of the autogenetic sovereign relies on the death of all things surrounding it, such as women, the economy, civil society, even the planet itself. With this penultimate chapter, Bratich shows that the implications of microfascism are anything but microscopic.

Having given his account of microfascism as a relevant force in today's world, Bratich can begin his discussion of micro-antifascist/anti-microfascist praxis, which is perhaps the most important part of the book. For Bratich, there is no sense in offering a philosophical analysis of microfascism. Given how prevalent microfascism is in today's world and the destructive effects it has, Bratich argues that it is necessary to discuss forms of micro-antifascist praxis in addition to any analysis.

While the idea will be attractive to the politically-oriented reader, the actual content of this chapter proves to be disappointing. Instead of offering real avenues for political praxis, Bratich simply presents more philosophical analysis under the guise of praxis. What the chapter provides is an exploration of what is the inverse of microfascism in today's world. Bratich does not guide the reader in ways to combat microfascism; he is content with outlining the philosophical counters or 'doublings' to it. This analysis culminates with Bratich's discussion of witchcraft. He argues that the witch is the ultimate inversion of the microfascist: where he seeks the abstract, she seeks the concrete; where he venerates death, she venerates life; where he flees mimesis and materiality, she flees hyperindividualisation and exclusion. This may be philosophically powerful, but where is the praxis? What is Bratich's practical advice to readers? To become witches? Or to integrate witchcraft into culture to compete with microfascist culture? If so, then how must this be done? What are the avenues to pursue for the anti-microfascist? Are they social? Institutional? Political? The closest Bratich gets to suggesting any practical approach is to 'reappropriate humour, play, and platforms to preempt forms of microfascism from crystallizing'. But again, this form of praxis is much closer to analysis than a practical handbook.

Outside of the substance of Bratich's book, there is another problem that arises when evaluating its practical ambitions. *On Microfascism* has a distinct formal issue. For a book that repeatedly reminds us of the importance of praxis, it is surprisingly inaccessible to the reader. This is not because the substantive ideas are exceedingly complex, but because the form in which they are presented is unnecessarily abstract and inaccessible, to the point where accessing the substance becomes its own challenge while reading. Despite Bratich's attempt to separate the book into three sections (gender, war and death), gender is always at the forefront. When discussing war, Bratich is in fact discussing the war against women. When discussing death, it is a death fuelled by gendered conceptions of the material, spiritual and social world. Because of this constant return to gender, the internal organisation of chapters three and four, on war and necrotics, becomes elusive and ambiguous. There is no argumentative line to follow; instead, Bratich gives more detailed and niche examples of the different gendered aspects of microfascism.

This movement toward the niche brings with it its own set of problems. Bratich indulges too heavily in philosophical neologisms and jargon in an endless effort to connect the different aspects of microfascism to gender in a novel manner. Many of these neologisms will appear a single time in the book and will never be referenced or used again. In more egregious cases, Bratich will make use of very specific jargon but will not explain the meaning of the terms he uses until twenty, thirty, or even forty pages later, if at all. There is a tragic irony behind the idea that one must be experienced in philosophy to even be able to read a book that so fervently preaches the importance of real-world praxis and practicality. And this is, ultimately, the biggest disappointment of *On Microfascism*.

Takin Raisifard

Crises and contradictions

'Marx and Capitalism', the Deutsches Historisches Museum, Berlin, February – August 2022

Rachel Pafe

In an August 1890 letter to Conrad Schmidt, Engels remarked: 'Just as Marx used to say, commenting on the French "Marxist" of the late [18]70s: "All I know is that I am not a Marxist".' Even during his lifetime there was a tension between what Marx himself wrote and thought and what his followers made of it. There is a similar tension, too, between Marx's ideas at various points in his life, which can sometimes seem diametrically opposed. The recent 'Marx and Capitalism' exhibition at the German Historical Museum in Berlin is a response to these tensions, more particularly between, on the one hand, Marx the man and, on the other, Marxism as a reaction to crises and capitalism in the nineteenth century, and as a political ideology in the twentieth century.

The exhibition responds to renewed mainstream discussions of Marx following the 2008 economic crisis, with a focus on the need to separate the contemporary relevance of Marx's thought from its abuses in twentieth-century Communist movements. But it equally questions Marx's applicability in the present, ending with a photo gallery of violent dictatorships and post-2008 anti-capitalist protest movements without explanatory text. The exhibition is keen to present the contradictions of Marx's thoughts and interactions whenever it can. However, it completely forfeits the dialectical leap to any overcoming of them, preferring instead to revel in them and signs of failure and obsolescence. As a consequence, it paints a portrait of Marx for a general audience that functions to dismiss him as an ultimately irrelevant figure, whose thought begins and ends in the nineteenth century. This picture and its shortcomings are particularly evident in the exhibition's shallow treatment of Judaism and antisemitism, colonialism, women's voices and Marxist thought.

Marx had many sides. Born to a formerly Jewish, converted Lutheran family in Trier in 1818, he was a philosopher, economist, historian, journalist, political theorist and Communist revolutionary. The exhibition tries to organise all this into a chronological timeline divided by main thematic clusters, ranging from Marx's thoughts on religion and ecology to journalistic and political responses to revolutions and violence in industrialised Europe and America. It describes how, after moving to Berlin in 1836, Marx married theatre critic and political activist Jenny von Westphalen, who was to become a key collaborator and editor of his writing. Berlin was the site of Marx's involvement with the Young Hegelians, where he was especially close to Bruno Bauer, with whom he co-edited Hegel's *Philosophy of Religion*. After completing his PhD at the University of Jena, Marx turned his attention to journalism, first in Cologne in 1842 and then in Paris in 1843. Marx's life is mainly explored through the articles and correspondence that he began to write around this time and which he continued to produce throughout his life.

In Paris, Marx was active in left-wing French-German journalism, met lifelong friend and collaborator Engels, and began his intensive studies of political economy. These activities forced him to move to Brussels in 1845, where he met other exiled socialists from across Europe. It was during this period that Marx and Engels refined their concept of historical materialism, were active with the Communist League, and wrote their 1848 *Communist Manifesto* in the shadow of the Revolutions of 1848 that roiled Europe. Marx established the *Neue Rheinische Zeitung* in 1848 as a means to interpret and comment upon this turmoil, but was soon forced into his final exile in London in 1849. Here Marx split with the Communist League over the issue of how to enact Europe-wide revolution, contributed to international newspapers and became interested in the United States. In 1864 he joined the First International and in 1867 he published the first volume of *Das Kapital*, the later volumes of which were published after his death in 1883.

This timeline is framed by an overarching concern for how Marx and his thought were affected by the crisis and instability caused by modern Europe's rapid industrialisation and its various discontents. It underlines that while Marx adapted and changed in response to each crisis, his thought, as the final panel on Marx's historical impact rather banally puts it, remained 'contradictory and fragmentary'. Such examples include Marx's simultaneous call for violent revolution and for cooperation with the revolutionary bourgeoisie in the struggle against monarchic rule. The exhibition also details how Marx coined the term 'capitalist mode of production' as a response to the first worldwide economic crisis in 1857, which Marx hoped would trigger a wider collapse, yet later distanced himself from this idea and instead admitted that crisis is built into capitalism itself. Beyond the obvious insight that Marx grew as a thinker and changed his mind throughout his life, these moments are presented as simply contradictory in character rather than as dialectical in their approach to strategy.

The exhibition is studded with a range of objects from the nineteenth century, including paintings, drawings, factory equipment, Marx's personal objects, several taxidermised animals and a chess game, as well as installations. Several large pieces of factory equipment dominate a large room in which raucous factory sounds echo across tattered red banners, and one can retire to a corner to experience 'the smell of capitalism', a heady mix of sweat, metal and money. While objects are intended to be didactic, they sometimes simplify concepts to the point of distortion, such as an interactive installation on surplus value in which viewers must pump water and receive only a trickle.

The exhibition's strategy for presenting contradictions is exemplified in the exhibition's first sections dealing with religion, antisemitism and 'The Jewish Question'.

It begins with young Marx's feelings about religion, detailing how he drew on Feuerbach's idea of religion as a human invention and saw all broader criticism as departing from the critique of religion. Marx's critique of the abuses of Christianity by European monarchs is used to underline his interest in religion as mainly a metaphor of illusion and control, useful for challenging the feelings of alienation and powerlessness elicited by capitalist modes of production. The following section places these broader thoughts on religion within the context of eighteenth- and nineteenth-century Jewish emancipation in Europe and rising anti-Semitism connected to restrictions on Jewish communities who were forced into banking and commerce. The close juxtaposition of the critique of religion and antisemitism sections seems to suggest that the thread of religion, so centrally important to Marx's broader societal critique, was inherently tainted by its casual use of antisemitic tropes that reinforced the precarious situation of Jewish people at this time. This section presents antisemitic cartoons, a picture of the Jewish grave of Marx's grandfather and includes Marx's letters to Engels in the 1860s in which he uses antisemitic language. Jewish socialist philosopher Moses Hess' *Rome and Jerusalem: A Study in Jewish Nationalism*, an early call for a Jewish nation state in response to European antisemitism, is there together with French socialist Alphonse Toussenel's 1845 *The Jews, Kings of the Epoch: A History of Finance Feudalism*, an antisemitic criticism of capitalism in the 1840s that describes Jews as parasites primed for world domination. It ends with a short overview of Marx's 1843 'Zur Judenfrage' (The Jewish Question) essay, in which he proposes that emancipation from Jewish concepts that have infected bourgeois society is the first step to a broader human emancipation in which all particular religions would cease to exist. In this section, as in the earlier examples, the 'contradictions' do not lead to any synthetic insight – for instance, a reflection on what assimilation meant for Marx.

In the Judenfrage corner, two white busts of Marx face off against each other. Quotes floating above each statue illustrate Marx's desire for Jewish assimilation as part of universal emancipation versus his use of antisemitic stereotypes that associate Jews with commerce. Certainly, the essay can easily be read as an example of antisemitism. 'What is the secular basis of Judaism', Marx wonders. 'Practical need, self-interest. What is the worldly religion of the Jew? Huckstering. What is his worldly god? Money.' Attempts to interpret Marx's relationship to Judaism typically either try to describe his thought as containing a concealed Jewish messianism or position 'Zur Judenfrage' as a document of Marx's antisemitism. But the exhibition fails to answer what looking at this small part of Marx's thought in a specifically nineteenth-century context actually reveals.

As Enzo Traverso argues in *The Jewish Question: History of a Marxist Debate*, Marx posits the Jewish Question as mainly an issue of the sublation of Judaism into a universal framework to create political equality between Jews and Christians in order to work on broader human emancipation. Marx does not mention the discrimination affecting Jewish communities. The Jew is rather a symbolic, supra-historical figure tied to banking and commerce. But Marx's desire to sublate Judaism has to be understood in the context of a broader generation of German-Jewish intellectuals who hoped for greater Jewish rights. This history was linked to the seventeenth- and eighteenth-century formation of a wealthy class of Prussian Jewish state bankers and 'court Jews' dependent on political sovereigns, and, subsequently, the creation of an intellectual middle class in the wake of various early to mid-nineteenth-century Jewish emancipation laws passed throughout the German states. Hannah Arendt describes this tension as one in which the status of the court Jews was kept in place while most Prussian intellectuals chose the path of converting to Lutheran Protestantism in the attempt to fully participate in German cultural and political life. Yet as convert Ludwig Börne (né Loeb Baruch) wrote several years after his conversion, 'Some reproach me for being a Jew, some praise me because of it, some pardon me for it, but all think of it.'

Marx, also a converted Protestant Lutheran, was part of this group of Prussian intellectuals who sought to escape their Jewish roots in the hope of equal participation. Despite these efforts, they were continually confronted with their Jewish past. It is in this setting that 'Zur Judenfrage' must be understood. On the one hand, it is part of a specific history of the desire for equality and assimilation on the part of nineteenth-century intellectuals who were never able to escape their associations with Judaism. On the other, it brings up the question of how 'assimilated' Marx could have ever become. Can Jewish radicals ever truly assimilate or do they just conveniently swap out one state of apostasy for another?

While one could argue that an exhibition on the entirety of Marx's life cannot devote such extensive attention to Judaism and antisemitism, the lack of detail is particularly striking given the exhaustive space that the downstairs 'Richard Wagner and the Nationalization of Feeling' exhibition devotes to völkisch antisemitism.

The German Historical Museum frames their Marx and Wagner exhibitions as part of their 2022 preoccupation with capitalism, stating, 'Like Marx, Richard Wagner was also a critic of the modern economy'. It likewise describes Wagner in language that strikingly echoes many of the upstairs descriptions of Marx, as a 'Composer and theatre reformer, court music director and festival founder, revolutionary and exile, entrepreneur and capitalism critic, debtor and anti-Semite.' The Wagner exhibition is voluminous and sensual in comparison to that of Marx. Diaphanous curtains hide nineteenth-century German cultural figures and soft pink neon words categorise the emotional nuances of Wagner's feelings on Germanness. The comparatively sparse nature of the Marx exhibition raises the question of why more space was not devoted to his side of the antisemitism debate. The juxtaposition of the two exhibitions runs the risk of normalising Wagner's racist antisemitism by perpetuating the idea that, from left to right, antisemitism was everywhere in the nineteenth century.

The failure to explore the nuances of Marx's thought extends beyond the lonely Judenfrage corner to the small colonialism and women's rights sections. These are treated as mere appendices to the canonical events in Marx's life, and are indicative of the exhibition's failure to discuss how Marxist thought shifted and changed in the years after Marx's death, especially with regard to feminism, colonialism, post-colonialism and race.

The 'Modernisation, colonisation, and global revolution' section of the exhibition juxtaposes Marx's 1851-1862 journalistic texts that supported the civilising mission of British colonial rule with his later condemnation in *Das Kapital* of the destruction and plunder enacted by European colonialism. Instead of referencing the various sites of colonisation, it includes Marx's 1853 article on British rule in India and a drawing of a British 'civilisation steam engine'. A discussion of Marx's later thoughts on colonialism would have provided an interesting point of intervention into the following 'Nature and ecology' section, which could have highlighted colonised lands as sites of the vast plunder of natural resources rather than speculating on Marx's infatuation with guano. It could have also been a chance to discuss Marx's relationship to the United States, abolitionism and the Civil War.

'The emancipation of women and social issues' section goes into more depth than the section devoted to colonialism, but likewise presents women's struggles simply as a topical issue. It states that neither Marx nor the First International could agree on the role of women in socialist movements. It presents documentation of women's strikes and interventions from Victoria Hull and Harriet Law, and underlines that, while Marx did support women's strikes, he argued that 'social issues' had to be solved before dealing with the 'women's issue'. This presentation does not include any discussion of the broader politics of the women activists who are cited here, something which is important in addressing figures such as Hull, who openly expressed support for eugenics, nor does it mention Jenny Marx, who is presented as her husband's faithful scribe and supporter throughout the exhibition but does not earn a place in the women's section.

The exhibition ends with a photo wall, including postwar German Social Democratic and Christian Democratic posters juxtaposed with a silken Stasi scarf that uses Marx's likeness. Marx then pops up internationally on photos of a banner on a Peking street in the 1970s, a banner from the 1975 Angolan War of Independence, and a meeting of the Khmer Rouge juxtaposed with pictures from the Occupy Movement, a Deutsche Wohnen & Co. enteignen banner, and a 2021 Migrantifa poster (referred to simply as a May Day demo poster). Interesting to note is that there is no mention of the political spaces Jews and No-Longer-Jews inhabit after the Shoah. The discussions of antisemitism brought up in relation to nineteenth-century Marx are just as important in a current context, as many leftist Jewish movements in Germany grapple with accusations of antisemitism in relation to pro-Palestine and BDS activism – although perhaps this absence is a blessing in disguise, as one could easily imagine a connection being drawn between Marx's Judenfrage and contemporary Jewish pro-Palestine activism.

The casual comparisons between such wildly divergent movements in the final section echoes the exhibition's overall tendency to present Marx as so contradictorily pro or anti that he ends up cancelling himself out. But it also speaks to a larger strategy of creating an ambivalent portrait of Marx, as a figure who may have some insights into capitalism but whose thought largely fails to hold up outside of a nineteenth-century context. Much of the story of Marxism after Marx is, of course, one of attempts to solve twentieth- and twenty-first-century problems using a theoretical framework that was created in response to the crises of the nineteenth century. Followers of all stripes have struggled to fully integrate these conflicting contexts, having to improvise, fill in blank spots, as well as violently project allegedly Marxian solutions onto suffering peoples. The exhibition fails to envision Marxism after Marx, to use Marx to productively illuminate the world after his death. It is 'Marxist' only in the sense that Marx would not have recognised himself here either.

50 years of *Radical Philosophy*

And 50 more to come!

Join us to celebrate.

Friday 4 November 2022, 18:30.

Toynbee Hall, 28 Commercial Street, London, E1 6LS.

eventbrite.com/e/50-years-of-radical-philosophy-tickets-426071299727

www.ingramcontent.com/pod-product-compliance
Lightning Source LLC
Chambersburg PA
CBHW082009090526
44590CB00020B/3409